# MEASURING CULTURE

JOHN W. MOHR

CHRISTOPHER A. BAIL

MARGARET FRYE

JENNIFER C. LENA

OMAR LIZARDO

TERENCE E. McDONNELL

ANN MISCHE

IDDO TAVORY

FREDERICK F. WHERRY

Columbia University Press    *New York*

Columbia University Press
*Publishers Since 1893*
New York   Chichester, West Sussex
cup.columbia.edu

Library of Congress Cataloging-in-Publication Data

Names: Mohr, John, author.
Title: Measuring culture / John W. Mohr [and eight others].
Description: New York : Columbia University Press, 2020. |
Includes bibliographical references and index.
Identifiers: LCCN 2019052336 (print) | LCCN 2019052337 (ebook) |
ISBN 9780231180283 (hardback) | ISBN 9780231180290
(trade paperback) | ISBN 9780231542586 (ebook)
Subjects: LCSH: Culture. | Culture—Research—Methodology.
Classification: LCC HM623 .M64 2020 (print) |
LCC HM623 (ebook) | DDC 306—dc23
LC record available at https://lccn.loc.gov/2019052336
LC ebook record available at https://lccn.loc.gov/2019052337

# CONTENTS

# ACKNOWLEDGMENTS

**B**ETWEEN his stately brown sport coat and cultlike following within cultural sociology, many people might have found John Mohr intimidating. But he quickly disarmed you with a kind of patient grace that made you feel as though you were the center of the sociological universe. For young scholars—as we all were when we started this intellectual adventure—John was our consummate ambassador to cultural sociology. Although we might have known him as a pioneer in the quantitative study of culture and social networks, we quickly learned of his keen appreciation for every other instrument within the cultural sociologist's toolkit. His mastery of numbers made it easy to forget that he was equally at home in discussions of Foucault and semiotics, and that he had an undergraduate degree in philosophy—a fact that would occasionally become apparent when he launched into discussions of Cassirer, Lewin, and Swidler.

Because of his panoramic perspective on the study of culture, within and beyond sociology, John was uniquely positioned to imagine this book. He spent the bulk of his career trying to corral cultural sociologists—a most unruly group of scholars engaged in everything from calculus to hermeneutics—to outline a series of principles and standards for the scientific measurement of culture.

There were numerous false starts. At the first meeting that John and Amin Ghaziani hosted to bring many of us together to discuss the measurement of culture, we learned of the several previous such meetings that had failed to generate a set of general principles, despite rich and vibrant conversations.[1] This time, we were told, would be different.

Our first meeting, in Vancouver, was as intellectually exciting as it was contentious. Articulating a way to measure culture would be no simple task. Was cultural sociology fundamentally about the measurement of meaning or cultural products? Could *all* forms of culture be translated into measurable categories? Could (and, indeed, *should*) cultural concepts be ordered according to levels of analysis? What *was* the relationship between interpretation and measurement? Hashing out these questions had us on the verge of shouting at each other on numerous occasions. If not for John, this book probably would have died on the sloping banks of the Pacific Northwest seven years ago.

We met again at a second conference at the University of California, Santa Barbara, in 2014, at a third meeting at the University of Notre Dame in 2015, and at a writing retreat at Teachers College, Columbia University, in 2017. Gradually, the experiment began to bear fruit. Based on our meeting at the University of British Columbia, the group created a special issue of *Theory and Society* edited by Mohr and Ghaziani; three of the participants came together to write a theoretical paper on cultural resonance; and we began to think that it might be possible to write this book.[2]

As the book slowly took form, some members of the original group pulled out of the project. It was a long process, and we were all overextended. Yet, instead of disbanding, the remaining group elected to write this book. We even added a member: Maggie Frye joined after a few participants kept bringing up her work, and everyone felt that her voice would make the book better.

The inaugural "Measuring Culture Conference," held at the University of British Columbia in 2013 (left to right: Fred Wherry, John Mohr, Jenn Lena, Iddo Tavory, Neil Gross, Amin Ghaziani, Ashley Mears, Ann Mische, Chris Bail, Terry McDonnell, Omar Lizardo, and Steve Vaisey).

Our goal was to write a volume in which a plurality of views could guide the agenda, allowing individual authors to dissent where necessary. This book was hardly an exercise in efficiency, but it does attempt to repair the deep disconnections among cultural sociologists who so rarely engage in conversations about how to measure culture. It is our hope that the hard-fought consensus achieved here will allow a future generation of cultural sociologists to avoid the same unproductive disputes about how to measure culture, or the very possibility of such an endeavor.

We lost John to amyotrophic lateral sclerosis (ALS)—far too soon—in August 2019. We dedicate this book to him, not only because it truly would not have been possible without his vision, encouragement, and good cheer, but also because he remained engaged in its creation even as his disease began to rob him of his ability to communicate. When he lost his ability to write, we began interviewing him—and reading his entire corpus—in order to channel him as we wrote the introduction and conclusion to this book. With the help of his friends and students, he read and commented upon these very imperfect impersonations with his characteristic grace and sharp insight. And as he entered the final stages of his disease, we learned to follow his example—not only his creativity and careful prose, but his ability to bring out the best in people and convince them that the very best science happens in collaboration with others.

This book also might not have been realized without the remarkable support of our editor at Columbia University Press, Eric Schwartz. Although John and Amin's original idea was to produce an edited volume, Eric pushed us to do something even bolder: trying to tackle one of cultural sociology's most daunting challenges with a single, unified voice. Although their names do not appear on the cover of this book, the words that follow were deeply enriched by Ghaziani, Ashley Mears, and Steve Vaisey—each of whom participated in one or more of the group's early conferences but ultimately decided not to join our effort in writing this book.

This book would also not be possible without the support of numerous professional organizations and universities. We are grateful to the American Sociological Association (ASA) for an Improvement of the Discipline grant that enabled John and Amin to arrange our first conference. We are also grateful to the University of British Columbia, the University of California, Santa Barbara, the University of Notre Dame, and Teachers College for hosting conferences where this book was conceived and developed. At Notre Dame, we are particularly grateful for support from the Department of Sociology, the Department of Anthropology, the Institute for Scholarship in the Liberal Arts, the Kellogg Institute for International Studies, the Center for the Study of Religion and Society, the John J. Reilly Center for Science, Technology, and Values, and the History and Philosophy of Science graduate program.

During conferences at the aforementioned institutions, this book benefited greatly from comments and feedback by the following people: Neil Gross (University of British Columbia); Jon Cruz, Simonetta Falasca-Zamponi, Craig Rawlings, Verta Taylor, and Sarah Thébaud (University of California, Santa Barbara); and Christopher Ball, Michael Jindra, Erin Metz McDonnell, and Lyn Spillman (Notre Dame). Marcus Mann and Friedolin Merhout helped us with the bibliography and footnotes when they threatened to bury us alive, Oscar Stuhler provided a useful reading of the first chapters of the book, Alex Kindel proofread the book, and Claire Sieffert saved us from many awkward phrases and nudged us to clarify our ideas. The reviewers of both the book proposal and the manuscript warned us away from possible pitfalls and offered crucial comments. Lastly, the book also would not have been possible without the kind support, inspiration, and participation of Paul DiMaggio, Robin Wagner-Pacifici, and Ron Breiger, who generously contributed their time to be interviewed for chapter four of this book and then patiently read draft after draft of that chapter.

# MEASURING CULTURE

# INTRODUCTION

## Why Measure Culture?

(N a small town in Texas called Crosby, a devout community lost the only thing more important to its collective identity than Christianity: American football) Like so much of the United States in mid-2016, the townspeople were embroiled in a controversy about the role of protest in sports, and specifically San Francisco 49ers quarterback Colin Kaepernick's decision to kneel during the national anthem before National Football League (NFL) games that year. When two members of the Crosby High School football team followed suit later that year, their coach abruptly suspended them from the team and demanded they remove their uniforms on the spot. Though the students' parents immediately protested that their children were engaged in a reasonable act of protest in the name of racial injustice and police violence, the high school coach interpreted the students' decision to kneel during the national anthem in starkly different terms. From the coach's perspective, the students had shown profound disrespect for people who gave their lives in service of the U.S. military—arguing in particular that Civil War veterans died in the service of racial injustice.

Controversies mirroring these tensions in Crosby played out across the United States and got an even higher profile in the lead-up to the divisive 2016 presidential election, particularly thanks to tweets by then-candidate Donald Trump. Although the subject of high school football may seem far afield from this book's title, the controversy about kneeling during the national anthem underscores human beings' remarkable capacity to attach different meanings to an act, an object, or each other. Indeed, meaning-making is at the center of human activity—in areas as diverse as health, the economy, and violent extremism. How, then, should we study it as social scientists?

As a core tenet of the human condition, meaning-making has received its share of attention. After all, anthropology's warrant—at least at one point—was the study of "culture" (a term borrowed from the German *Kultur* and turned into a more-or-less analytic category); the entire field of cultural studies is dedicated to it. In our own part of the intellectual world, sociology, the study of culture has been part of the canon since Max Weber and Émile Durkheim, and it has evolved through the work of Norbert Elias and many others since. As a formal analytic center that focuses our attention on the world, however, the history of the term is checkered.

In its current iteration, the study of culture is most strongly associated with the subfield of *cultural sociology*, which emerged in the United States in the 1980s (with some strong Continental influences). Though some parts of this subfield study the social processes that enable the creation of cultural products such as music and art, the core issue concerning the field is increasingly the study of meaning—and, more specifically, what it means to study meaning "scientifically." Key to this agenda is the development of theories and methods that explain how people assign meaning to events, objects, individuals, or groups, as well as how people interpret and live through such meanings themselves. As sociologist Robin Wagner-Pacifici writes, cultural sociologists thus aim to "[know] their objects from the inside-out as well as from the outside-in."[1]

Over the past four decades, cultural sociologists have amassed an impressive array of theoretical insights and modes of empirical investigation about how people create and interpret the meaning of the world around them. A central theme of this work is unpacking what meaning-making actually entails. Culture has turned from something that everybody in a given society has—whether that society is defined by national boundaries, language, or history—into a more stratified and segmented category. In this view, culture is not only the environment that enables the meaningfulness of social life but also a more specific set of scripts, narratives, embodied practices, and schemas. Precisely because of this theoretical and empirical segmentation, the scientific study of meaning-making has flourished across many different social arenas, from the study of social class and identity to the study of health behaviors or violent conflict.[2] Yet, beyond this weak consensus, a thousand flowers bloom. And while we are all for blooming flowers (what kind of monsters wouldn't be?), this should be the *beginning* of a disciplinary conversation, not its end. As sociologists, we feel that we need to know both exactly what to look at within a social setting, and—just as important—*how* to look at it.

## THE DUALITY OF INTERPRETATION AND MEASUREMENT

For all of the theoretical progress that cultural sociology has made, the methodological promise of cultural sociology has yet to be realized. Though cultural sociologists routinely engage in lengthy discussions about the definition of culture, much less attention has been paid to the question of how it should be measured or to the relationship between our theories and our methods. What aspects of the meaningful environment can be encoded within binary, nominal, and continuous categories? What do we gain and what do we lose when we operationalize culture via such imperfect calibrations?

One of the strongest assumptions we make in this book is that culture is not an "amorphous mist" or a collection of meanings that inherently defy measurement, as sociologist Gary Alan Fine once warned.[3] While some of us see ourselves as card-carrying interpretivists, we also assume that interpretation is patterned, and that these patterns can be analytically captured and translated into measurable form—albeit to varying degrees, and always at some cost. In other words, we resist the temptation to argue that cultural meanings are so closely tied to social construction—and that social construction is so multilayered and subtle—that we will never be able to produce a generic set of methodologies that facilitate comparison of meaning-structures across social contexts. Instead, we will argue that even data produced within the most qualitative traditions in cultural sociology—such as ethnographic observation or qualitative interviews—become amenable to more quantitative techniques as soon as they are externalized in the form of field notes or interview transcriptions, not unlike what Paul Ricoeur called "second-order externalizations."[4]

On the other hand, to deny hermeneutic interpretation's central importance in the study of meaning-making is equally misguided. To try and do away with interpretation and focus on so-called hard facts is actually quite woolly headed. To put it in its strongest form, *there can be no measurement of culture without interpretation.* Defining our problem as that of the duality of interpretation and measurement is thus the second most important assumption of this book. Interpretation, in its most basic form, is the process in which sociologists reconstruct that which is known or understood between people. Interpretation and measurement are thus intertwined in the very project of cultural sociology.

As we have foreshadowed, cultural sociologists are certainly not the first scholars to attempt to formalize a logic of meaning that iteratively transubstantiates interpretation and measurement. Theologians, philosophers, and scholars of the humanities have worked toward this goal for millennia. And, even if we conceive of this project more narrowly, we are far from the first to tread this path in the past century's humanities and social sciences. The literary theorist Kenneth Burke, for example, famously argued that the reason why one should study literature is that the arts are the result of human beings' attempts to give a reflective voice to their experience by telling stories.[5] To understand literature, for Burke, is to understand the templates that human beings have sought to make sense of their own experiences. Similarly, cultural sociologists have been much influenced by anthropologists such as Claude Lévi-Strauss, Clifford Geertz, Mary Douglas, Marshall Sahlins, and Fredrik Barth. And while these scholars are often labeled as interpretivists, some of them were formalizers who would make the most hard-nosed empiricist among us blush. To give only one example, Lévi-Strauss's calculus of myth and kinship is a form of measurement whose formalism rivals concepts that would be dreamed up by a network theorist years later. *Boundary*, as an analytic term, owed its power to its binary, and eminently measurable, form.[6]

Moreover, the sociology of culture draws on still other fields. While its character as *cultural* sociology leads it to borrow from the humanities and other interpretive disciplines, its character as cultural *sociology* means that it also draws on more scientistic tools and styles of knowing. Cultural sociologists borrow epidemiological tools and heuristics from the friendly demographer next door, computational advances such as network models, and even techniques developed by psychologists, political scientists,

*Caution*

and computer scientists. Perhaps because of its intermediary position, cultural sociology *must* reflect on the balance between interpretation and scientific measurement. It is not unlike Geertz's recollection of an Indian myth about how the world rested upon the back of an elephant, which rested in turn upon the back of a turtle. With Geertz, we agree that there are cultural "turtles" all the way down (even if few of us think that there are *only* turtles there).[7] Meaning can never be explained solely by nonmeaningful variables. While other kinds of explanations are often crucial for understanding meanings (e.g., political economy or network structure), other *meaningful* explanations are always part of the analytic story we tell. This is true in two senses: first, that meanings always arise historically from other meaning structures, and second, that any act is predicated on a deeper meaning structure, whether theorized as "schemas," "discourse," or a more embodied language, such as that of "habitus." Yet, as cultural sociologists, we need to dwell a little longer on the metaphor. If there are turtles there, we want to know what they look like and how we should go about studying them. Do we check their weights? The curve of their shells?

Thus, while the history of the social sciences is littered with explorations of the boundary between formalist and interpretivist understandings of social life, cultural sociology is uniquely positioned to articulate a new set of principles.[8] This book is not merely another call for the integration of qualitative and quantitative traditions within cultural sociology, nor does it purport to offer a new theoretical synthesis for the study of culture. While some of us may laud these efforts, our ambition is not so grand. Instead, our goal is both less imaginative and more generative: to outline *how* cultural sociologists can combine interpretivist and formalist approaches in the study of culture in an age of perhaps unprecedented methodological innovation.

We find that cultural sociologists routinely make ad hoc decisions about how to navigate the boundary between formalism and hermeneutics as ways to understand meaning-making. Yet it is not necessarily that cultural sociologists disagree about such decisions on theoretical grounds as much as they reside in methodological silos and do not think outside or in between them anywhere near enough. We believe that articulating the landscape of measuring culture is necessary not only to standardize the unruly nature of methodology in the field but also because our empirical and theoretical imagination depends on it. In the chapters that follow, we discuss and integrate research that blends interpretive and formal approaches to studying meaning-making processes that occur at the individual and subconscious level, all the way up to broader discursive fields, interactions, and networks. In so doing, we aim to enliven researchers' imaginations as they encounter problems in the field. By integrating the different kinds of things that sociologists of culture look at and the ways they go about formalizing them, we hope to inspire better research.

To understand how this plays out, we can return to the example we began with—taking a knee as a form of political protest in athletics—and the categorical sanctioning of this practice. There are different modes of interpretation—different levels of analysis, and consequently different modes of measurement—that we can construe when we approach this scenario as sociologists of culture. We can ask about taking the knee as an icon: What makes the image resonant? What turns it into an aesthetic-political performance? We can take aim at the discursive strategies employed by those taking a knee and those who condemn the practice. Who are their audiences? What kind of agency do they have? What acts do they describe? How do they delineate the boundaries between *us* and *them*? We can ask about whether and how the reactions to taking a knee become morally embodied. We can ask about the context within which a *deviant* form of meaning-making emerges: the small groups, such as internet forums, through which ideas crystallize and spread virally across the ether. That is, we can look at the ways that ideas themselves travel. How is the particular aesthetic of civil disobedience marked, and how did the reaction to taking a knee itself spread—both from the fringe and from the political center?

Each of these questions forces us to think about the appropriate mode of measurement. Indeed, a number of authors in this book made their careers by dancing across different modes of measurement. We can think about ways to formalize discourse and measure the dramatic structure of the situation that various actors enact through Galois lattices; we can trace Facebook pages and online conversation coverage through network techniques; we can even measure the meaning of objects such as knees or footballs themselves. Like any object worth our attention, a dizzying array of paths appears to be available—so many, in fact, that we can become confused about how to actually move forward.

By thinking systematically about what we actually do as sociologists of culture, we can even come to realize—as all sociologists do at one point or another—that the options we have are themselves patterned. And, in that way, we become both more aware of what we *can* do and what we *don't* end up answering for. While long and involved research projects may move among different modes of measurement, different levels of analysis, and different environments of meaning-making in order to fully solve a research problem, most research projects and researchers are more limited. This book is meant to open researchers' imaginations to the full range of options they have and to make them more aware of their blind spots.

## A BRIEF HISTORY OF MEASURING CULTURE

As we have mentioned, the study of meaning-making has deep roots within sociology. The antecedents of cultural sociology today were born in the canonic traditions of Max Weber, Georg Simmel, and Émile Durkheim, along with certain strands of Marxian sociology. From Weber, sociologists of culture have distilled the audacious claim that the subject-topic of sociology *is* meaningful action, placing meaning at the very center of the discipline. From Durkheim comes the idea that the architecture of normative structures is a causal force in the world, as well as an early rendition of the binary classifications that human beings use to distinguish objects—such as totems—or groups. Durkheim shaped the rise of structuralism in linguistics and anthropology. The work of Lévi-Strauss—and other structuralists—took up the structural assumptions of Durkheim's *Elementary Forms* and ran with them to develop structuralist semiotics and formal methods for analyzing cultural meanings through the examination of the relations that connect cultural elements into larger structures. Culture, in this tradition, was imagined as a grid of relationships among meanings.[9]

If cultural sociology's theoretical basis was born out of European hermeneutical and structuralist traditions, its methodological roots lie deep in the formalism developing in the United States at the fin de siècle. This included the empirical work on race relations, immigration, and poverty of Jane Addams, W. E. B. Du Bois, Robert Park, and Ernest Burgess. Though these scholars were not engaged with the formal analysis of meaning-making in the sense we develop in this book, they were collecting data on individuals' beliefs, aspirations, and understandings of social systems that would later become central to cultural sociology. Their image of modernity as the challenges of urbanization and immigration was deeply "cultural." It was about people making meaning as they moved from small communities into an urban world of strangers and marginal men (The alienation of the city was not primarily an economic relationship, as it was for Marx, but rather an existential, meaningful relationship.)

At the same time, and through similar historical processes, American social science was discovering the public more broadly.[10] The systematic measure of public opinion did not exist until sociologists began to develop the concept of personal attitudes, which conveyed a sense of how a person's deep structure of meanings and orientations has direct consequences for action in the world. Sociologists William I. Thomas and Florian Znaniecki were the first to theorize and measure attitudes in their *The Polish Peasant in Europe and America*.[11] By 1925, both Floyd Allport and Emory Bogardus published independent approaches to constructing "attitude scales" using survey data. Later developments by Louis L. Thurstone, Rensis Likert, and others produced rapid advances in using social surveys to measure subjective experiences, including cultural orientations, values, systems of meanings and beliefs, and individual heuristics for interpreting social situations.[12]

The formalization of meaning-making accelerated around the time of World War II through a number of projects that were initiated during—and in service of—the war effort. This included Samuel Stouffer's work *The American Soldier*, which focused the study of attitudes on different kinds of soldiers in different units, including their motivations and their emotional states.[13] But, crucially, it also included the invention and rapid development of methods of content analysis through the work of Harold Lasswell, who directed the experimental division for the study of wartime communications established at the Library of Congress during World War II.[14]

It began as a matter of propaganda—how to read and code the enemies' positions effectively when taking vast corpora of newspaper articles from Germany, Italy, Japan, and other Axis countries, looking for patterns, and trying to discern the attitudes of Axis powers. But like Stouffer's research, the work on quantification took on a life of its own. After the war, Lasswell led a number of pathbreaking studies that created the modern science of content analysis. In addition to his pioneering work on word frequency analysis, he explored the linkage of word meanings to heart rate and other physiological markers as people were speaking or reading words. Wartime funding also supported many social scientists who would go on to lay the groundwork for the measurement of culture as we know it today. The most prominent of these was Paul Lazarsfeld at Columbia University, whose work on public opinion created a groundswell in the growth of modern quantitative social science. His work was also notable because he saw no distinction between qualitative and quantitative data.[15] Instead, Lazarsfeld argued that all data begin as qualitative observations and move through ever-more-abstract forms of quantification. This is perhaps why some of his most influential work on social networks and mass persuasion transitioned seamlessly from in-depth qualitative interviews with individuals about their media consumption and political attitudes toward quantitative studies of larger social structures that enable "opinion leaders" to mediate messages designed for the public.[16]

Meanwhile, after the war, theoretical frameworks for the study of culture and meaning-making became wrapped up in the broader ambition of prominent sociologists, such as Talcott Parsons, to develop a general theory of human behavior. Social meanings were a key component of Parsons's model of adaptation, goal attainment, integration, and latency (AGIL), with culture being the linchpin of latency. But Parsons parceled out culture to anthropologists. Indeed, the rise of cultural anthropology was partly an outcome of the premature aspirations of Harvard's Department of Social Relations. Separating out topics of inquiry among the disciplines, Parsons and Alfred Kroeber—one of the most important anthropologists of his time—formally divided the loot of their disciplines' labors:

> We therefore propose a truce to quarreling over whether culture is best understood from the perspective of society or society from that of culture. As in the famous case of heredity "versus" environment, it is no longer a question of how important each is, but of how each works and how they are interwoven with each other. The traditional perspectives of anthropology and sociology should merge into a temporary condominium leading to a differentiated but ultimately collaborative attack on problems in intermediate areas with which both are concerned.[17]

While high-minded, this was a disciplinary low point for the sociology of culture. Culture was, simply, none of sociology's business. Thus, even when the discipline of sociology soured on the project of grand theory, the elimination of the study of culture and meaning-making from sociology reverberated throughout the discipline. While the great sociological critiques of Parsons in the 1960s all focused attention on meaning-making (e.g., Herbert Blumer's *Symbolic Interactionism*, Peter L. Berger and Thomas Luckmann's *The Social Construction of Reality*, and Harold Garfinkel's *Studies in Ethnomethodology*), sociologists by and large embraced noncultural explanations that emphasized the role of social structures, network structures, and theories about resource dependencies.[18]

Outside of sociology, however, considerable progress continued to be made in the measurement of culture and meaning.

This includes Charles Osgood's pioneering work on the semantic differential—searching for a formal way to analyze meaning as a system of paired associations between standard questions that could be used to describe concepts and terms. It also, crucially, includes Kurt Lewin's field theory, as well as cognitive anthropologists such as Roy D'Andrade and Dan Sperber's strategies for developing a theory of "an epidemiology of representations."

What might be termed the "modern era" of cultural sociology began in the late 1970s and exploded in the 1980s. Like so many disciplinary shifts, cultural sociology experienced simultaneous discovery. From France, the work of Pierre Bourdieu, featuring a deeply consequential account of the stratification of meaning-making, was being translated—sometimes literally—into the language of American sociology, influencing pioneering work by Michèle Lamont and others on symbolic boundaries and social inequality. Richard Peterson and his colleagues were developing new theories about the production of cultural products such as popular songs by organizations and market actors, and—while these studies were not focused on the study of meaning but rather on the production of meaning clusters—they brought culture back into sociology. Wendy Griswold's "cultural diamond" organized cultural analyses, drawing attention to the sociological role of interpretation in cultural methods and to the measurement of intention and reception of meaning. Jeffrey Alexander was reworking the Parsonsian synthesis and reclaiming culture for sociology in the process. Ann Swidler fused a pragmatist sensibility with the question of culture in her classic paper "Culture in Action: Symbols and Strategies." Paul DiMaggio, Woody Powell, Lynne Zucker, Roger Friedland, and others inserted meaning into the heart of sociology with the construction of "new institutionalism," which was deeply influenced by Garfinkel's ethnomethodology and Alfred Schütz's phenomenology.[19]

Although Harrison White is not usually remembered as a participant in the so-called cultural turn within sociology, his work in the 1970s and 1980s was another key inspiration for the field, and indeed for this book. He moved to transcend the formal structuralism of social network analysis as he began to consider the study of identities and social categorization within markets. This work was expanded into a full-bodied theory of culture in *Identity and Control*.[20] Key to this work is the notion that categorization is constitutive of social networks, or what White called *catnets*.[21] This work proved to be the inspiration for a new generation of influential cultural analysts who drew upon the methods and theories of network analysis, such as Ronald Breiger, John Mohr, Kathleen Carley, and Peter Bearman.[22]

The marriage of cultural sociology and network analysis helped usher the former subfield into the sociological mainstream, and the remarkable increase in digital data in recent years may propel it even further.[23] The era of computational social science offers an unprecedented wealth of text, image, and audio data produced on social media sites, as well as massive efforts to catalog human history.[24] These new wellsprings of data create an even more urgent need for the integration of formal and hermeneutic approaches.[25] Though text, audio, and image data naturally lend themselves to hermeneutic analysis, there are billions of data points produced each day on any one of the largest social media sites alone. Fortunately, computational social science has also produced a new suite of tools for analyzing these data.[26] And, importantly—as we shall see—these new techniques are not simply more sophisticated forms of regression or linear modeling. Indeed, these new techniques require a balance of inductive and deductive reasoning to calibrate machine learning models that are capable of identifying patterns that could expand the range of questions that cultural sociologists may ask for years to come.

## OVERVIEW OF THIS BOOK

As the preceding brief history describes, cultural sociology has matured into one of the largest subfields in sociology, expanding into nearly every other subfield in the discipline.[27] As of this writing, the sociology of culture section is the second-largest section of the American Sociological Association (ASA). Despite its ascendance, cultural sociology faces a critical challenge, as we mentioned at the outset of this book: the extensive catalog of theories of culture that we have created is far weightier than the list of tools and procedures presently available to test them. *Measuring Culture* provides a programmatic statement on the measurement of culture that moves debates beyond qualitative and quantitative boundaries and among theoretical traditions. It proposes concrete strategies for measuring culture across levels of analysis, in its different manifestations (e.g., textual versus material culture), and for cultural processes that are both implicit and explicit. More than just a call for mixed-method approaches, we advocate measurement strategies that make legible the interrelations among cultural forms and facilitate the identification of cultural mechanisms in explanation.

As we have noted previously, cultural analysis has historically been a site of diverse and creative strategies of specification, formalization, description, and quantification in the social sciences. However, this proliferation of perspectives and analytic strategies can generate problems of communication and coordination, both across different scholarly communities and between scholars and the lay public. One perennial issue is the ambiguity of the very term *culture*, which resists a consensual, unitary definition. This perceived lack of conceptual clarity and analytic specification opens up the field to methodological criticism from social scientists that expect more clearly delimited concepts.

( If critics are right, our failure to develop consensually shared analytic and measurement strategies for cultural analysis can produce
three problems/First, the lack of common yardsticks for measuring culture can lead to the problem of scholars speaking past each
other. This is at least in part the cause of heated debates between
quantitative and qualitative researchers and, more recently, between
ethnographers who study action and interviewers who study discourse.[29] Second, without standard measures, it could prove difficult
to build upon past work and refine theories *as a field.* Third, culture
has a dual character: both a subjective reality embodied in persons
and an objectified reality out in the world. Bridging the research
on embodied and objectified aspects of culture, each of which often
relies on distinctive methods and skills, has proved difficult.)

Rather than seeking to compel the field to converge around
a set of standardized measures, this book instead advocates for
an iterative approach that embraces diverse measurement strategies and specifies the research questions to which each strategy is
most usefully applied. For this reason, we call for a multipronged
approach to measurement in the sociology of culture. The methods deployed by the scholars in our group include close textual
readings, ethnography, focus groups, interviews, survey analysis,
network mappings, and automated text mining.

As we show, the contributions of one measurement approach
should be understood in dialogue with other approaches. Stan-
dardization is not the goal; rather, we seek productive dialogue
across different ways of tackling measurement problems, the kind
of dialogue that yields insight into the phenomenon of interest.
To understand culture and its contexts and effects, we must often
come up with creative solutions rather than traditional or habitual
ones. Such creativity involves borrowing techniques from proxi-
mate fields, putting measures in conversation via triangulation, and
inventing and adapting approaches to data gathering and analysis.

Over the course of our conversations and arguments, we identified a few shared assumptions on which our work is based. First, the authors share a realist bent: we assume that data depict actual things and processes in the world. While we know that there will always be, as U.S. secretary of defense Donald Rumsfeld so famously proclaimed, "unknown unknowns," and that our measurement does not simply mirror the phenomena we study, we nonetheless assume it represents—however imperfectly—real things and processes in the world.[29] We also assume that measurement is an enterprise that can be engaged by using a range of methods, which vary in their scope, techniques, and assumptions.

Precisely because of this wary realism, we recognize that all forms of measurement involve hazards, including the necessary reduction of information that occurs when we collapse any kind of measurement category. In this sense, all research and measurement strategies—whether ethnography, interviews, surveys, or computational methods—reduce and even distort social reality in the effort to represent the world. Different methods then afford distinct angles of vision, providing insight into aspects of the social world that are hard to see using other methods.

Lastly, this ecumenical view is translated in what we think we should measure. We argue that measuring culture is about cultural elements' *quality* (e.g., their content, form, and distinguishing characteristics) and *quantity* (which can be assessed using a range of methods from simple counts to advanced statistical modeling). It is also about the *relationship* among cultural elements (which can be mapped and charted) and the *processes* by which cultural elements are generated, reproduced, transformed, or dissolved over time.

If measurements are just representations of the world, then every representation is good for something, but not for everything.[30] We advocate a theoretically informed approach to cultural analysis that questions the opposition between quantitative and qualitative approaches, showing how hermeneutic and computational methods complement and inform each other.[31] In the chapters ahead, we will show how the rich nexus of theoretical and methodological approaches described in this book can be used in a dialogic fashion to shed light into causal mechanisms and provide better explanations of the workings of culture in the social world.

The first three chapters of this book describe the state of the art in measuring culture at three levels of analysis. Chapter 1, "Measuring Culture in People," first reviews current approaches to measuring culture when individual people are the main source of data, examining how culture can be measured in people's thoughts, speech, and actions. Particular attention is dedicated to delineating measurement strategies for declarative or publicly articulated forms of meaning-making, as well as deeper subconscious or embodied cultural processes. Chapter 2, "Measuring Culture in Objects," discusses how to measure culture within objects such as texts, pieces of art, or other physical items. Particular attention is dedicated to how human beings interpret objects and to how the meaning of objects spreads across social systems. Chapter 3, "Measuring Culture in Social Relationships," discusses the measurement of culture at more compounded levels of analysis, including social interactions, networks, and fields.

Each of these chapters discusses the tension between interpretivist and formalist traditions in the measurement of culture at one of the three levels of analysis, reviews the history of measurement in that tradition, and discusses best practices for future studies that aim to measure culture at these levels. These three chapters, taken together, provide an overview of modes of work and the state of the art of formalization in cultural sociology. This is a "general sociology" taken on the level of culture. By taking this broad canvas approach to the sociology of culture, the chapters also aim to refract the work that sociologists do more generally. If we hold, with Weber, that people are suspended in webs of meaning, then the sociology of culture is but a specific angle from which to see sociology more generally.

Chapter 4, "Pivots and Choices in the Process of Research," takes the accounts outlined in these first three chapters and sets them in motion. Having differentiated levels of analysis in the measurement of culture, we then approach the more complex question of how cultural sociologists move between levels of analysis when they measure culture. Because examples of such multilevel measurement of culture are scant, we take a deep dive into three exemplary projects: Paul DiMaggio's work on political polarization; Ann Mische's work on political activism in Brazil; and John Mohr, Ronald Breiger, and Robin Wagner-Pacifici's collaborative work on U.S. national security statements through automated text analysis. Using in-depth interviews with the authors of each of the aforementioned projects and a reading of their entire corpus, we present a narrative and analytical account of how each of them developed their multilevel approaches toward the measurement of culture.

The final chapter, "Conclusion: The Future of Measuring Culture," identifies best practices in the measurement of culture, outlines concrete measures that future scholars can take to ensure they capture the duality of interpretation and measurement, and discusses some of the limitations of our analysis. We conclude by discussing the future, with a particular focus on the promise of computational social science. Our goal is to convince the reader that the landscape of the sociology of culture is shifting. Increasingly, sociologists reach out for sophisticated computational tools and modes of measurement to answer old questions and discover new ones. This shift, we believe, does not come at the expense of the kind of qualitative work that sociologists of culture have been engaged in. Historical comparative work, ethnography, and interview research will continue to be crucial for the sociology of culture. There is no computational apocalypse on the horizon. Yet, as the possibilities for measurement develop, and as ways of automating analysis of language and images become more sophisticated, the palette of possibilities that sociologists of culture have to choose from expands. The question is how to approach this change and how to make the most out of it.

This book is intended primarily for those of us who are empirically engaged with questions of the sociology of culture—an increasing number of practitioners, whether or not they think of themselves as card-carrying sociologists of culture. For them, the book should fulfill a few functions: surveying the land and showing the kinds of interpretive and formal decisions that we make as we work through an empirical problem. As we do so, we hope to jog our sociological imagination instead of keeping ourselves siloed in the confines of our favorite method.

Lastly, an intellectual community is made not only of individuals but also the multiplex relationships among them. As our community of inquiry continues to expand, we hope that this book will allow people to appreciate not only what they can (and can't) do but also how other research—potential and actual—relates to it. Like meaning itself, our research is part of a matrix of similarities and differences that give it meaning. To use another relational metaphor, a mosaic of projects and approaches may each have value in themselves, but they crystallize as a larger image when we see how they fit together. And, like most human things, the mosaic is a reflexive structure that shifts as we become more aware of it. It is our belief that, by being more aware of the mosaic structure and our location in it, we can craft better sociological projects and, on a broader level, a better sociology.

# 1

## MEASURING CULTURE IN PEOPLE

**W**E begin by looking at the measurement of cultural processes and patterns that can be observed in individuals. At first glance, this may seem like a strange point of departure for this book. As we have already discussed, culture is a hard concept to define. Yet most—if not all—sociologists would agree that (the study of culture and meaning-making centers on how social life is structured by *extra-individual* forces.) And yet, as we will show, much of our evidential basis for what culture is and how it operates rests upon observations of how individuals internalize such social processes and change their behaviors because of them.

We structure this chapter around how culture can be measured by observing people as they *think*, *talk*, and *act*. We then show how these fundamental human capacities can be connected to culture through methods of observation, documentation, and analysis. In each section, we aim to identify both the content (or "what") that constitutes culture and the process (or "how") that enables such forms of meaning-making to come into being. This is because it is difficult—if not impossible—to discuss how people talk without paying attention to what they are saying, and the same goes for analysis of thought and action.

*Problem*

We recognize that there are methodological stakes in the ground, and sociologists have never reached consensus on how culture should be measured in people. In each section, we document past and present controversies about measurement. We take a pluralistic perspective on method and include discussions of exemplary work that has observed culture in individuals using participant ethnography, in-depth interviews, focus group discussions, surveys, experiments, wearable devices, and data collected for purposes other than social research.

At the same time, we are not agnostic as to what is the best match between a methodological approach and particular forms of culture. Accordingly, each section favors some methods over others. To investigate how people bear the mark of culture in thought, talk, and action, we argue that it is necessary to *isolate* each type of observation about a person from other types, and some strategies are better at this than others. Researchers who focus on the links between culture and thought should use surveys, experiments, and interactive data collection formats that bypass speech and (often) conscious thought. Analysts of culture in talk should turn to formats that provoke reflective self-articulation partially bracketed from action—most notably the in-depth interview and focus group discussion, but also formal speeches. And scholars of culture in action should use data that unobtrusively monitor people as they routinely go about their business in the world, elicited from either participant observers or technological enterprises that collect data on us without our noticing.

# THOUGHT

## *History of Measurement*

What can we learn about culture by measuring what and how people think? Conceptions of culture as shared patterns of thinking have been foundational to sociological inquiry since the consolidation of the field in the late nineteenth and early twentieth centuries. This includes the Germanic tradition, centered on shared thinking as "ideas," which was fundamental to the work of both Marx and Weber, despite their disagreement about ideas' causal import.[1] Shared patterns of thinking were also central to the French neo-Kantian tradition, organized around the notion of *représentations* (representations).[2] This theoretical perspective culminated in Durkheim's sharp demarcation between individual and collective representations and his associated definition of *sociology* as the science in charge of studying *représentations collectives* (collective representations).

The tradition of theorizing culture as shared thinking extended into the mid-twentieth century in the work of Karl Mannheim and Ludwik Fleck, who developed the systematic sociological study of professional knowledge and thought communities.[3] Alfred Schütz would later extend this approach to the conceptualization and study of so-called everyday knowledge by merging Weber's interpretive sociology of ideas and the continental philosophical tradition of phenomenology.[4] This led sociologists Peter Berger and Thomas Luckmann to a synthesis of Germanic, Durkheimian, and phenomenological traditions around the notion of *The Social Construction of Reality*—a formulation that remains more or less canonical to this day.[5] People construct social reality via the development, transmission, and institutionalization of shared patterns of thinking across generations.[6]

Despite its deep roots in classical sociology, measuring culture as patterns of thought within people is not without its pitfalls. Decades of research on survey interview techniques, social psychology, and cognitive science show that people either misrepresent or misunderstand their own thoughts and intentions.[7] For example, on an online dating site, users whose profiles stated that they had no preference for dating people from the same racial or ethnic background (in answer to a question posed by the site) tended to *enact* preferences toward same-race partners, based on which profiles they selected to investigate further.[8] In addition, people's reports on their own attitudes, beliefs, values, and conceptions are sometimes labile, context-dependent, and changing based on seemingly irrelevant extraneous conditions.[9] This poses strong challenges to the reliability and validity of certain ways of capturing what people think. We will concentrate on two such high-level challenges, which have attracted scholarly attention in cultural sociology and highlight the promises and pitfalls of measuring thinking traces in persons.

First, some critics of studying thinking in people note that it is by definition a first-person, nonobservable phenomenon, and thus outside the purview of empirical cultural sociology.[10] One response to this line of criticism is that thinking might be private, but it leaves external (and thus measurable) traces. For instance, people leave behind explicit traces of what they think in documents, diaries, memoirs, or other archival records. Some approaches to cognitive sociology rely heavily upon such objectified thinking records as sources of data and measurement.[11]

A second criticism of studying thinking in people is that the theoretical tradition most strongly associated with this—mid-twentieth-century functionalism—was widely viewed as a failure. Functionalist theorists made unsustainable empirical assertions, such as presuming that people could internalize complex systems of symbols, values, and ideas,[12] and left behind no credible measurement program.[13] From this perspective, focusing on people's thoughts and ideas as causal drivers of action is a red herring, given that external contexts and institutions are easier to measure, and often also have a stronger impact on action.[14] However, this view runs counter to strong empirical evidence that what people think does causally shape their actions.[15] Just because (thinking is hard to measure does not mean that we should give up on trying to capture it, as it is unlikely that a purely external-ist analysis will provide a complete account of the role of culture in action) Or, to paraphrase Mary Douglas, dispensing with the study of thinking processes along with the functionalist theoretical perspective is like cutting off one's nose to spite one's face.[16]

Nevertheless, cognitive science's emergence and consolidation in the 1970s and 1980s brought bad news for those who equated thinking with explicit statements or consciously accessible pro-cesses measurable via self-reporting, because it was discovered that much thinking is not conscious.[17] This has led some to resort to different ways of capturing thinking in people, ways that try to bypass self-reporting as the royal road to measuring culture in people. Creative borrowing of theories and techniques developed by social and cognitive psychologists during the last two decades for measuring implicit thinking patterns is thus one of the most active areas of research in cultural sociology today.[18]

The other major input from the cognitive sciences comes from observing that when people think about any domain, they seldom do so via single attitudes or beliefs. Instead, underlying frame-works, which are referred to as _schemas_, link these unit elements into an organized _network_ of associations.[19] Cultural knowledge about any domain thus comprises such networks of associations between concepts. When these frameworks are shared across people, we can speak of groups sharing a cultural schema, which organizes their thinking within a domain.[20]

## Measuring What People Think

The debate about how to measure people's thinking was reopened by a now-classic paper by Stephen Vaisey,[21] which helped to introduce sociologists to "dual process models" developed in cognitive and social psychology.[22] The basic idea of dual process models is that people think via both deliberative (slower, conscious, reflexive) and nondeliberative (fast, unconscious, implicit) pathways. These two thinking pathways operate via different mechanisms and may have distinct causal effects.[23] Vaisey linked this distinction to classic work in the theory of action, such as Bourdieu's notion of habitus and Anthony Giddens's distinction between practical and discursive consciousness.[24] Vaisey's paper changed the conversation because it connected the conceptual dual process argument to a basic measurement point: if thinking happens via distinct processes, then different methods of eliciting thinking will be more or less equipped to measure one or the other. Some methods will be more likely to access discursive consciousness and more deliberate thinking, while other methods will be more likely to access nondeliberative thinking.

To show this, Vaisey juxtaposed the structured (or open-ended) interview and the forced-choice survey item, positing that the former triggers deliberative thinking while the latter leads to nondeliberative thinking. He argued that we should expect more equivocal, open-ended, and thus less coherent statements of thinking when people speak extemporaneously, as is typical within qualitative interviews. He contrasted this with the forced-choice survey item, which prompts people to make a "gut" choice between stated options (e.g., "agree" or "disagree" that sex before marriage is wrong), even if they were conflicted about it at an explicit level. He then showed that the latter were better predictors of subsequent behaviors (e.g., having premarital sex as a teenager). This indicated that there was a stronger link between nondeliberative thinking patterns and action than cultural sociologists realized at the time.

Yet Vaisey's argument drew the mapping between methods and types of thinking in too stark a way, suggesting that interviews access *only* deliberative cognition, and that fixed-response questions in surveys mainly access nondeliberative cognition. These led analysts to take Vaisey's original point as a blanket argument for the superiority of surveys over interviews for measuring culture in people. This was an implication that was forcefully challenged by those who pointed to skilled researchers' ability to extract implicit patterns of thinking and feeling from interviews.[25]

We are now in a better position to clarify some of these issues. First, there is no one-to-one or mutually exclusive mapping between methods and deliberative or nondeliberative thinking processes. Some methods will be tilted to one process or the other, but all methods capture traces of both.[26] Thus, we can only make *relative*, not absolute comparisons among methodological approaches.[27] Second, fixed-response questions in surveys are less sensitive to nondeliberative cognition than Vaisey proposed.[28] As psychologists Russell Fazio and Michael Olson have argued, survey responses may be especially sensitive to measuring nondeliberative thinking under special circumstances (e.g., time pressure, low motivation).[29] Under normal circumstances, however, the reverse is more likely: surveys are more likely to measure deliberative thinking because they are on the direct side of the "direct/indirect" method divide that is now well established in cognitive and social psychology.

Srivastava and Banaji[30] elegantly demonstrate this point by comparing direct and indirect measures of the same cultural content (the "collaborative" self-concept) and then linking these measures to actual patterns of action through a study of collaborative behaviors in an organization. Their results supported Vaisey's theoretical point that nondeliberative thinking has a stronger link to action than deliberative thinking. But rather than using a forced-choice survey to tap nondeliberative thinking, they used an indirect measure—a version of the Implicit Association Test (IAT) developed by social psychologists to assess implicit cognition. This test takes advantage of the fact that it takes people less time to sort stimuli into categories when the associations are consistent with our implicit stereotypes, and thus we can rely on automatic cognition.[31] Srivastava and Banaji found that their indirect measure correlated strongly with collaborative behavior, whereas direct self-reports about being a collaborative person show little or no net correlation with this outcome.

Srivastava and Banaji's work elaborates and generalizes Vaisey's general findings on the relationship between thinking processes and action, but it also relativizes his methodological distinction in an important way. One way to reconcile these observations is to think of different methods as being arranged along a continuum of sensitivity from the deliberative to the nondeliberative. Along this continuum, specific methods such as unstructured interviews could be labeled as more (or less) sensitive to deliberative thinking, although they also can be calibrated to capture implicit thoughts and feelings.[32]

## Nondeliberative Thinking: Sociological Applications

More recent work has extended the use of indirect measurement strategies to topics more directly related to the study of culture as shared patterns of thinking. In an inventive analysis, Rick Moore uses a combination of direct and indirect measures  to examine how religious identity shapes how people evaluate social categories.[33] The direct measures in his analysis include explicit ratings, and the indirect measures include the amount of time it takes respondents to make such ratings. Building on research on implicit cognition in social psychology, Moore argues that the speed of evaluative judgment is an index of whether individuals are producing responses via nondeliberative thinking. Evaluations that take longer to produce may indicate that deliberative thinking processes are overriding the initial nondeliberative responses.[34]

Moore collected direct ratings of four concepts associated with religiosity (i.e., religion, atheism, spirituality, and Christianity) from a small sample of respondents. Half of this sample identified as "evangelicals" and the other half as "atheist." Moore obtained direct ratings by asking each participant to rate how much a set of thirty-nine words and short phrases from a free-association exercise were associated with these four conceptual categories (the words and phrases included "close to God," "science," "freedom," "hypocrisy," "New Age," and others). Moore's key finding is that while evangelicals made explicit distinctions between the "Christianity" and "religion" categories (being more likely to apply negative descriptors to the latter), their patterns of indirect responses told a different story. Evangelicals were as quick to link "religion" to positive descriptors as they were to link the same words to the "Christianity" category. This represents a dissociation between the ambiguity and categorical distinctions made by evangelicals in their direct responses and the patterns of thinking evident by looking at their indirect responses. Despite their explicit ambiguity regarding organized religion, evangelicals have a gut reaction to the category that is positive.

Andrew Miles's research on the link between values and action provides another example of using indirect measurement strategies to measure thinking in people.[35] His strategy is to use "cognitive load" techniques to deplete the resources required for deliberative thinking. For example, Miles asks respondents to remember an eight-digit number while answering certain questions in his survey. The basic idea is that, with cognitive resources for deliberative thinking temporarily "down," evaluative and behavioral responses can be made only via nondeliberative pathways, partially isolating the mechanism that drives behavioral responses. Responses from participants subject to cognitive load can then be compared to those made by participants under normal circumstances. Using this design, Miles shows that participants who are high on a "self-transcendence" values measure[36] are more generous toward others in an economic ultimatum game, but only when they are under high cognitive load.

Overall, the suite of indirect measurement techniques developed by psychologists that could be adopted by sociologists for measuring culture in thought is large and continually expanding.[37] Brian Nosek and colleagues identify at least twelve distinct indirect measurement strategies, most of which can be implemented in computer-assisted survey research platforms such as Amazon's Mechanical Turk.[38] In a recent contribution, Miles, Charron-Chénier, and Schleifer argue for the particular relevance of one such technique, the Affect Misattribution Procedure (AMP), for effectively isolating the work of nondeliberative thinking.[39] They compare the predictive validity of the AMP against the more popular IAT in three sociologically relevant domains (racial attitudes, politics, and morality), and their findings show that AMP outperforms the IAT in terms of predicting nondeliberative attitudinal and behavioral responses. Miles and collaborators conclude that the AMP represents a relatively untapped measurement resource for sociologists—one that can complement and expand traditional and direct measurement techniques aimed at capturing nondeliberative thinking.

## THE INTERPLAY BETWEEN NONDELIBERATIVE AND DELIBERATIVE THINKING

Recent theoretical work challenges the compartmentalization of deliberative and nondeliberative thinking as isolated compartments of human cognition.[40] Instead, these studies indicate that both types of thinking typically interact in a dynamic process that unfolds over time. Although nondeliberative thinking is faster, deliberative thinking—given the time, opportunity, and motivation—can override nondeliberative responses, which in turn often creates a new round of nondeliberative thought.[41] To account for this dynamic, Cunningham and collaborators have developed what they refer to as the "iterative reprocessing model."[42] This approach has received convergent support from neuroscience and artificial intelligence research.[43] This work is only beginning to make forays into sociology, however.

A recent contribution by Karen Cerulo provides an example of how traditional methods for capturing deliberative thinking can be recalibrated to measure the interplay of deliberative and nondeliberative thinking.[44] Drawing on the iterative reprocessing model, Cerulo has participants react to an emotionally powerful and socially significant sensory stimulus (namely, brand-name perfumes). While people are not directly aware of the sources of their immediate gut reactions to perfumes, they are reflectively aware of the second step in the iterative reprocessing cycle: their explicit reaction to the initial nondeliberative thought process. Thus, direct measurement methods used at the moment that people react to powerful stimuli can capture both the reflective element of initial reactions and subsequent attempts to reinforce or override the initial response. Using this strategy, Cerulo establishes strong race and class connotations associated with different fragrances. She also discovers attempts by some participants to reprocess these reactions using their own deliberative thinking—or the reflective reactions of other persons engaging in the same evaluative acts.

## Schemas

A key presumption of classic work in social and cognitive psychology is that people's understanding of a given domain is not piecemeal or disorganized. Instead, thinking is structured via underlying schemas internalized by people.[45] Measuring schemas from interviews, survey responses, and other material opens a window into how people's thinking is organized.[46] More specifically, we define *schemas* as a set of associations between concepts in memory acquired from experience and used for the purposes of categorization, recognition, and filling-in of missing information.[47]

The measurement of schemas in sociology was jump-started by a key contribution from Goldberg—a paper that, like Vaisey's before it, was notable for making both a theoretical and a methodological point.[48] Goldberg's methodological agenda is to encourage readers to see cultural schemas at a higher order of abstraction than specific beliefs, attitudes, or values.[49] That means that people whose attitudes are opposite from each other, in terms of their evaluation of a given set of objects, can share cultural schemas, thus organizing their thinking about a domain using the same overall framework. In other words, they can share the same basic facts about a social problem, even if they disagree vehemently about how to solve it.

In the United States, for example, both strict liberals and staunch conservatives strongly associate *big government* with *taxation*, and *taxation* with *redistribution* of wealth from the top income earners to the rest of the population. This network of associations forms their schema for thinking about government fiscal policy, despite the fact that liberals and conservatives disagree about how to deal with all three issues.[50] It is because this set of associations is *shared* that liberals and conservatives can argue about this domain in a coherent manner. Put differently, a person who associated big government with taxation but saw no link between the size of government and income redistribution would have trouble communicating with traditional liberals and conservatives, even if they shared the same evaluation of these elements.

Goldberg formalized the study of schematic thinking in such relational terms. To figure out whether two people organize their thinking about a domain in similar or dissimilar ways, he proposed that individual survey responses could be arrayed as a vector of schematic associations that people have among items in the survey. A criterion for similarity across survey responses can thus be conceived as a way of grouping people into classes based on shared schemas. Using the domain of musical taste and the General Social Survey's 1993 culture module as his empirical example, Goldberg argued that a measure that he referred to as *relationality* met these requirements.

The idea behind thinking about survey responses in relational terms is simple. The goal is to compare response vectors produced by each pair of respondents, while ignoring the directionality or valence of each response. For instance, let us say that three musical genres (e.g., opera, country, and rap) are rated by each person from -2 (strong dislike) to 2 (strong like), with zero being neutral. Suppose also that one respondent rates the genres -2, 0, and 2 (opera hater, country neutral, rap lover, respectively), and another rates the genres 2, 0, -2 (opera lover, country neutral, rap hater). Using Goldberg's measure, these two respondents can be classified as sharing the same schema as the absolute values of their conceptual oppositions to one another: $|(|-2| - |2|) + (|0| - |0|) + (|2| - |-2|)| = 0$. Perhaps the schema here is one distinguishing "high art" from "commercial music."[51]

Using this approach, the schematic distance between every pair of survey respondents can be computed. Standard clustering techniques can then be applied to the resulting distance matrix to elicit groups of people sharing the same schema. Class partitioning can then be validated by looking at within-class correlation networks between responses and by linking schema-classes to sociodemographics. Goldberg refers to this analytic sequence as Relational Class Analysis (RCA).[52]

This type of analysis has been used in a variety of settings to measure schemas in people, including political belief logics, cultural tastes, patterns of thought about markets and the economy, and cultural logics about the link between science and religion.[53] Although this approach has been applied across a wide range of topics, the extraction of schemas from survey responses is a technique in its relative infancy. A variety of validation and methodological challenges remain at each step, from the choice of distance criteria to the selection of the clustering technique and cluster validation. In addition, the substantive link between schematic class membership and patterns of action has been only a sporadic focus of research efforts thus far, and as such, this area is ripe for future development.[54]

# TALK

## History of Measurement

What can we learn about culture from listening to what people say? We must exercise caution here because people's accounts of their own behavior cannot always be trusted. As C. Wright Mills once quipped, "[T]he differing reasons . . . [people] give for their actions are not themselves without reason."[55] What we say is influenced by our shared understanding of the world and by our efforts to manage how we appear in front of others. Nonetheless, a critical set of voices within sociology has long advocated for spoken language as a crucial way to measure culture.

The study of culture in talk has been greatly influenced by the work of Ferdinand de Saussure,[56] who claimed the social world is *structured* by systems of meaning rooted in language. Rather than focusing on what words and gestures concretely denote, the structuralist philosophical tradition focused on the underlying system of organization that makes languages intelligible. According to this tradition, language transmits the social to the individual and serves as a mediator between lived reality and abstract ideas.

By the 1960s and 1970s, the structuralist tradition in linguistics came under attack by a diverse set of theoretical perspectives collectively referred to as *poststructuralism.* This challenge consisted of two main critiques: feminist theorists argued that nonmale perspectives had been overlooked, and political theorists (most notably Michel Foucault) argued that power is wielded through language.[57] What these critiques shared with structuralism, however, was a focus on language and speech as influential sites of meaning production and contestation.

Shortly after the heyday of poststructuralism in linguistics and philosophy, cultural sociologists turned to spoken language as a primary source of data on how shared systems of meaning are developed, transmitted, and internalized by individuals.[58] Meanwhile Jürgen Habermas was advocating for a focus on language and talk as the main sources of social integration in modern societies.[59] Collecting speech data from individuals—most often through in-depth interviews—became the preeminent method in sociology at the time. In an editorial in the *American Journal of Sociology*, a leading journal, Benney and Hughes proclaimed that "sociology has become the science of the interview."[60] In the early 1980s, Brenner estimated that ninety percent of social scientists used interview data.[61]

Yet debate continued about the link between talk and action.[62] The most recent iteration of this long-standing debate about whether, or when, sociologists should trust what people say was ignited by two ethnographers, Colin Jerolmack and Shamus Khan, in their article entitled "Talk Is Cheap." Summarizing decades of social scientific research and critically examining several influential interview studies in cultural sociology, Jerolmack and Khan concluded that "what people say is a poor predictor of what people do,"[63] though this point was disputed even as the article was published.[64]

This debate is orthogonal to our purposes here; we are concerned with how to measure culture in thought, talk, and action, not how one type of observation predicts another. We describe how we think sociologists can best measure how culture shapes action in the next section. Our view is that the best way to measure culture via talk is to focus on elements of culture for which a connection to observed behavior is not even of interest. Instead, the cultural elements best expressed via talk are representations of planned or idealized patterns of action. In these scenarios, rather than being a weak proxy for what people do, *what people say* is the whole point of the matter.

### Measuring What People Say

Listening to what people say is an ideal method for measuring two types of culture in individuals. The first type is *aims*—an umbrella term encompassing what we strive to do (our ambitions), who we want to become (our ideals), and what we hope will happen to us (our desires). The second type is collective *narratives*—stories that people tell to develop a common understanding about the social world or to make sense of important events. These are not the only two types of culture that can be measured by focusing on what people say as a source of data. Indeed, speech is a fundamental component of interactions *among* people, and thus talk will show up again in chapter 3, which discusses how sociologists can measure culture in interactions. However, aims and narratives can be captured in traditional interview settings because the analytic focus is on the organization of meaning in speech—and not necessarily the presumed linkage of interview responses to unobserved patterns of action.

*Aims*

Talk is ideal for measuring aims for precisely the same reasons that scholars have critiqued the use of talk to measure culture more broadly. Because the futures we imagine and the things we strive to achieve are not directly observable in present actions, the study of how culture influences people's aims is not subject to what Jerolmack and Khan refer to as the "attitudinal fallacy"—the misconception that people reliably tell us about what they do.[65] Only the most agentic theory of social action would posit that people's actions are accurate indications of what they want to accomplish or who they want to be. If we know what people want, we can sometimes discern patterned differences in subsequent outcomes on the aggregate level; conversely, observing differences in outcomes does not lend much insight into what people want.[66] Instead, the link between our aims and our actions is often disrupted by both real and perceived structural barriers, as well as by the inconsistency of our energy and focus.[67] This matters because people's success or failure to achieve their aims affects their subjective experience of their romantic relationships, their satisfaction with their careers, and their sense of personal identity more broadly.[68]

Recording what people say is ideal for learning about how culture influences people's aims because ambitions, ideals, and desires are located firmly (though not solely) on the discursive, intentional, and conscious side of cognition. As Ann Mische writes, "Even if we engage in automatic cognition 'most of the time,' we need to pay attention to the potentially important role played by periods in which people do stop and think projectively—and yes, critically and deliberately—about what might . . . happen in the future."[69] In other words, aims reflect deliberate attempts at self-fashioning. People are also told what to strive for, both explicitly and implicitly, through interactions with institutions such as schools and the media. From a young age, people are encouraged by school curricula and educational materials to choose a career goal that best represents who they are, and to strive for it with a singular focus.[70] The self-help industry encourages us to contemplate imagined futures so that we can jump-start more efficacious and triumphant versions of ourselves.[71]

How can we use our observations of what people say to better understand how culture shapes what they strive for? Scholars attempting to do this are confronted by two main challenges. First, aspirations are by definition unrealized. Because aspirations have not yet happened—and perhaps never will—they can be difficult to measure. Second, it is difficult to link what individuals say about their imagined futures to cultural representations of success. Next, we briefly introduce two recent studies that use in-depth interviewing to examine idealized futures as a site for cultural theorizing and that work through these challenges in innovative ways.

In a pathbreaking book, *Living the Drama*, David Harding tackled the challenge of how to elicit detailed responses about the aspirations of young men by inserting a series of structured mini-surveys into his otherwise unstructured in-depth interviews.[72] Interviewing sixty African American boys in Boston, Harding borrowed questions from the National Longitudinal Survey of Adolescent Health to solicit respondents' educational aims in terms that could easily be compared with one another. He then asked a series of follow-up questions to move beyond these simple statements and gain a richer understanding of their imagined futures—how important these goals were to them, how informed they were about potential pathways, what they pictured when they imagined a successful person, and whom they viewed as role models in their community.

This approach allowed Harding to uncover a key cultural mechanism: the level of heterogeneity of cultural models that youth are confronted with in a particular context. In poor neighborhoods, boys are exposed to multiple and contradictory models of what success looks like. As a result, they frequently jump from one model to another and cannot construct a linear path toward a successful future. In contrast, youth in more advantaged neighborhoods are exposed to a smaller and more congruent set of ideas about what it means to be successful. These young men therefore articulate more coherent future goals.

In her work among secondary school students in rural Malawi, Margaret Frye confronted the second methodological challenge: how to link discussions of individual-level aims to culture.[73] She proceeded in two steps. First, she asked people to talk about their aspirations, as well as to reflect on the obstacles standing in their way. Paradoxically, she found that her interviewees almost unfailingly insisted that their chances of success hinged primarily on their own behavior and determination—even as they described external circumstances that made their goals almost impossible to achieve. In a second step, Frye gathered newspaper articles, school curricula, and promotional materials from nongovernmental organizations (NGOs) representing youth striving for ambitious future goals in order to construct a cultural model of educational success reflected in these documents. By *pivoting* from the talk produced by students to the cultural objects distributed to them, Frye was able to highlight the shared cultural meanings undergirding the students' imagined futures. Because these cultural materials so heavily emphasized future optimism, future aspirations were essential to the students' self-identities, even as they recognized that this optimism was unfounded. Expressing future optimism allowed students to claim a moral identity of "one who aspires."[74]

## Stories and Narratives

Listening to what people say is also ideal for identifying how the stories that they tell about our social worlds are created. These stories—often referred to as "collective narratives"—are typically defined in opposition to circumstances or actual experiences.[75] As Charles Tilly writes, "[T]he actual causal structure of social processes . . . usually contradicts the logical and causal structure of standard stories."[76] Unlike the randomness of real-life experiences, narratives contain sequences of events that are "emplotted": they are knit together according to a morally consistent logic.[77] Eschewing the multidimensionality of real people, collective narratives involve essentialized stock characters such as hapless victims or tragic heroes.[78] The difference between what people say and what happened is not a problem to be overcome when examining collective narratives—instead, it is an outcome of interest.

In studying collective narratives, cultural sociologists attempt to identify the reinterpretation of reality as it occurs through the act of narration.[79] These retellings are prominent during times of personal crisis or rapid cultural change—as sociologist Francesca Polletta writes, "[W]e turn to narrative to comprehend changes that shatter our routines and threaten our sense of self."[80] Such retellings can also be observed when individuals are asked to describe themselves to others outside their social communities. Lena and Lindemann[81] observe that professionals working in the arts field who graduated from art programs refuse to identify themselves as "artists," because within the artistic community, this term is often used to connote honor or social roles rather than an occupational category. Yet these narrative retellings rarely unfold in full during everyday life interactions: because telling a story takes longer than other kinds of conversational offerings, people are unlikely to launch into narrative mode unless they are implicitly given permission to do so.[82] As a result, the in-depth interview, along with other instances where the analyst is observing an individual talking at length, is an ideal format for examining collective narratives.

What can a focus on collective narratives—as observed through talk—tell us about culture? First, collective narratives can provide a strategic way to measure what Gabriel Abend[83] terms the "moral background": which topics can be evaluated in moral terms, and which cannot. This is because collective narratives reveal how individuals connect particular experiences with more general normative principles. Second, researchers can examine the misalignments between cultural understandings and external conditions when narratives break down—or contradict themselves—and observe how people respond to these discrepancies.[84] Third, collective narratives enable researchers to gain insight into which characters and which sequences of events are most powerful and influential in context, by focusing on different accounts of the same event—not unlike the Akira Kurosawa film *Rashomon*.[85] Once identified through talk, narratives can be assessed in this way in terms of whether and when they drive people to action.[86]

Yet scholars who study stories to understand culture face two unique challenges. Because narratives are composed of standard plot structures and stock characters and adhere to conventional stylistic genres, it is often hard to disentangle how culture is transmitted through each of these elements.[87] Second, it is difficult to study *changes* in the relationship between the stories we tell and the worlds we live in—for example, moments when narratives become less salient due to events that reveal their inaccuracy and undermine their resonance.[88]

In their analysis of how college students interpret narratives about campus sexual assault, Polletta and her collaborators tackle the first empirical challenge: how to disentangle the effects of *plot* from those of *character*.[89] Conventions of plot shape our expectations for how the story will end through normative assumptions about what "usually happens," whereas conventions of character shape expectations about how people "normally behave." To examine how these two types of assumptions shape how people respond to stories, Polletta and her colleagues wrote a series of stories about campus sexual assault that conform to different conventional plot structures (e.g., heroic versus tragic). The stories all contained the same biographical information about the protagonist (a female college student who attends a party with her friends and drinks enough to feel impaired, but not intoxicated), but in each version, she is given different personality traits. Through sharing these stories with students during focus group discussions,[90] the authors found that people usually use plot to make sense of stories *unless* the main character's description does

not fit with dominant status expectations. When the female protagonist was assertive and confident, for example, respondents
interpreted the stories based on gender norms rather than the
conventions of the story's plot structure. This study thus explains
how cultural expectations are transmitted through plot versus
character, as well as how these different elements influence how
stories are understood by others.

Eva Rosen tackles the second empirical challenge (how to examine changes in the congruence between collective narratives and
people's lived experience) through an analysis of the stories that
people tell about their neighborhoods.[91] Her research includes
in-depth interviews about people's responses to neighborhood
violence, as well as ethnography.[92] Rosen finds that narratives
allow people living in poor and crime-ridden neighborhoods to
develop a sense of belonging and stability in the face of unsafe
conditions—until a violent event shatters their narrative of how
a person can survive in their neighborhood. In these cases of narrative rupture, residents often move to similar neighborhoods,
restoring a narrative of safety, even if they don't achieve upward
mobility. This combination of methods allows her to pivot from
what people say to what they do, and also to develop a theory of
the relationship between narrative and behavior.

Hijab

## ACTION

### *History of Measurement*

Even though practices were the last fundamental human capacity to be incorporated into the culture tent, they are as analytically and empirically consequential as thinking and talk. Indeed,
the rise of "practice theory" and the revival of interest in the

American pragmatist tradition of social theory in recent years have brought renewed attention to measuring culture in action.[93] Rather than viewing actions as manifestations of high-level ideas or values—or as disembodied elements embedded within a semiotic or discursive code—scholars argue that practices can carry cultural meaning in their own right.[94]

But at the risk of refrain: measuring practices in people is not without its challenges. In contrast to most elements intuitively thought of as cultural and available via self-reporting or structured linguistic records, it is unrealistic to expect that people will have pristine reflexive access into the mechanisms governing their practices.[95] As Michael Polanyi once observed, seemingly simple practices such as riding a bicycle presuppose a tremendous amount of knowledge by a person that would take a long time to articulate.[96] Yet people ride bikes without awareness of the large store of knowledge that the practice presupposes. In Polanyi's words, practices are rooted in "tacit" rather than explicit knowledge.[97] That is, practices are encoded in a format that is difficult—if not impossible—to redescribe through explicit statements and instructions.[98] This is why self-reporting strategies are poor tools to measure practices in people. While self-reports provide (partial) perspectives "on" action, the effective study of practice requires more direct observation of people "in" action.

Practice also has a nonarbitrary (and, some would say, fundamental) relationship to the human body and its environment.[99] Practices are inherently embodied; linguistic elements are not. This represents a crucial difference. Any strategy for measuring practices requires access to people in natural settings where they engage with other persons and objects. So-called default measurement settings—such as lab experiments or the interview—are less effective precisely because people are not observed interacting, practicing a craft, using tools, and so on.[100] The status of practices as being irreducible to sayings—coupled with their embodied and situated nature—narrows the suite of measurement strategies that make them accessible to the analyst.

## *Measuring What People Do*

We argue that two families of methods are best suited to measure culture *as* practice in people. The first, the "experience-near" approach, is participant observation.[101] This is perhaps the oldest method for measuring culture in people in the social sciences.[102] This strategy was revived around the late 1990s and early 2000s by sociologists inspired by the "practice turn" and Bourdieu's[103] emphasis on the fundamental embodiment of cultural patterns. Sociologist Loïc Wacquant, an early and forceful proponent of this approach, describes the "culture" of the boxing gym he studied by noting that it

> is not made up of a finite sum of discrete information, of notions that can be transmitted by words and normative models that would exist independently of their application. Rather it is formed of a diffuse complex of postures and . . . gestures that . . . exist in a sense only in action.[104]

Measuring culture as practice in people, therefore, sometimes requires that the people doing the measurement themselves become embodied "participants" in the milieu by trying to acquire the relevant practices.[105] By experiencing the process of learning new practices, each person doing the measurement becomes one of the people on which practices are captured.

The second strategy to measure action in people is composed of a more recent suite of techniques for the passive and unobtrusive recording of behavioral traces. This includes data extracted from online social media platforms, from portable computing and communication devices (e.g., tablets, laptops, smartphones), as well as smartwatches and other wearable devices.[106] These platforms and devices can function as remote mobile sensors, generating streams of time-stamped event data on rates of social interaction (e.g., via voice calls, texts, and other digital channels), patterns of spatial mobility, sleep habits, and physical activity, among other behavioral and social traces. Although not without significant limitations, which we discuss later in this book, these methods can provide at least partial windows into people's practices.

## *Acquisition of New Practices*

On the "experience-near" end of this continuum, several sociologists have used participant ethnography to gain an intuitive and personal understanding of what it means to acquire new practices.[107] By working alongside others to develop the skills and master the routines and bodily dispositions involved in a trade or activity, this methodological strategy foregrounds the embodied nature of culture and allows the reader to observe how people come to adopt ways of moving and acting that appear natural in a given social world. We identify two major sources of variation in this body of work. The first is whether the set of practices are *embedded in formal organizations* or are *adopted independently by autonomous actors*. The second is the extent to which the researcher enters the scene as an *insider*, with the same background assumptions, bodily dispositions, and social conventions as the people whom they study; or as an *outsider*, approaching the scene with a greater sense of unfamiliarity and confusion than typical practitioners.

Next, we profile three studies occupying different positions vis-à-vis these two sources of variation. These positions in turn create different but related methodological challenges. The first challenge—which is particularly vexing for researchers who enter their study settings as outsiders—is how to isolate practice from discourse. How do we link action with culture without asking people to reflect on their behavior, or without observing stated norms and expectations? The second challenge—which is particularly germane to those investigating communities they are more familiar with—is how to adopt a long-term perspective on culture and action, and how to connect practices observed in one moment to more enduring systems of movement and behavior that people develop over the course of their lives. Such a long-term perspective requires a sense of detachment and objectivity that can be difficult for insiders to achieve. The third challenge—which is particularly salient for researchers studying autonomous practices outside organizational structures—is how to think about practices when they are both cultivated and enacted in private, outside cohesive communities or organizational settings.

The now-canonical example of using participant ethnography to examine the acquisition of new practices is Wacquant's account of how he learned to be a boxer.[108] He tackles the methodological challenge of how to investigate bodily movement as a sociocultural process—how to isolate what people do from what they say or think. Wacquant highlights how his unfamiliarity with boxing and his outsider status in the gym—his being "a perfect novice"—enabled him to make connections between his embodied experience of learning to box and the moral culture of the gym where he learned.[109]

The set of practices that Wacquant investigates are embedded in the formal organization of the boxing gym—with its strict regimens for training and moral expectations placed on all members.

Through an immersive participant ethnography involving over two-and-a-half years of daily practice in the gym, Wacquant documents how his own body and the bodies of other gym members moved during individual practice, sparring, and competition. These patterned movements are themselves a form of culture: shared routines and habitual responses that convey unspoken meaning to fellow boxers. By taking the reader through specific episodes in painstaking detail, Wacquant reproduces the sensations of his practice: the sounds and smells of the gym, the fatigue in his muscles, and how his arm movements during punches slowly became more purposeful and less tentative.

Rather than observing other people's actions and interactions, he "deploy[s] the body as [a] tool of inquiry and vector of knowledge." Wacquant shows how boxing's structured postures and movements, as well as the strict discipline of practice, comprise a shared moral vocabulary for gym members—one that is primarily enacted, not articulated. As he later wrote, his account is a sociology "not *of* the body . . . but *from* the body."[110] This account develops a theory of how culture can "exist in a sense only in action, and in the traces that this action leaves within (and upon) bodies."[111]

Matthew Desmond's book on wildland firefighting offers a contrast to Wacquant's account of the boxing gym, in terms of the researchers' relationships with their study sites.[112] While Wacquant entered the gym as a novice and cultural outsider, Desmond capitalized upon his previous experience fighting wildfires and his shared upbringing with the people he is studying. This insider status allowed Desmond to investigate how practices can simultaneously be *novel* (gained through formal, organizationally mediated activities), and *habitual* (incorporated from early childhood through routine experiences).

Building on the work of Bourdieu, cultural sociologists have theorized how culture shapes what people do through two

related, but distinct, concepts: _specific habitus_, or the development of highly specialized embodied knowledge about a particular practice; and _general habitus_, or the deeper dispositions
and habits that develop slowly over time and that people carry
with them from their past. Desmond sought to examine how
these two types of culture interact during crises, such as when
firefighters must work together quickly to contain the threat of a
wildfire. Methodologically, he pivots between a deep analysis of
his coworkers' upbringing—gleaned primarily through in-depth
interviews—and an analysis of how team members come to
effectively fight fires together—obtained via participant ethnography. The ethnography focuses on how the team members establish community, train and discipline one another, and coordinate
their actions during times of crisis. As he traced the practices and
routines that he observed backward in time, Desmond also draws
heavily from his own embodied experience: "My body became a
fieldnote, for in order to comprehend the contours of the wildland firefighting habitus as deeply as possible, I had to feel it
growing inside of me."[113] What people do when they fight forest
fires is shaped by how they came to be there in the first place,
Desmond argues. His work shows that firefighters developed a
cohesive response to a major threat not because of the formal
training they received from the forest service but because of their
similar upbringing. "As country boys," Desmond writes, "they
came to the organization already ready to fight fire . . . with nearly
instinctive proficiency."[114] Desmond's analysis thus addresses the
second challenge—how to connect fleeting patterns of action to
the long-term acquisition of habits that accrue throughout the
life course.

Both Wacquant and Desmond highlight the intense social
bonds between the people they study and the formal organizational structures in which these people are embedded as crucial to

the acquisition of shared practices. Through her analysis of fashion modeling, Ashley Mears addresses the third methodological challenge: how to study people's adoption of a common set of practices and bodily dispositions when they are working on their own, outside stable communities and formal training systems.[115]

Mears approaches her setting as an insider, having previously worked in the modeling industry. And yet her account lacks the natural fluency and social comfort of Desmond's, due to the autonomous and individual nature of modeling. The social interactions that Mears describes between models and others in the industry—bookers, agents, photographers, and clients—are fleeting, hierarchical, and glaringly impersonal. Agents advise them to achieve a specific bodily measurement, but do not explain how to do so. Models spend hours standing in line, only to be quickly dismissed by a client for being "just not right." Designers poke models with pins without acknowledging they are humans and not mannequins. Yet the "look" that models strive to achieve is *cultural*—as Mears writes, "[I]t represents not just a person or an individual beauty but also a whole system of knowledge and relations among people."[116]

How do models gain a shared set of behavioral norms and bodily manipulations within this anomic system? To answer this question, Mears spent two-and-a-half years as a fashion model, documenting all her interactions and her own efforts to transform her body to achieve a more desirable look. To place these intensely personal experiences within a broader social system, she also interviewed people occupying various social positions within the industry: bookers, clients, agents, and other models, all of whom achieved differing levels of professional success. Moving among these various perspectives, Mears shows how models learn new practices passively, via having others objectify them. Again and again, people physically manipulate their bodies to get a better angle, apply makeup or cosmetics to minimize their flaws, and fabricate their bodily measurements and ages on industry documents to make them seem more desirable. Mears describes how "these daily confrontations with objectification . . . form a set of work routines and expectations through which models learn to embody the 'right' look or, at least, to stay beyond the parameters of the 'wrong' look."[117] This research shows how the acquisition of new practices can occur in *social situations* when people are left to figure out on their own what they are expected to do.

## Microactions

When measuring culture via observing what people do, it is not always necessary for a human to make the observations. Actions can be specified at different levels of description. For instance, a person sitting in front of a computer might be "trying to get an academic job," "writing a book," "typing," or "tapping keyboard keys with their fingers at a fast rate."[118] These descriptors would cover the same pattern of bodily movements, but would differ in terms of how they fit into a larger story. Human observers would most likely use the first three descriptions depending on context, and would be unlikely—unless they were obstreperous or joking—to use the last. This is because it is easier to fit action described at a higher level into a broader meaning framework, such as "I need to get tenure to advance my academic career," featuring elements discussed here with thinking and talk, such as beliefs, values, frames, narratives, or aims. [119]

While novel data collection techniques based on unobtrusive monitoring can capture all kinds of action patterns, we argue they are best positioned to measure culture in people as it manifests itself in *microactions*. Other forms of big data, especially those geared toward archiving text, are better suited for measuring culture as discourse in larger institutional fields in partial independence from people (see chapter 3).

Capturing microactions presents important, but not insurmountable, challenges for the sociological observer. The reason is that microactions are lines of activity that occur at very restricted temporal scales. Microactions can thus accumulate rapidly, with as many as hundreds or thousands occurring within a span of a few hours. Microactions may also be so ingrained as habits that the person being observed might not have the ability to articulate them either. As such, not even the most adept or well-trained participant observer would be likely to capture or "code" them.

Even as they so often go unnoticed, microactions can aggregate up to form larger social patterns that are of interest to cultural sociologists. They represent "micro" versions of patterns of behavior used to accomplish pragmatic goals of interest to sociologists, such as evaluation, boundary drawing, categorization, decision-making, and affiliation. Therefore, while the unit of measurement is still the person, the relevant microactions have an inherent interactional component because they are usually directed at other people, and as such are *social* microactions.[120]

How have sociologists begun to meet this observational challenge? Because microactions are produced in real time, unobtrusive monitoring emerges as the best way to capture cultural processes revealed via microactions in people, as once anticipated by Randall Collins.[121] This monitoring can be done either with the help of increasingly available *wearable* devices, such as smartphones, fitness devices, microphones, and skin-conductance devices, or by exploiting traces of microactions left behind in online platforms.[122] Next, we present recent examples of both approaches.

McFarland, Jurafsky, and Rawlings set out to study how the experience of "clicking" with a prospective romantic partner happens in real-life courtship situations.[123] To do so, they equipped 110 individuals (graduate students at an elite West Coast university) with small audio recorders worn on a shoulder sash and asked them to participate in 1,000 four-minute "speed dates." The data were augmented with pre- and post-surveys, and the outcomes amounted to a subjective assessment of having clicked with the discussion partner. They drew upon Collins's theory of interaction ritual, which emphasizes microactions associated with rhythmic entrainment, mimicry, and tone of voice as signaling either successful or unsuccessful solidarity-producing communication events.[124]

The relevance of the McFarland et al. study for measuring culture is that they could capture a variety of microactions by extracting sonic features such as pitch, "energy" (loudness), and duration from the digital sound file of each participant's conversation. They also captured the number of words emitted per second and such paralinguistic cues as laughter and interruptions. They find that these features help predict clicking and willingness to date, adjusting for differences in actor-level attributes and sociolinguistic aspects of the conversation (e.g., interruptions, self-markers, hedges, etc.), and that these patterns (e.g., using loudness to signal excitement) differ systematically between men and women.)

Ingram and Morris followed a similar strategy to find out whether people would actually "mix," or engage in discussion with each other, at cocktail parties.[125] They invited approximately 260 managers who were taking part in an Executive MBA program at an elite New York City business school to attend an informal gathering described as a "mixer" (120 accepted the invitation, and 92 showed up). The invitation explained that participants were expected to "[a]ct normally. Talk to whomever you want to, while enjoying food and drinks."[126] To capture who interacted with whom unobtrusively, they equipped each person with a wearable device developed at the Massachusetts Institute of Technology (MIT) Media Lab, which was the size of a large smartphone. Each wearable device recorded when it was in relative proximity to the other ones for at least one minute. The relevant microaction was mixing. Premixer networks and other individual attributes were measured prior to the event.

Ingram and Morris found that there was much less behavioral mixing than would be expected, given participants' reflexive statements about trying to meet new people. About ninety-five percent of attendees expressed the premixer goal of meeting and interacting with new people. Premixer rates of interaction and positive feelings predicted who interacted at the mixer (and how long they stayed in proximity), though previous negative feelings had no effect. Notably, however, sociodemographic homophily did not predict who interacted with whom. The only attribute predicting interaction at the mixer was having the same gender, although this effect declined over time. Finally, participants who had similar levels of physical attractiveness were more likely to interact at the mixer, and this effect increased over the duration of the event. Ingram and Morris's study shows how microactions relevant to the construction of social networks can be captured unobtrusively, yielding sometimes compatible, but at other times surprising, results compared to direct ways of measuring sociability.

Finally, a study by Kevin Lewis decomposes the often-studied process of mate choice and associated outcomes, such as romantic homophily (preference for sociodemographically similar others), into its constituent microactions using digital footprints left behind on an online dating platform.[127] He used data from self-described "straight" and "single" active users on the site during a three-month period in 2010, who lived in the New York City area. The outcome considered by Lewis was sending messages via the site's electronic messaging platforms to others who had piqued their interest. He also measured the number of replies to these messages. These represent microactions constitutive of the early stage of relationship formation in heterosexual romantic links.

In contrast to Ingram and Morris's results, Lewis finds strong homophily, especially for prospective dates of the same race. There are also fairly strong effects for messaging others in similar income brackets and the same religious background. Matching on education turns out to be spurious, a by-product of matching on the aforementioned dimensions. Users also display very strong preferences for extending initial feelers to same-occupation others—an effect that dwarfs that of other sociodemographic similarities. In addition, a variety of behaviors and attitudes indicative of lifestyle matching (e.g., smoking, views about dogs, desire to have children) also predict who is selected as an initial communication partner.)

Once these factors are considered, the gross effect of most sociodemographic characteristics is attenuated. Lewis's measurement approach is useful because it allows us to see patterns usually described in terms of broad-brush outcomes (e.g., romantic or marital "homogamy") play out at the initial stages of communicative microactions, largely reproducing large-scale patterns of division and segregation.

## CONCLUSION

This chapter has set out to show how culture can be measured by observing people. Our discussion was not about a set of cultural concepts themselves, but rather around the things that we can observe about a person—their *thought*, *talk*, and *action*. This focus allows measurement choices and considerations to remain at the forefront of our discussion. In each case that we examined, we highlighted the methodological challenges that researchers confront when observing people, and we also introduced some exemplary research that shows how scholars can confront these challenges.

This chapter's structure also has some drawbacks. We neglected strategies to measure some important cultural phenomena that can be observed in people—most notably emotions and feelings.[128] Particularly egregious was our omission of Arlie Hochschild's field-defining work, which showed that how people experience and express their emotions are shaped by "feeling rules" that circulate within institutional cultures, such as airlines.[129] More recently, sociologist Eva Illouz[130] has foregrounded the extent to which emotions are produced by broader cultural trends, such as the representation and marketing of romantic love. We also neglected more complex cultural constructs that encompass multiple types of human capacities. These include identities, which are constructed in both thought and talk and which both reflect and drive our actions; as well as categorization processes like racial attribution and stereotypes, which shape how we perceive the world.[131] Finally, while we focused on the content of what people say, there is also a rich body of literature that examines contextual variation in how people talk, and specifically how they change their way of speaking in relation to audiences and related identity concerns (known as "code switching").[132]

### Looking Ahead

As noted at the outset, this chapter has focused on measuring culture in people. This requires a certain degree of analytic bracketing of people's embeddedness in broader contexts. When sociologists think of how people are embedded in these more encompassing structures, they generally think about individuals' placement in relation to other people, thus focusing on interactions, social networks, and other mesolevel structures. Another way of thinking about how people are linked to larger macrolevels is to see them as parts of larger networks of discursive meanings, or as part of institutional fields with relatively long histories and their mechanisms of reproduction. These are prime sites for measuring culture above and beyond people, and we thus return to these levels of analysis in chapters 2 and 3. Yet, to paraphrase French social theorist Bruno Latour, people are embedded in larger social and interactional contexts that include a world of objects.[133] The questions of what an object is and how culture is embodied in objects pose important problems for the project of measuring culture. The next chapter turns to this challenge and offers some promising solutions.

# 2

## MEASURING CULTURE IN OBJECTS

Gucci's black balaclava sweater was all over the news, and not for the reasons its designers intended. The sweater's neck featured a cutout for the mouth of its wearer, outlined in bright red lips against opaque black wool. The pale model donning the high-fashion blackface amplified the offending signal. François-Henri Pinault, Gucci's chief executive officer, apologized and pulled the sweater from store shelves. Brief history lessons were provided on the blackface makeup used to humiliate African Americans for the entertainment of whites in the 1830s. The object and the histories it stirred, Pinault stated, did not reflect the company's commitment to diversity. Gucci's *mea culpa* followed Prada's December rollout (and rollback) of black caricatures that the company's spokesman insisted were not meant to be racist, though they resembled the characters in the 1899 children's book *The Story of Little Black Sambo*, written when the violent backlash to the emancipation of black slaves was at its height.

As this example demonstrates, cultural objects can carry great social and political significance. But as the example equally illustrates, there can be conflicts and other differences over how we interpret objects' meanings. What gave this object, but not others with similar shapes and color schemes, the cultural power to cause racial trouble? How were the object's characteristics tied to particular collective identities, and how might their salience be weighed? Measuring and understanding how multiple, divergent meanings emerge are essential tasks for cultural sociology.

Our focus in this chapter is far-ranging. We begin with clothes by way of example to help illuminate what we mean by "an object," as well as what it means to measure an object. Measuring "clothes" or even "fashion" is as complex a topic as any.[1] What makes a single piece of clothing worthy of praise or repudiation? What do clothes' meanings say about human dignity, social inclusion, or racial hatred? And, more generally, how do we, as social scientists, study objects' meanings? What makes these meanings, and their objects, cultural? Starting from seemingly mundane objects, as these questions show, leads us to wide and deep sociological questions.

To measure meaning through objects poses a particular challenge for sociologists: the problem of interpretation. Unlike literature scholars or art critics, sociologists have an allergy to scholars assigning meaning to objects. If we did, our noncultural sociologist fellows would deem our work too subjective, and therefore illegitimate. More important, speaking *for* objects is also an issue within cultural sociology. Given that we recognize objects as polyvocal (or multivalent), assigning meaning to an object does violence to our data because it makes objects appear more determined than they really are. It is for this reason that Wolff argued that sociologists of culture are "inhibited": a fear of subjectivity has led us to disengage from objects' content.[2] Instead, we have preferred to measure *people* and *their* interpretations of objects, principally using their interpretations to understand how meaning-making is shaped by participation in groups. This renders objects as mere Rorschach-like inkblots, reflecting people's shared understandings of the world.[3] Here, we offer a different path—one that takes objects seriously, and their form, content, and qualities as measurable and essential to theorizing meaning.

In this chapter, we provide some starting points for such inquiries. To that end, this chapter is not organized around the concepts that sociologists use to theorize the relationship between culture and objects, such as commemoration, authenticity, iconicity, or boundary objects. Instead, we discuss the measurement of cultural meaning along three dimensions. First, we begin with techniques that have been used to measure observable qualities of objects, such as their color, weight, height, depth, durability, tactility, and sound. These material qualities of objects are what distinguish and differentiate them from other objects and allow us to identify and categorize them. Second, much like living things, objects have a temporal life cycle. At the simplest level, they have stages of production and consumption. Someone produces an object, and another person consumes and discards it, applying meaningful interpretations during this process. Finally, objects are talked about, acted on, and in some cases they themselves act. Objects have what we could think of as properties such that they themselves are actors in the world. Like other active agents, objects shape human behavior.[4]

But let's return to where we started: clothes. One of our first considerations in measuring objects should be to define the qualities of the objects themselves. Qualities of objects allow us to distinguish between them. How is a sweatshirt different from a sweater? How is a suit that is black different from a suit that is pink? People interact with other objects in the production and reception of clothing. When producing clothes, people use computers and pencils to design garments, machines to manufacture them, and cameras and printing presses to promote their existence. Consumers utilize computers, televisions, and print media to familiarize themselves with various products, visit glassed-in storefronts to observe what garments are for sale, purchase clothing using credit cards and cash, and store them on shelves and closets before and after use. Fashion is a system that depends upon multiple objects to facilitate production, distribution, and consumption. Each of these objects is potentially relevant to the study of culture: collective understandings of trends and technical knowledge about materials constrain what garments are made, and thus, what kind of garments we can use to visually display our identity. In parallel, collective understandings of the ways that our identities can be displayed through fashion enable the creation of particular garments. In fact, cultural systems help us determine if what we are observing is a fashion or clothing object at all—we might decide the object is instead garbage, a joke, or a piece of art to be exhibited in museums. Herein we see the material, temporal, and action-oriented properties of fashion objects.

Put differently, measuring culture through objects provides us with a way to get at some of the most pressing theoretical and empirical questions in the sociology of culture because objects are immediately observable. Objects are "explicit" or "public" parts of culture.[5] In objects, culture is externalized and materially embedded. Once material, objects stabilize, or at least canalize, human action. Objects can therefore tell us a great deal about culture and are central to the transmission of culture. And, more practically, as objects are removed from the flow of action and interaction, they are often easier to observe than the people and organizations that produced them. However, one danger of studying objects is that they appear stable in their meaning, so scholars might affix a certainty to the meaning of objects that is not in fact there. This is a measurement challenge, in that objects do not carry meaning, but rather *potential* meanings. We can take stock of objects' qualities or the presence and distribution of particular interpretations of those qualities, but qualities and interpretations are not the same thing. Instead, meaning emerges in the production and consumption of objects—when objects are put to use.

How, then, do objects act in the world? Our approach to this question affects how we measure objects. Often cultural sociologists treat objects as representations or symbols of things out in the world. We then constrain our measurement of objects to what they denote or connote. When we do this, there is the danger of treating objects as too stable or static in their meaning—to confuse the object with the sign it embodies. We should be wary of assuming that objects are one-to-one facsimiles of ideas or things out in the world, or the culture in people's heads.[6] Objects vary in how exact they are in their representation. When objects are identified as representations, they necessarily summarize and alter the idea or thing they represent. When making a representation, people select elements to emphasize while ignoring others, arrange elements in different ways, and translate elements from one medium to another.[7] The features of an object that are present (and absent) and the multiple *denotative* features of that object are heuristically distinct, and any presumptive alignment between them is a contingency that we can and must establish through empirical investigation. The point here is that when we seek to measure an object, we should be attentive to what it means, but we cannot do so without considering what elements get represented (and what gets lost), how they are represented, and the consequences of those representations. Indeed, sometimes the impetus to assess meaning immediately can foreclose the empirical strategies that deepen and validate our interpretive analyses.

Bruno Latour shifts our attention away from objects as totemic representations or nodes in a meaning system in order to consider how cultural objects are consequential in lines of causation.[8] The question becomes less about what an object represents and more about what an object *does*. We require measures that observe how people put objects to work and how objects make certain kinds of work possible. In addition to measures of objects as representations, we need strategies to measure objects as actants in our theories of culture in action.[9] If Latour is right that objects are the "missing masses" of our social explanations, improving our measurement of objects (and of objects in action) will make cultural theories of action better. To do so, sociologists need to measure objects at different moments in time and take objects on their own terms. But first, what exactly *is* an object?

## WHAT IS AN OBJECT?

Wendy Griswold, a pioneering sociologist of culture, offers a useful definition of a cultural object in her book on renaissance revivals.[10] Objects, she states, are "shared significance in form."  This concise definition encompasses two arguments. First, the meanings that we attach to form must be socially shared, rather  than personal and idiosyncratic. The *sharing* of significance is what makes it cultural. In this sense, cultural objects exist in people's heads and in communicative action as the shared meanings they associate with things in the world. Second, people attach  meaning to *form*. Importantly, when Griswold refers to form, she means a material instantiation in the world. Even more abstract cultural objects such as a play or a ballet performance must be "perceptible."[11] In other words, they have material qualities; even so-called virtual or digital objects like streaming music, which people may imagine are not physical, are perceptible. Ideas must be externalized in material form—whether speech or electronic ones (1s) and zeros (0s)—and those material qualities matter in their diffusion and interpretation.

To measure a cultural object, it must be *durable*. Objects vary in their durability. Carvings in stone are immune to destruction by many means; paper objects, in comparison, are quite easy to destroy. Objects can be joined together when they offer more-or-less-durable forms of representing the same content— a dance performance described in a diary or captured on photographic paper may be less durable than a digital video image stored on three independent hard drives. In cases like this, the temptation may be to treat the diary, the photograph, and the digital video as different media in which the same "thing" is fixed. But as we will demonstrate in this chapter, taking the measurement of objects seriously means recognizing that the alignment of this performance's *meaning* across various media is contingent upon social action.

Also, as a shared significance in form, the study of objects relies on *perception*—evaluating the presence and absence of objects and, secondarily, of their other qualities. Perception, in turn, is mediated through our senses, meaning that measurement operates through subjective experience and bodily capacities, not unlike those described in the previous chapter. More than any other sense, sociologists rely on vision as the medium of measurement, but seeing is itself a socially shaped activity. How people divide the color spectrum is mediated both by culturally specific categories (e.g., where to draw the line between green and yellow) and biological faculties (e.g., vision acuity and capacity—color blindness being another position on a spectrum of color-perceptive capacities).[12] To measure cultural objects, then, analysts must consider whether they are perceiving the same object as the group they seek to understand.

Lastly, by way of introductory remarks, it may make sense to think of measures of the object *in situ*. This line of thinking is inspired by the work of anthropologist Mary Douglas, who famously argued that the definition of *dirt* is that it is matter out of place. Shoes are not "dirty" in and of themselves, but they may become so when they are placed where they do not belong—such as on a dinner table.[13] According to Douglas, objects cannot be defined absent such context. Concretely, we cannot know if we have identified a "dirty" object until we have some empirical grasp on how our subject population defines the system of rules. Measuring objects thus necessarily involves iteratively measuring the system of symbolic meanings within which they are literally objectified.

## *The Material Qualities of Objects*

In this section, we focus on the variety of techniques available to cultural sociologists to measure meaning by using objects such as pieces of clothing, written documents, or pieces of art. Let us begin by thinking about an obviously "cultural" object—a novel. By refusing to take for granted that a novel is an abstracted narrative, and instead noting that it is also a book, a "bag of words,"[14] and cover art, as well as a thing that may be passed around, read from, decorated, or preserved (ritually and physically placed out of circulation), we are able to confront the question of which *qualities* of objects "count" for our various projects in the sociology of culture.

In most cases, sociologists treat these measures of qualities as measures of meaning. For example, heavy books may suggest more "weighty" content, text size and the presence or absence of serifs can make the content more or less legible, and a book's dog-eared pages and a weakened binding indicate that it is well loved. Measuring an object's particular qualities is well-trodden terrain in the sociology of culture. As a strategy, content analysis of texts tends to dominate the measurement of objects and their qualities.

In some situations, however, we treat texts and objects as a static and stable series of words to be counted at our peril.[15] One object isn't always the "same" as another. As Hutchison has shown, depending on which edition of Shakespeare's *Quarto* one reads, the sonnets break across pages in different places.[16] He argues that while the words are identical, their physical manifestation on the printed page can radically change the emphasis and meaning of the "same" poem. To "correctly" measure meaning or interpretation, then, the researcher should know which of the various objects referred to as "the *Quarto*" was read and include measures of line breaks.

Objects also change over time, and their material qualities can give way to entirely different meaning systems. For example, Rose-Greenland measures audiences' reactions to Greek and Roman marble statues that have been restored with colored paint, as measured by forensic scientists.[17] We think of these statues as white because modern audiences do not know that they were painted in the era of their creation. In this paper, Rose-Greenland shows that color perception is an unstable and contestable phenomenon. The negative valuation of the resulting objects— which were "ruined" in most viewers' minds—illustrates the link  between material and symbolic culture. As these two are often tightly coupled, vigilant attention should be paid to them in order to yield independent measures of each.

Measures of objects' material characteristics can facilitate an analysis of patterns in their use. White and White note that the introduction of paint tubes made different styles of painting (*plein air*) possible and reduced the amount of time that artists needed to spend mixing colors.[18] Similarly, DeNora demonstrated that Beethoven's success as a writer and composer depended upon the availability of a new instrument: the pianoforte.[19] This object was better than the harpsichord at producing both loud and quiet sounds, and these differences correlated with audiences reporting a greater range of emotional responses. She argued that in this case, the innovation of a physical object promoted particular meanings, social relations, and reputations within a field.

Focusing on the materiality of objects in this way often means that when measuring cultural objects, we most centrally measure qualities including magnitude, location or position, and sensual qualities like smell or texture. As Simmel famously argued:

> The development of sense impression . . . [is] a means of knowledge of the other: what I see, hear, or feel of the person is now only the bridge over which I get to them as my object. Just as the voice of a person has a quite directly attractive or repulsive effect on us, independently of what the person says . . . the same is probably true with regard to all sense impressions: they lead us into the human subject as its mood and emotion and out to the object as knowledge of it.[20]

Insisting on the primacy of sensual identification of social life, and objects in particular, is uncommon within the sociology of culture. And yet, using our senses is fundamental to the measurement of any sociological phenomenon.

Our reliance on vision as the dominant sense for measurement has led scholars of culture to miss information retrieved from other senses. To give only one of many possible examples, one could study food cultures by analyzing patterns in photographs that restaurant-goers take of their dishes, but while this would surely be interesting, it would be an impoverished way to understand food. Yet the measurement of taste, smell, or the textural dimensions of objects remains underexplored (both theoretically and empirically). As a way of orientation, here are some points of departure.

Tasting food involves texture, aroma, and pleasure responses to sensate information. The biological study of gustatory sense and olfaction, as well as the central nervous system's response to pleasurable (or displeasing) tastes, has generated very little attention from sociological research. Instead, sociological research is employed to study how contextual and social factors like attitudes and beliefs, neighborhood resources, and economic factors affect food preferences and consumption. Sociologists of culture have particularly been interested in food rituals, how dining practices are shaped by cultural context, and the development and operation of professional food preparation and consumption.[21]

Still, while earlier generations of sociologists largely ceded the measure of taste to other disciplines, sociologists of culture recently benefited from interdisciplinary research to identify the distinctively *social* character of this phenomenon. For example, Leschziner and Dakin measure the evolution of food tastes by analyzing patterns in cookbooks and other guides to eating and cooking; they find that gastronomy's growing autonomy from other disciplines has led to a shift from focusing on food's (real or imagined) therapeutic properties to new epistemologies of the eating experience.[22] Even in this case, biological predictors are captured only in an attenuated form, as they percolate into guidebook writing. We can safely assume that there are types of "taste" that are systematically omitted from secondary data sources. Sociologists are, as yet, unable to directly measure the biological features of taste.

The human sense of smell has also been largely ignored in discussions of measuring culture, apart from Cerulo's study of perfume fragrance described in the previous chapter. In reviews of research on the topic, Synnott and Low have argued that, with the exception of Georg Simmel and Berger and Luckmann, sociologists have neglected the study of odors.[23] The potential impact of olfactory measurements on our understanding of meaning-making and sociability is quite large. There is evidence that sociologists are implicitly using "measures" of smell to advance their arguments: ethnographers report on the greasy-smelling diner, the urine or bleach smell of a hospital, or the tobacco smell of a pub.[24] This evidence can provide a great deal of explanatory power, particularly in qualitative research, but it is rarely subjected to systematic, direct measurement.

Our sense of touch is similarly neglected by sociologists, but it is particularly important for measuring meaning. In her analysis of art museums and botanical gardens, Mangione provides a useful model. Art museums'"look, don't touch" approach offers a very different experience to visitors than do botanical gardens with "touch gardens."[25] Based on observations of object-person interactions, and comparing them across organizational contexts, she argues that we can identify distinct dimensions of value. Measures of touch and people's routinized interactions with objects may also give us evidence of and insight into "tacit knowledge," or the skills, knowledge, and experiences that people have, but find difficult to express in words (and therefore, are impossible for a sociologist to measure using text).[26] This may be critically leveraged in cases where repeated touch is a relevant indicator of skill, as in Richard Sennett's study of craft production.[27]

Finally, cultural sociologists have begun to examine our sense of hearing. In order to listen, humans must be in proximity to a sound-making device. Sound waves interact with the environment as they travel to the ear, and then within the anatomy of the ear, and finally individuals initiate a set of mental processes in response. These processes of the mind are triggered by an individual's willingness to be attentive to sound input and to generate meaning.[28] Like the other senses described in this section, we are largely limited to measuring individuals' reports of sensory activation, rather than the biological response itself. We can, however, usefully differentiate between primary and secondary categories that individuals use to measure sound. For example, we make distinctions between sounds that require our attention (e.g., alarms) and those that do not; sounds linked with action (e.g., fleeing a building or marching) and those that are not; and so forth. We sort sounds into broad categories, such as singing, talking, or mechanical.

In short, as these examples illustrate, the measurement of culture via sensory information does not yet correspond to the sheer volume of information that humans receive about their environment from these channels. Future collaboration with natural and human scientists could expand our capacity to develop both measures and theories of such sensory data.

## *What to Do with Material Qualities?*

Once an object's material qualities have been observed and identified, a core objective for sociologists of culture is to understand classification and categorization processes.[29] Such work has focused on connections between the activity of sorting and its consequences for identities, hierarchies, and power. For example, in Norbert Elias's foundational study of etiquette manuals from the sixteenth century, he examines two types of objects—appropriate for the table, or inappropriate—as indicators of so-called civilized behavior. He details the introduction of the fork to the table in Italy, and then in France, England, and Germany. He argues that the shift from communal eating, where food is eaten by hand, to solitary eating, in which such intimate contact is anathema to a sophisticated person, reveals a much broader insight about the social organization of societies.[30] At least two types of objects in this example are central to his measurement of civilization—the presence or absence of the fork on the table, and the content of the etiquette manuals themselves—which provide data on prescriptions of appropriate behavior while dining.[31]

Similarly, anthropologist Victor Turner focuses on rituals that allow individuals to forsake an older classification system in favor of a new one, like baptisms or other initiation rites. The boy arriving at his bar mitzvah leaves a man, and the baby leaves her baptism as a member of a religious community in good standing. Socialization into communities involves inculcation into relevant classificatory orders. For example, following the work of Lévi-Strauss, Marshall Sahlins examines how animals—and parts of animals—are sorted into "edible" and "inedible" categories.[32] Categorization into these groups is culturally and historically contingent. Eating meat from cats is prohibited in Judaism and Islam, but it can be found on restaurant menus in Switzerland, China, and Vietnam. Under changed social circumstances, food classifications can rapidly change, as when the Siege of Leningrad resulted in Russians breaking their prohibition on eating dog meat. In short, studying the process of sorting objects into acceptable or unacceptable can reveal the organizing principles of a community.

Perhaps the most fundamental way to categorize objects is to begin with a simple distinction between being and nothingness. This may not be as simple as it sounds. Consider, for example, the "I know it when I see it" feature of fashion and taste described by sociologists including Blumer,[33] Mears,[34] and Godart and Mears.[35] Each argues that the determination of whether a fashion object or body *exists* is a classification of primary importance. The measurement question that emerges, then, is what makes a fashion model an object: the distinctive attributes of them as an object (e.g., body type, facial features), or the act of categorizing them as a model?

Such a focus on classification sensitizes us to stratification systems. First, as we already noted, classification systems are taught over the life course. Children often learn the Linnaean classifications for living objects and learn how to sort particular examples into domains, kingdoms, phyla, classes, orders, families, genera, and species. In the process, they learn to identify contested or confusing classifications: that whales are not fish, but mammals; and that ratites and penguins are birds that cannot fly. Furthermore, learning the sorting systems used by others—and fitting them to the contexts within which they are relevant—is an important part of the socialization process. For example, we may learn that knowledge of genera may be of great value in a biology class, but it would be deemed pretentious in casual conversations with friends. This example also illustrates the relationship between categorization and ranking processes—in this case, "higher" and "lower" orders of classification.

Second, however, a focus on categorization opens up different axes of variation. Object-sorting systems are always multidimensional, and any number of them can be deemed relevant in particular social situations. For example, the ordinary sorting process for popular music involves allocating songs and musicians to genre groupings. That same ordinary process involves several prior sortings: a distinction between music and noise (a battle that both jazz and rap lost, initially), and between the familiar and not. Once one is certain that some collection of noise is music—and that it is familiar music—genres can be identified. The refinement and content of those categories depend on the listener's depth of knowledge. Yet in-depth knowledge among experts can also create new classification struggles. In her study of rap music, sociologist Jennifer Lena identifies four dominant sorting systems that experts use to define rap: data on record sales (where genre was defined by chart-builders); data on radio airplay (where genre was defined by station-identification); data from record store owners; and finally, data on compositional elements (e.g., the existence of spoken-word lyrics). By demonstrating that each of these indicators of song genre yields different groups of songs, she illustrates the multidimensionality of object-sorting systems, even within a single field of endeavor.

Moreover, sociologists can measure both emic and etic classification systems for objects, where *emic* classifications refer to  native designations and *etic* refers to measures generated from social scientific classifications. Some sociologists have rejected the use of etic measures, for instance when humanists "define genre in terms of form or content similarities."[37] In other cases, however, emic classification systems are seen as incomplete descriptions of variation. Sociologist Viviana Zelizer argues that money and other gift objects are circulated in all intimate relationships, and that such relationships "defined the appropriateness of one sort of payment or another."[38] However, in cases where those money exchanges were involved in legal disputes, the court's definition of the situation governed the fate of those funds. Emic definitions of the money's significance—as payment for services, or as a gift—were misaligned with the classification system employed by legal authorities, opening up opportunities for contestation.[39] Sociologists studying culture should be careful to attend to circumstances in which they are measuring an object according to classification principles that are expressed by users, or leveraging sociological classification sets that are unfamiliar to most users.

In many cases, physical objects are category markers, in the sense that they form a boundary between that which belongs in the class and that which is outside it. Ordinary objects are reclassified as art when they appear in a frame or on a pedestal, either of which serves to demarcate the "profane" of everyday life from "sacred" artistic space.[40] An even more basic example is the geopolitical boundaries of nations, which define who is a citizen, as Durkheim and Weber both recognized.[41]

Despite the long tradition of such study, there is no robust and generalizable theory of dynamic change within classification systems, although notable efforts have been made in the study of social movements, nation building, and cultural fields.[42] Yet, observing patterns in how human groups identify the presence of objects, sort them into categories that are then associated with traits, and then engage in disputes over that sorting, are basic activities in the measurement of objects. Research into the sorting of objects often highlights disputes about how or why objects are viewed as members of a group, and this leads us to consider research on those disputes over boundaries.

Cultural sociologists also often use the term *boundary* in a symbolic sense, following the work of the anthropologists Douglas and Barth. Much recent work has focused on measuring the existence and functioning of "boundary objects."[43] Boundary objects are tools used by multiple communities of practice (e.g., science and the arts), and that are viewed by community members as useful, while having different meanings in each community.[44] The measurement of boundaries, then, focuses on how different communities attend to different qualities of the same object.

## *The Temporality of Objects*

Objects serve as repositories of culture, the "frozen remains of collective action."[45] Some objects, though, are more frozen than others (by which we mean more or less durable). Bound up in material, objects carry symbolic content forward through time, making it available for analysis and measurement.

Some objects are easier to pull out of the stream of action and history than others; they are more or less durable, more or less available. Archives, museums, libraries, and government agencies collect and store objects for us to analyze, but many objects are never collected or preserved. Some of the most durable objects tend to be commemorative. Thus, for example, sociologists Robin Wagner-Pacifici and Barry Schwartz analyze the qualities of a war memorial, the discourse surrounding the production and reception of the memorial and the objects that people leave at the Vietnam Veterans Memorial site to measure genre, ambivalence, and commemoration.[46] As they show through the analysis of both material form and historical texts, the Vietnam War posed a "genre problem" for those who wanted a public symbol to commemorate the conflict. Feelings of ambiguity over the American defeat, moral controversies over the justifications for the war back home, and the treatment of veterans upon their return all made for a challenging commemorative project that would not easily fit into the traditional genre of monument-making. Traditional war memorials include "statues of fighting men, obelisks, arches, granite monoliths" with physical qualities like "vertical preeminence, grandness of size, and lightness of color, with national symbolism."[47] For the Vietnam Veterans Memorial, Wagner-Pacifici and Schwartz thus needed to map the range of objects that constitute the field of memorials, measure the types and intensity of the interactions people had with the memorial, and count and classify the objects that people left at the memorial.

Not all objects are so well preserved. Objects vary in terms of their preservability—we lose important dimensions of the cultural world when the objects or content most integral to those dimensions are unavailable for analysis. Sometimes this has to do with the materials themselves. At other times, the preservation of an object is an outcome of its social location. The history of objects is the history of winners. In other words, there is an elite bias in object preservation; people tend to preserve objects of the wealthy, the educated, and the victors of war. Given this bias in institutionally preserved culture, we have to be careful about elite biases in our analysis of culture. Sociologists, too, attempt to freeze culture by embedding observations in objects, which might introduce other biases into our analyses. We make a distinction, then, between objects produced by the people we are interested in studying and objects we create in the process of observing people. In cases where people (nonsociologists) do the "freezing" themselves (as in the analysis of books, photographs, newspaper stories, or furniture), bias may come from the availability of objects to study, or sampling bias. In cases where researchers freeze ephemeral cultural activities and action into forms that we can analyze (e.g., speeches into audio recordings or transcripts; a movement's street theater into field notes or video footage; and accounts of the structure of ritual), we must be attentive to those translations and the biases they entail.

An object's physical attributes affect its ability to influence human life and to exert particular kinds of influence. The physical deterioration of a red ribbon affects what interpretations viewers can make of its significance.[48] Similarly, the decay of an art object, like Leonardo da Vinci's *Portrait of a Man in Red Chalk*, can make the original illegible.[49] But at what point does decay, alteration, or transformation of an object change the very nature of the object? When does a da Vinci painting become just another piece of parchment? Cultural objects have "life histories" and "biographies."[50] Their qualities change over time as materials decay, or as art preservationists attempt to stabilize the wood frame of a painting, retouch parts that have lost their color, or construct elaborate environments of glass, light, and air that minimize decay. At some point, the da Vinci work may no longer be worth exhibiting, limiting people's access to it and reducing its capacity to influence.

These insights have real consequences for measurement. The danger of measurement is *assuming that the object in front of you*

*is the same as the object used by the people you are studying.* Objects
are "unruly."[51] As McDonnell has shown, AIDS organizations
assume everyone understands the denotative meaning of red ribbons is simply "AIDS awareness." That assumption doesn't hold
for Ghanaians who associated the symbol as meaning death and
danger, given the use of red decorations for funerals.[52] For that
matter, some material qualities of red ribbons are more durable
than others. Red dye fades quickly in the sun, leaving a pink or
white ribbon, which further changes the interpretive possibilities.
Put simply, a red AIDS awareness ribbon doesn't always stay red
or give hope to those aligned with the cause. The lesson here is
that we may need to measure the "same" object differently over
time and context, and be attentive to differences across communities producing objects and those consuming them.

The survival of a physical object can also influence the survival
of other forms of culture. For example, Lang and Lang's study
of painter-etchers reveals that the survival of art objects influences the likelihood that the artists will enjoy a posthumous
reputation—that the objects they create will continue to circulate in ways that affect meaning.[53] Moreover, the artists' ability to
maintain and preserve records of their work during their life is
correlated with preservation, correct attribution, and reputation.
That is, the extent to which artists act to preserve and distribute
their creations can determine the extent to which those objects
shape meaning or facilitate social relationships in the future.

As historians remind us, if we measure past cultures only
through the objects that have lasted, we will generate a biased
sample, overrepresenting the cultural influence of those in power.
In this sense, there is often an elite bias in measures of objects,
simply because the objects are physical manifestations of the
power to preserve and to affix culture into more durable media.
Objects need to be archived, preserved, and collected to become

available for analysis, and in this sense, archival processes are key to durability. This is equally true of digital objects. Online content is not subjected to centralized or standardized preservation, and preservation can be costly. These are serious concerns, as knowledge is not accessible and transferrable unless it is transcribed into objects.[54] Alternatively, studies of present cultures may wish to prioritize the study of old objects that have been maintained. Objects that last longer often require institutional effort to maintain, suggesting they remained culturally relevant to those communities that support their preservation.

## Objects and their Connections

As we will discuss further in the next chapter, sociologists often analyze the relations among objects themselves, as well as the material and ideational attributes tying objects together. This relational perspective supports more structural approaches that reveal broader meaning systems. In this portion of the chapter, we examine how sociologists have measured the relational qualities of objects, focusing on four ways in which objects are typically measured: the relationship of objects to one another; the interpretation of objects and how those interpretations influence the production of other objects; the diffusion of objects across individuals and groups; and the utilization of objects to spread ideas and practices and to identify categories.

In this, we follow Griswold's influential "cultural diamond" framework, where she connects cultural objects to their social world, those who produce these objects, and those who receive them.[55] Griswold's diamond orients us to the social links between people and objects: how objects are produced, diffused, and consumed, and how these relations in turn shape social worlds. To fully account for the social role of objects, Griswold argues that scholars should measure links across all points of the diamond. To answer this challenge, sociologists have taken different approaches to this "complex," from measuring the various objects across a field[56] to following a single object as it travels through stages of creation, production, and reception.[57]

# MEASURING OBJECT PRODUCTION

## *History of Measurement*

Where do objects come from? One thriving stream of research within the sociology of culture is comprised of those scholars who focus on the creation of cultural objects. This production of culture perspective emerged in the 1970s and is anchored in two distinct impulses: a desire to study the meaning-making of workers in creative industries, and an interest in how the actions of object-creators affect consumers' patterns of meaning-making. In this next section, we thus explore measurement issues that affect those studying production systems and the broad organizational contexts within which they take place, as well as the measures of creativity that dominate most studies of creative work at an interactional level.

## *Measurement Choices and Challenges*

### MEASURING OBJECTS IN FIELDS
White and White's classic study of the emergence of nineteenth-century French impressionism already contained the germinal

elements of what would later be called "the production of culture perspective."[58] Rejecting prevailing theories of revolution-
ary social change and genius artists, they demonstrated that the
advent of the novel art historical style called *impressionism*—the
creation of novel art objects—was a complex social invention.
They attributed the decline of the French academy system
(and the rise of the gallery system that supported impression-
ists) to changes in artistic style, technology and training, critical discourse, ideology, and organizational form and function.
Almost sixty years later, production of culture scholars continue
to emphasize technological innovations, organizational change,
legal conditions, career structures, understandings of consumer
demand, and industry structure in explaining the production of
meaningful objects.[59]

One of the key debates within this subfield concerns the proper
measurement of novelty. Because many production of culture
scholars seek to understand the social conditions for innovation,
identifying robust measures of newness is of paramount concern—
whether one is interested in new ways of doing (or institutions),
new understanding of consumer desires, or new products. Many
sociologists have tackled a field in which object novelty is particularly vexing to measure: music production. While in the strictest
sense, every recording, album, or MP3 file is new at the moment
of creation, sociologists seek to document situations when products are *meaningful* in their novelty. This type of novelty could
involve the invention of a new genre category, the innovation of a
new production technique (e.g., the use of autotune to adjust the
pitch of singers' voices), or major shifts in the construction of an
entire bundle of songs (e.g., a trend in rock music).

The measurement of musical novelty was initiated by Richard
Peterson and David Berger, who sought to characterize the diversity of popular music, broadly defined, to determine whether

independent (and smaller) labels were better at spotting and developing new talent and new forms of music.[60] They measured musical diversity within the "Hot 100" *Billboard Magazine* music charts (which captured both sales and airplay on radio stations) in two ways: as a count of the number of Top 10 and number 1 singles on the charts in any year (a kind of measure of "churn" within the elite), and a count of the number of new artists. Peterson and Berger concluded that independent, smaller labels were serving as "talent scouts," identifying, producing, and distributing more diverse music than their major label peers. In 1992, Paul Lopes sought to revise and update those findings; he argued that organizational and institutional structures within record companies mediate the association between market concentration and musical diversity. He replicated Peterson and Berger's measures of diversity and added a measure of genre innovation, noting the chart appearance of artists working in new styles. While he argues that counting the number of new artists on the charts is an imperfect measure of musical novelty, this approach has been used in later analyses.[61] However, there is growing skepticism of this measure which equates new producers with new music, because it likely overestimates the number of new performers who deviated from the strong institutions that govern popular music creation.[62]

Given the evidence that *Billboard Magazine* created genre designations to service its business model rather than solely on the basis of musicological or sociological indicators of novelty, sociologists sought alternative measures of object novelty.[63] One pathway was to decompose songs into their constitutive elements and identify the introduction and diffusion of new elements as measures of innovation. For example, both Kim de Laat and Jennifer Lena (working separately) replicate the earlier analyses of diversity on the *Billboard* charts, but include musicological characteristics (e.g., lyrics, chords, melody, and beat pattern) among their measures of innovation.[64] Such measures perform adequately when utilized within a bounded genre, and yet few sociologists of music agree that genres have universally agreed upon boundaries.[65] That is, as Lena says, "[t]reating genres and the boundaries around them as natural and inevitable effaces their core sociological attributes by portraying something constituted through dynamic relations as something objective and extra-social."[66]

The future of measures of object novelty, optimal differentiation, and specifically of innovation in music most likely lies in a combination of sociological and musicological qualities.[67] As streaming services like Spotify proffer categories of choice to users that incorporate both prior user behavior and musicological similarity, they can be used to refine our understanding of the degree to which object qualities qua qualities can or should be sufficient to measure innovation. As we return to below, another solution has been to turn attention toward patterns in the reception of the object by audiences, looking for indications that receivers believe novelty has taken place.

## THE PRODUCTION OF CULTURAL OBJECTS AS A COLLECTIVE ACT

How do the actions of object creators affect patterns in meaning-making? In the previous section, we explored this question in the context of large, quantitative data sets. Here, we consider the measurement practices of those who qualitatively explore creative communities. For continuity, we explore the same measurement quandary addressed in the previous section: what methods we can use to detect novelty.

Howard Becker's *Art Worlds* is perhaps the most popular text on creativity from a sociological perspective, and early in that book, he illustrates the difficulty of measuring innovation at the micro-level.[68] As he relates, a sculptor was interested in creating a lithographic print—a creative task with which he had limited experience—so he requested the assistance of a printer. Cooperative links like this one are essential to creating objects, as Becker argues at length. Thinking that he was making an image that would simplify the printer's work, the sculptor used large blocks of color. The lithographer explained that the printing process would necessarily leave roller marks, which are viewed as indicators of poor craftsmanship. This example neatly illustrates how task-specific definitions of quality, as well as the cooperative links between object creators, affect what objects get made (by whom, how, and when), and how their meaning is then interpreted.

Just as we explored in the previous section, creators and sociologists alike are interested in identifying objects that have significant meaning-making potential before production and distribution take place. If notions of craftsmanship provide one limiting feature, the danger of imitation provides another. Creative workers seek to balance conformity and originality, as important studies of artists,[69] chefs,[70] and rap musicians[71] have shown. This notion—that peer esteem is built from achieving an ideal balance between conformity to existing objects and innovation—is at the center of both theories and measurement within this subfield.

As best we can determine, the majority of research has been done on professional object creators; when sociologists have studied amateurs, it has mainly been the work of qualitative scholars. Take, for example, sociologist Corey Fields's[72] study of a knitting circle: his objective is to understand how this group, comprised mainly of young, professional women, yoke their identity to objects strongly associated with elderly women. While Fields is conducting research, the "Vegan Fox Fur" pattern excites group members "because no one had seen anything like it before," and this novelty "and its clever reinvention of a traditional item embodied the ethos of the group." Group members also selected patterns from well-known designer brands, like DKNY, instead of older or less chic patterns to create objects that differ from those created by "grandma" knitters ("not crap like *Grandma's Knitting* or *Knitting American*," said one member).[73] The importance of materials to the collective identity work of the group was also demonstrated in their invocation of a hierarchy of yarn retailers, where "independent yarn shops" that sell "natural fibers" and "fashion" patterns are promoted as the most suitable vendors for members of the group. In short, he argues, "Objects, in this instance yarns and patterns, played a central role in the reconstruction of identity."[74]

The fashioning and refashioning of objects in the service of individual and collective identities brings the importance of measuring objects into focus. In-depth, qualitative study of the small-group creation of objects demonstrates little evidence that there exists a simple set of measurement practices that can be adopted by scholars working in different contexts. Yet the diffusion of practices across multiple groups is important to understanding cultural objects, so in the next section, we return to the world of large data sets to understand how such diffusion has been measured.

## MEASURING DIFFUSION: OBJECTS IN TRANSIT

The study of the conditions and mechanisms that specify patterns in the flow of social practices across individuals, groups, and organizations unites many subfields in sociology. Within the sociology of culture, scholars study the diffusion of rumors, beliefs, cassette tapes, labeling systems, and many other forms of material and nonmaterial culture. In this section, we focus solely on measurement issues that concern the transfer of objects between social positions. To understand how culture works, it is often essential to trace how objects move, flow, circulate, and get picked up by people and communities. The "diffusion of innovations" approach offers a well-honed model for this objective.[75]

Some objects encounter great obstacles to diffusion, while others exist within a system that promotes a relatively frictionless process. Digital technology allows more books to diffuse more quickly, and at a lower cost to the consumer, than when only print books were available. Recording and radio made possible the transfer of sound across space and over time.[76] Private access to satellite technology has made possible the global diffusion of television programming.[77] Telephones, fan magazines, online community spaces—these are just a few of the technologies that have facilitated the growth of global ties between individuals and the fomenting of transnational communities.[78] Thus, while the measure of diffusion can amount to what is essentially a count of objects arriving at a destination, it can also include measures of the attributes of the material infrastructure upon which diffusion depends.[79] These measures include relatively abstract dimensions of the material infrastructure that affect the diffusion process, like organization size or market structure, both of which have demonstrably affected the spread of innovations like styles of popular music.[80] For instance, Ferguson[81] demonstrates that the availability of train travel made new and fresher ingredients available to Parisian chefs, encouraging the maturation of the field of gastronomy.

The introduction of objects to new social contexts can result in an adaptation of their uses, and therefore, changes to our measures. For example, studies of youth cultures sometimes measure changes to commercial objects as indicators of symbolic resistance via appropriation.[82] Terry McDonnell finds that Ghanaian women who are given access to condoms transform them into jewelry.[83] Measures of the adaptive uses of objects also feature in studies of "invented tradition" included in the famous collected edition by Hobsbawm and Ranger.[84] Barry Schwartz[85] counts the presence of images of President Abraham Lincoln in World War II propaganda as an indication that the meanings of the two wars were being "keyed" to one another. Kuipers[86] provides an excellent model for studying this, observing the practices of French, Italian, Dutch, and Polish translators as they take different approaches to adapting television shows for their particular publics. Some use subtitles, some overdub, some adapt the script, and some translate the language as closely as possible to the original. Tracing the process of diffusion makes clear how difficult it is to treat all instances of *The Nanny* as the same. This insight—that adopters might also be adapters—is an important sociological insight that the diffusion of innovations approach can sometimes miss. As objects move through social worlds, the complexity of cultural flows shouldn't be overlooked.[87] The question this raises for measurement is: when can we treat our object of study as the same across instances, and when do we need to treat the object as different across sites of reception?

In some studies, the diffusion of objects to new contexts is itself used as a measure of their changed meaning. For example, the specific books reported to be in the sixteenth-century miller Menocchio's possession at the time of his inquisition trial as a heretic are "measures" that cultural historian Carlo Ginzburg[88] uses to understand how his unique religious worldview was formed. Similarly, the adaptation of objects to their use as art is important to studies that examine the rise of the concept of art in the United States.[89] The diffusion of objects is also a measure of the spread of particular notions of authenticity, and participants in communities themselves "measure" authenticity via the presence of "authentic" objects.[90] Consider, for example, how measures of the presence of smoke, cheap beer and whisky, broken and dirty furniture, and poor sound systems are indicators of the authenticity of particular blues clubs.[91] Also consider the white, middle-class audiences for whom the broken and the dirty are highly salient to the blues. Or take Frederick Wherry's observation that the materials that artisans use in production, their rituals, and their reluctance to pursue export opportunities in the global market all serve as indicators of authenticity in Thai and Costa Rican handicraft markets.[92] Measures of the use of objects are employed here as well; Peterson describes how the ritual practice of kicking off her shoes on stage illustrated and reinforced the "hard core" country authenticity of singer Loretta Lynn.[93]

## MEASURING OBJECT CONSUMPTION

### History of Measurement

What do people do with the objects they receive or purchase? How do they interpret objects? How do they adapt objects to their own practices and purposes? These are the overarching questions addressed by studies of consumption, reception, and taste. The major theoretical traditions in sociology have had a great influence on how object significance is measured and interpreted. Those working from Marxist and post-Marxist positions tend to focus on the narcotizing effects of entertaining objects, as well as on how elements of capitalist production are hidden from view during consumption.[94] Those scholars influenced by Durkheim and other structuralists identify features of objects that highlight group identity and activity. Those in Weberian and neo-Weberian traditions may identify homologies that link the consumption of particular objects to the social position of consumers. The last of these approaches is perhaps best exemplified in Bourdieu's research, as well as in the rejection of a taste and class homology by those researching the "omnivorousness" of contemporary tastes.[95]

The measurement of consumption has its roots in anthropological work on material cultures.[96] Much of this work is ethnographic. Scholars have counted the numbers and types of consumer goods in people's homes.[97] Others examine the cultures that emerge around stuff, from scooters to television shows to books, and how the qualities of these objects come to symbolize group commitments. Other work in this area focuses on how people incorporate objects into ritual, which in turn symbolizes the group and structures participants' belief systems.[98]

In the late 1980s to early 1990s, studies of reception demonstrated how different groups can interpret the same object differently. This work often combines measurement of the object itself and its capacity for polyvocality, along with measures of audience reception. Measures of reception have included the measurement of themes discussed in other objects like critical reviews, or by measuring people's interpretations through interviews, focus groups, or observations of discussion groups like book clubs.[99] Future measurement (and theoretical) challenges for reception studies include how to capture alternative mechanisms of polyvocality beyond group membership, as well as how to measure the consequences of reception.

## Measurement Choices and Challenges

### MEASURING IDENTITY THROUGH CONSUMING OBJECTS

The objects that people consume can offer an indication of their identity. For example, in a classic essay, "Possessions and the Extended Self," Belk demonstrated how the sense of self was intricately tied to mundane and emotionally charged material belongings.[100] On the basis of a wide-ranging review of the general psychological aspects of the importance of possessions, he demonstrated that it is "an inescapable fact of modern life that we learn, define, and remind ourselves of who we are by our possessions."[101] Belk drew out lessons for understanding consumption and directed his gaze on collecting, pets, gift giving, organ donation, and the care and disposal of goods. If goods and chattels constitute an extension of self and are responsible for "generating meaning in life," then in a world characterized by an abundance of commodities, the significance of possessions intensifies.

Interviewing people about the objects they consume, Holt showed how people in different social positions have specific and typical orientations toward material objects and cultural activities, and thereby different types of cultural experiences.[102] He demonstrated, for example, that persons with high cultural capital apply critical judgment to all cultural forms, informed by cosmopolitan standards, and engage in leisure with a view to self-actualization, whereas those with low holdings of cultural capital apply referential criteria, informed by local context, and treat leisure as a form of autotelic sociality.[103]

Work on fan cultures and material cultures both bring insight into the work that objects do to facilitate a sense of belonging.[104] Jenkins studied Trekkies and other intense fans of popular culture. The measurement innovation that he offered was to do more than observe their practices of consumption, but also to analyze the objects they produced. Consumption inspired fan fiction and communities of circulation that allowed people to express feminist readings of pop culture, thus in turn creating more inclusive fan cultures. He shows how this productive consumption also feeds back into the industry.

Following in the footsteps of Csikszentmihalyi and Rochberg-Halton, Miller conducts innovative studies of people's connections to the everyday objects in their lives.[105] In his book, *The Comfort of Things*, Miller examines objects and collections people have around their homes. He visited homes along a single London street, offering insight into the range of relationships with objects that can be found in a single community. Miller accounted for people's everyday objects, as well as most precious things, observing the sources of social interaction and connection among families through their consumption of objects. *Blue Jeans*, by Miller and Woodward, takes this a step further, demonstrating how blue jeans can make "ordinary" identities outside of ritual and sacredness.[106]

## MEASURING OBJECTS IN ACTION

When do cultural objects shape belief and behavior? Stated differently, how can we measure the "cultural power" of objects?[107] This work on the role of objects in action follows a more Weberian approach. Schudson points toward a number of mechanisms of cultural power, with each requiring different kinds of measurement. For instance, for an object to affect lines of action, it needs to be available to people. This is Schudson's notion of "retrievability": how easily the object retrieved is put to use. One could measure retrievability through diffusion or the spread of objects over time and space. Widely diffused objects could be considered indicative of cultural power, or a pure measure of power—in that widespread diffusion can speak to dominant organizations' ability to impose the object upon publics.[108] Retrievability does not necessarily mean that an object was actually retrieved. The fact that an object diffused doesn't necessarily give an indication of how it was put to use. In this sense, retrievability is a better measure of the *potential* for cultural power. More widely reproduced and diffused objects have more opportunities to be incorporated in action, but further evidence is needed to know how these objects are put to use.

Once available, objects sometimes resonate with people, such that they use the object, or interaction with the object leads to novel lines of action.[109] Why some objects resonate (in some situations, for some people), whereas others do not, is an ongoing area of theorization that needs better measurement to be empirically tested. Measuring the experience of resonance itself has long been a challenge, given that resonance is often inferred from outcomes rather than observed firsthand.[110] Observing people's emotional reactions when interacting with an object both offers a measure of the presence of resonance and can indicate what qualities of the object, the situation, or cultural schemas encourage resonance.[111] Alternatively, Bail takes a macro approach to measuring resonance when observing whether the range of discursive variation predicts how engaged people are with organ donation advocacy organization pages on Facebook.[112] To do this, he uses topic models of the pages' posted content, finding that more variation (to a point) leads to more engagement. These findings mirror Griswold's argument that (some, but not too much) ambiguity can give objects cultural power.[113] She finds that objects that elicit consensus around its topic but support divergent interpretations tend to be valued more in the literary field because they encourage more debate and discussion. To measure ambiguity, she examines the agreement and dispersion of thematic categories across critics' reviews of George Lamming's novels.

Following Griswold and Gell, we can measure the cultural power of an object by tracing people's intentions for an object through to their reception and consequence.[114] With such an approach, measures of intended meaning can be compared to meanings made by audiences. The successful *alignment* of audiences' meanings and actions with the intentions of those who made or mobilize the object offers another measure of cultural power.[115]

Thus, for example, art historian Michael Baxandall's influential research on the production of fifteenth-century paintings in Italy offers a model for how to measure changes in status by studying objects.[116] For some time, painting commissions were dominated by a desire for ultramarine-colored paint. Patrons and artists negotiated over the quantity and quality of ultramarine contracted in the work, as the vibrant blue was recognized as expensive and conferred status upon the patron who commissioned the work. Over time, the rising nouveau riche could afford expensive pigments, and they commissioned or bought works using ultramarine, with the consequence that the color ceased to indicate the possessor of such a work was an "old money" patron. In an effort to retain the elite signaling value of artistic objects, the wealthiest patrons began to promote the artistic skill of painters they supported, not their choice of materials. This, in turn, helps explain changes in taste—the shifting "period eye."

### Looking Ahead

This chapter has addressed the measurement of objects and how sociologists employ such measures to understand meaning and significance in shared social life. As we observed throughout the chapter, the relationship between people and objects is mediated by social structures, often referred to as *fields, networks,* or *relations.* The bridge between objects and relations is quite short.

For example, consider the fact that innovative objects can encourage the rise of new technical competency. Technically competent producers and users can be understood as a network, or, in some cases, a field. In the next chapter, we turn our full attention to how relations between various social actors, including things and people, can be measured at multiple levels of analysis.

# 3

# MEASURING CULTURE IN SOCIAL
# RELATIONSHIPS

**P**REVIOUS chapters of this book have outlined strategies for measuring culture by examining attributes and practices of individual people, as well as the material qualities of different kinds of objects. As we have seen, many of the building blocks of cultural analysis and measurement have developed via efforts to observe, categorize, and compare the individually and materially grounded dimensions of culture. Culture, however, not only is constitutive of persons and things, but also shapes our relations with one another. These interpersonal relations can be conceptualized at different levels—in the interactions among people in face-to-face settings; in the way that these relationships can be abstracted into patterned connections and exchanges between people and groups in social networks; and in the dynamics of broader social fields.

Across these levels of analysis, cultural processes are key to the emergence and evolution of social relations, whether these are composed of ties between individuals, groups, objects, practices, or discursive elements (or some combination of these). It is, therefore, important to develop strategies for measuring the cultural dimensions of these relational configurations (i.e., for making these cultural processes visible, intelligible, and amenable to comparative analysis), while noting recurring patterns of co-occurrence and covariation.

Our focus on the cultural dimensions of relational configurations builds upon—and moves beyond—a historical debate that has sometimes been framed as an opposition between relational and attribute-based approaches to the study of social life. This opposition was announced with great rhetorical flourish in a series of programmatic statements over the past half-century. In the 1970s and 1980s, Ronald Breiger, Kathleen Carley, Mark Granovetter, Bonnie Erickson, Nancy Howell, Barry Wellman, and others helped consolidate the emerging social network approach in the social sciences by declaring the primacy of relations over categories and attributes.[1] In their pathbreaking *American Journal of Sociology* article on blockmodeling techniques, White, Boorman, and Breiger declared that "the presently existing, largely categorical descriptions of social structure have no solid theoretical grounding."[2] In 1988, Erickson critiqued sociology's reliance on individuals to understand attitudes (and thus, culture): "People do not form attitudes in direct response to their attributes. Attitudes are maintained, or modified, primarily through interpersonal processes . . . they occur largely within the boundaries of social networks."[3]

In the 1990s, Mustafa Emirbayer and Jeff Goodwin expanded on this principle by describing the "anti-categorical imperative" of social network analysis, which "rejects all attempts to explain human behavior or social process solely in terms of the categorical attributes of actors, whether individual or collective."[4] Following sociologists such as Pierre Bourdieu, as well as the philosopher Ernst Cassirer, Emirbayer then took this argument a step further in his "Manifesto for a Relational Sociology," which contrasted "relational" and "substantialist" perspectives. The latter "takes as its point of departure the notion that it is *substances* of various kinds (things, beings, essences) that constitute the fundamental units of all inquiry."[5] In contrast, relational approaches put these substances in motion by taking *transactions*—unfolding, relational processes rather than static ties—as the starting point of social action.

In a way, this was an old sociological insight: meanings, as well as groups and identities, are always relational since they are defined through their differences. What was important about this moment in social science was that it called for ways to ground not just our theories but also our methods in a relational perspective. In other words, it is not simply that social life is constructed through relationships by definition, but that attempts to model and measure social life need to measure such relationships, which raises a series of challenges to social scientists' conventional methodological toolkit.

We recognize that there are many ways to measure social relationships—some are measured very close to the concrete settings of observed action, while others are much more abstract, aggregated together, and detached from their specific contexts. As in previous chapters, we do not see an opposition between hermeneutic and computational approaches. Even deeply interpretive approaches to the study of social interactions observe presences and absences, note repetitions, make comparisons, and search for relational patterns and associations. Formal and computational methods for the study of interactions, networks, and fields do these same things, if at a higher level of aggregation and abstraction from context. Moreover, even the more abstract end of the spectrum requires interpretation. The use of formal mapping techniques or quantitative modeling does not relieve researchers from the fundamentally hermeneutic tasks required at each stage of the analysis, from case selection to unit and coding choices to the development of an intelligible story of what it all means for understanding and explaining the social world.

In what follows, we give examples of the measurement of the cultural dimension of relations that vary on this hermeneutic-computational spectrum, describing context-grounded techniques for observational counting and pattern location, as well as sophisticated quantitative techniques for mapping and dimensional analysis. We begin at the more concrete end of this spectrum, examining the measurement of relations within interactions. We then move to techniques for mapping and analyzing the cultural constitution of social networks, followed by systematic approaches to studying the cultural dynamics of social fields.

## SOCIAL INTERACTION

### *History of Measurement*

People construct, transmit, and reinterpret meanings in interaction. Rather than thinking about meaning as something that is lodged inside people's cognitive capacities or as the larger societal codes they grow up with, the interactionist tradition has focused on the situational emergence and malleability of meaning. In this regard, interactionism followed an American pragmatist tradition that saw meaning not as a frozen construct, but as an ongoing accomplishment. As Charles S. Pierce, the first architect of pragmatism, put it, meaning-making is a triad comprised of the signs we use and the objects that provide the grounds for these signs, but also—and crucially—the effect these sign-objects have on ongoing actions and interactions.[6] This focus on the temporal movement of meaning was sharpened and placed in interactional context by Herbert Blumer.[7] In an influential essay, Blumer talked of three tenets of interactionism: (1) meaning is constantly being constructed; (2) meaning is constructed in interactions, and (3) meaning is modified—or sustained—through subsequent chains of ongoing interactions. This reworking of the pragmatist insight is inherently relational. Patterns of meaning do not reside "in" actors—even if their habits are crucial for understanding what they bring to the interaction. Rather, meaning resides in the back-and-forth *among* actors; meaning emerges and changes in ongoing relations.

This pragmatist focus on the back-and-forth of meaning was complemented by another intellectual movement—that of ethnomethodology and conversation analysis (CA). Ethnomethodology, which emerged in the 1960s and was influenced more by phenomenology than by pragmatism, has been singularly focused on the local production of meaning and order. That is, it is an analytic strategy that asks how people sustain and create their world anew in each instance, while bracketing what we think we know about the actors.[8] Within this stream of research, some of the early proponents of ethnomethodology gravitated toward asking how we create meaning and order in the back-and-forth of conversation. This approach, developed mostly by Harvey Sacks and Emanuel Schegloff in the 1970s, sought to pinpoint the emergence of meaning in the minutest moments of interaction: in the overlap in actors' speech, in the way they repair their own utterances as an interaction unfolds, and in milliseconds of silence and indrawn breath. Importantly, conversation analysis made a methodological-theoretical choice: the meaning of utterances cannot be assumed in advance. Only in retrospect, as the interaction unfolds, does meaning become solidified. And thus, even though they began from a different starting point, conversation analysis ended up quite close to interactionism: assuming a radical flow of meaning and a relational approach to what meaning looks like.

While both interactionism and ethnomethodology deal inherently with meaning-making, the fundamental building block of any theory of culture, they seldom mention "culture"; they are wary of the kind of abstraction that this term implies. Originally, both interactionism and conversation analysis were suspicious of any attempt to abstract and quantify observations. Indeed, Blumer's text takes aim at the quantification of social science, railing against the language of attributes and variables. Rather than abstracting meaning from the situations in which it emerged, he wanted researchers to stay within the situation and capture the complexity of its unfolding. In-depth ethnographic and historical analyses were seen as the way to do justice to processes of meaning-making, and the second Chicago school that he was instrumental in developing was mostly comprised of ethnographers.[9]

This reluctance to derive abstract insights from analyses was even more stark in the case of ethnomethodology. Focused on the local production of order and action, the analytic power of ethnomethodology was lodged in the analysis of each specific case. Schegloff, one of the primary architects of conversation analysis, was adamant that attempting to abstract patterns and quantify them is extremely problematic.[10] Any translation of the ongoing production of meaning into measurable units, he argued, risked shifting the analysis from forms of action into a content analysis, where we count the occurrence of specific words or conversational gestures. And, in such a translation, the context of the production of any specific marker in which we are interested gets lost. It makes little sense to ask, "How often do people laugh?" noted Schegloff, if we do not know how often there was an opening for such laughter in interaction. It also makes little sense to ask how often people laugh as a measure of sociability when laughter can be a marker of different forms of action, and when people may always use *different* markers to construct the *same* action. Measuring the action alone is insufficient for interpretation; only with measures of context can we achieve reliable interpretations of its meaning.

And yet both traditions include important countervailing forces. For interactionism, the potential for quantification stems from the assumption undergirding some of its most exciting research programs: the idea that specific situations generate patterned, practical pressures, and thus produce patterned responses. To take a couple of classic examples, because the interaction between taxi drivers and passengers is fleeting and anonymous, the passengers tend to treat the driver as a "nonperson," while the driver will try to categorize clients based on very few clues so that she can know how to interact with them—and how much money she can get out of them.[11] Likewise, because doctors weren't obligated to tell patients that they were dying, and their job was easier without managing the terror of death, a large part of the drama of dying was centered around the control of this information and the "awareness contexts" it engendered.[12] Despite interactionists' reluctance to recognize it as such, this assumption—that institutional pressures on the creative back-and-forth of interaction tend to result in patterned meaning-making—opens up possibilities for both abstraction and quantification. We can assume that the situation is the same in important ways, and we can try to see whether the situation is resolved in similar ways across instances.

Something similar happened in conversation analysis. From quite early on, researchers wielding this approach were interested in tracing the basic building blocks of talk-in-interaction. And, despite some misgivings, identifying such building blocks gives rise to possibilities for quantification and abstracted measurement—particularly in the era of big data, when transcripts of conversations have become ubiquitous (even if they do not capture the same level of detail that could be measured in interpersonal settings). Moreover—especially as conversation analysts gravitated toward analyzing specialized talk in institutions such as court-talk, doctor-patient interaction, or

911 emergency calls—they found themselves echoing the symbolic interactionists' account of institutional pressures leading to patterned responses. That is, conversation analysts described how each institution had its "institutional fingerprints," and although they assumed that institutions are constantly created anew through interactions, the specific pragmatics of these settings shape conversations in predictable ways.[13] This in turn broadens the possibilities for measurement, including through the use of formalization and quantification (e.g., by aggregating turn-taking dynamics in institutional settings).[14]

## Measurement Choices and Challenges

Despite the suspicions of some scholars in this tradition regarding quantification, the most rudimentary form of measurement arising from interactionism can be glimpsed in cases of "ethnographic counts."[15] Relying on the predictable patterns and pressures in the settings they studied, some ethnographers used quantification as the most compelling forms of evidence that they marshal to make their case. The classic example of such ethnographic counts comes from the work of Donald Roy.[16] In his classic study of piecework machinists in a Chicago factory, Roy described how workers learned to "game" their work quota—that is, how they learned to limit their production as their skill increased, and how they learned not to work too hard on piecework assignments that didn't pay well.

The point Roy makes, and which ties it to the sociology of culture rather than only to measurement, was deceptively simple—rather than a *homo economicus* interested in simply maximizing profit at any given point, the machinists were acting and calibrating their work productivity in constant relation to how they assumed management would react if they worked "too well." That is, machinists constantly worried about management finding out that they could produce more units per minute and reacting to this discovery by decreasing piecework payment amounts, thus making them work harder for the same money. Importantly, the crux of Roy's evidence comes from a juxtaposition of moments of meaning-making in which machinists talked to each other with meticulous quantification of productivity per hour, both of his own work as a participant-ethnographer and that of others in the factory.

Ethnographic counts are also prevalent in recent ethnographic texts. For example, Moskos's work on policing shows how ebbs and flows in arrests don't emerge from a natural activity of police work, but rather from police officers deciding to position themselves in specific places with the intention of achieving predetermined arrest quotas.[17] As he argues, criminal statistics are thus a better measure of policing decisions than of the types and locations of crime. Another example can be seen in Lara-Millán's recent work, which describes how medical professionals manage care for the poor by expediting some patients and delaying others. Importantly, Lara-Millán begins his paper by telling the reader the number of observations, and uses the quantification of interactional outcomes throughout. Thus, for example:

> Of these discretionary decisions, nurses used time-of-arrival 20 percent of the time, criminal stigma 38 percent of the time, and police/jail arrivals 20 percent of the time. Grouping the last two categories together, which constitute the crime control dynamics described in this article, accounts for 58 percent of all discretionary decisions. Thus, when no medical criteria present themselves, nurses are much more likely to invoke criminal stigma or to choose a police arrestee than to simply pick the next patient in line.[18]

In each of these examples of ethnographic counts, the unit of analysis is a particular recurring situation. Whether these are the rhythms of work described by Roy, the arrests described by Moskos, or hospital admissions decisions described by Lara-Millán, the ethnographic text is centered on the situation. This, of course, is only one variant of interactionist research. Others focus on how communities are constructed in multiple sites of action or how careers unfold over time—that is, how meaning is made in relation to different situations and moments. And although here, too, there are openings for measurement, these tend not to be where the force of the argument lies. Measurement becomes a powerful vehicle for the development of the argument when ethnographers are focused on the structure of similar situations, where it is the repetition of moments—rather than the juxtaposition of different ones—that structures the text.

This affinity between measurement and situational recurrence has also motivated conversation analysis practitioners to move toward formal measures. Heritage and his colleagues,[19] for example, show that doctors receive systematically different responses from patients depending on how they construct their questions. As doctors and patients try to align with each other, they send subtle cues: using the word *any* (as in the sentence, "Do you have any more problems . . . ?") tends to generate a negative response, while using the word *some* tends to generate a positive response. By looking at subtle conversational shifts, researchers were thus able to point to larger emergent effects on an outcome that many in the medical world spend much time thinking about—how to get patients to divulge more information. And, as opposed to most earlier modes of conversation analysis, the power of the analysis here rests on quantitative measurement. Once you have access to a large number of cases that operate similarly—a convenient feature of institutional settings—then quantification becomes possible. While the structures of microinteractions are culled from qualitative, in-depth analysis of brief moments of interaction, these structures are then scaled up.[20]

Recent work by David Gibson proceeds in a similar vein, showing that the stakes of such interactional patterns may be quite dramatic.[21] Analyzing recordings of conversations of the high-level American committee that discussed how to react to Soviet nuclear missile bases under construction in Cuba, Gibson shows that these discussions were, importantly, shaped by conversational structures. Actors were often following conversational structures rather than responding to the task at hand, sustaining the smoothness of interaction at the potential expense of nuclear holocaust. And, again, while he deals with minute moments analyzed in painstaking detail—such as the tendency of speakers to continue the line of reasoning offered by the last speaker, rather than what may be most pertinent for the task at hand—these moments add up, creating a larger effect. In this case, measurement does not mean simply scaling up, but rather showing how the accumulation of many small microinteractional moments shapes the contours (and outcomes) of a high-stakes situation.

Lastly, while conversation analysis is well situated as a method for systematically measuring interactions, recent technological and social changes are opening new avenues to measure interactional emergence. Thus, another front in the measurement of interaction has arisen with the increasing ability to scrape data off the web.[22] As people exchange text messages in digital settings, a new arena for the study of meaning in interaction is becoming available.[23] Like face-to-face interactions, internet conversations are not only sites in which people present themselves, but also places where their thoughts and feelings take shape. These sites thus promise to return sociologists to the basic interactionist notion of the flow of meaning: how meanings emerge and shift over iterations of action and interaction.

To take one recent example, Bail, Brown, and Mann show how various communicative styles ebb and flow on the web.[24] Returning to previously intractable questions of mass persuasion, their study focuses on how cognitive, emotional, and social styles of communication on Facebook provide openings for social advocacy groups. And although their major focus is how advocacy organizations stimulate public discussion about social problems, no less interesting are their intermediate findings: the emotional tone of interaction varies rhythmically as the interaction between actors modulates the conversation. Looking at data from over 46,844 Facebook posts, the authors report how emotions spread and deepen, then give rise to a counterresponse that mitigates the first emotional response, thus generating predictable emotional rhythms. Emotional tones, like meanings, are interactionally emergent. They gain their potency, but also their predictable staleness, from their location within chains of meaning-making. And thus, with new forms of communication and measurement, "old" interactional insights can be approached and measured in new ways.

## SOCIAL NETWORKS

### *History of Measurement*

The highly sophisticated quantitative techniques that make up today's network science might seem, at first glance, to be antithetical to the rich interpretation that we often associate with cultural analysis, or even to the back-and-forth of interactional analysis. Some cultural sociologists are skeptical of what they see as the reductionist character of most network measurement tools, in that they take richly layered processes and turn them into matrices of ones (1s) and zeros (0s) that then can be analyzed for formal properties such as density, connectivity, or centrality. Moreover, network scholars often produce graphs and visualizations that are so complex that it is hard to remember how they are tied back to the more legible dynamics of interaction contexts or cultural texts.

Nevertheless, culture and networks have a long history of methodological linkage, which has produced a number of distinct measurement tools. Social network analysis traces its origins back to anthropological studies of kinship and community relations, as well as psychological studies of interpersonal and intragroup relations. Early movement toward measurement could be seen in the attempt to formalize patterns of interaction observed in group behavior, such as Jacob Moreno's sociometric mappings in the 1930s (with the famous sociometric "star" prefiguring later, more sophisticated measures of network centrality).[25] Likewise, Fritz Heider's psychological research on balance in interpersonal relations—and his early formalizations of congruence (or the lack thereof) between positive and negative relations—laid some of the groundwork for the mathematical analysis of triadic interactions by Dorwin Cartwright, Frank Harary, and others in the 1950s, as well as for subsequent experimental work by James Davis and others in the 1960s and later.[26]

The point is that the measurement of network relations developed out of attempts to formalize the patterning of social interactions, and thereby move toward a more abstract structural phenomenology, aligned with Simmel's approach to understanding the formal properties of modern life.[27] A similar pattern in the push toward formalization out of observational research can be seen in the Harvard community studies by Elton Mayo and colleagues. These researchers used sociograms—visual displays of social network relationships—in a number of famous work-place and community studies in the 1930s and 1940s, including a follow-up study of the famous Hawthorne factories where experimenter effects on work productivity were first observed.[28] W. Lloyd Warner and Paul Lunt, as well as other researchers, also used sociometric analysis to make sense of patterns in observed interactions in the well-known "Yankee City" studies and the "Old City" study of urban communities in the Deep South.[29] Some of the core measurement concepts in network analysis developed from these observational studies, including the analysis of cliques, of core-periphery relations, and positional class analysis, which prefigured concepts like structural equivalence and methods such as blockmodeling.

Lastly, from yet another direction, a group of anthropologists at the University of Manchester began taking the metaphorical concept of "networks" or "webs" of relations in a more systematic and abstract direction—that is, from observation of social inter-action toward formal measurement. Members of what became known as "the Manchester School"—including John Barnes, Clyde Mitchell, and Elizabeth Bott—began experimenting with the use of graph theory to move the anthropological toolbox for kinship mapping in a more complex and formal direction.[30] More attuned to their fieldwork than to abstract theories, they "paid less attention to the formally institutionalized norms and institutions of a society, and rather more to the actual configurations of rela-tions that arise from the exercise of conflict and power."[31] At the same time, they saw these formal methods as continuous with more qualitative kinds of data collection. For example, in Bott's influential study of family networks and gender roles, she com-bined repeated family interviews (in which she requested accounts of social ties) with direct observation and longitudinal commu-nity engagement.[32] In combining these qualitative techniques with innovations in graph theory, the Manchester anthropologists drew on earlier mathematical approaches to social structure— particularly the use of algebraic and matrix techniques for studying interlocking role sets as patterns of relations—which was key to articulating a particularly *relational* approach to measurement.

Building upon these innovations, network analysis took a leap forward in the quantitative measurement of social relationships with the pioneering work of White and his students at Harvard in the 1970s. Widely read studies by Nancy Howell Lee and Mark Granovetter showed the utility of systematic network techniques for studying variability in outcomes (i.e., in searching for jobs or abortion providers), while articulating foundational mechanisms for subsequent network theories (such as Granovetter's notion of "the strength of weak ties").[33] White's group further experimented with the use of algebraic and matrix techniques, extending Siegfried Nadel's earlier insights into interlocking role sets through their work on "role algebras."[34] They also pioneered techniques for analyzing "structural equivalence" such as blockmodeling—i.e. ways of identifying structure within social networks that helped usher in more "positional" approaches to network analysis, beyond those based on direct ties.[35]

Although the Harvard School pioneered by White was critical for the development of the field of network analysis as a whole, its importance for the study of culture and networks is less well known. As with earlier work in graph theory, the techniques developed at Harvard in the 1970s and 1980s emerged out of attempts to systematize and contextualize the study of social interactions—not unlike those described in the previous section of this chapter. In other words, network methods are in fact deeply cultural in their origins, and in the past few decades they have been applied in quite innovative ways to the mapping and measurement of cultural relations.

## *Measurement Choices and Challenges*

Cultural analysts have taken a number of very different approaches to understanding the link between culture and networks.[36] These approaches differ in whether they understand the interplay between networks and culture as *causal, descriptive*, or *co-constitutive*. We will briefly sketch several of these approaches to give a sense of the choices facing researchers who seek to use network approaches to cultural measurement.

### SHOWING CAUSAL RELATIONS BETWEEN
### CULTURE AND NETWORKS

First, researchers can use network analytic techniques to investigate causal relations between networks and culture. The focus here is on understanding ways in which networks shape or channel various kinds of cultural processes, from flows of ideas, innovations, and practices to the historical emergence of new cultural identities, protest repertoires, or macrostructural formations.

One classic approach to this can be seen in diffusion studies. In the previous chapter, we focused on measuring the diffusion of objects, but ideas, norms, and practices also spread through and across social spaces. Influential studies of the diffusion of innovation—such as those by Katz and Lazarsfeld; Coleman, Katz, and Menzel; and Burt—demonstrate how cultural elements can flow through networks via mechanisms as simple as interpersonal contact or through more complex processes, such as opinion leadership, broadcasting effects, normative pressure, or competitive mimicry.[37] This conception of cultural values or practices as flowing through networks can also be seen in theories of the critical mass in social movement analysis, as well as in studies of influence in small worlds, such as work by Duncan Watts and colleagues.[38]

This approach has some limitations, as it sees networks and culture as fundamentally different from each other; networks are merely conduits for culture. Researchers measure the ways in which cultural elements (such as ideas, opinions, values, tastes, innovations, protest repertoires, and other things that we generally deem to be "cultural") travel through external networks, which in turn determine how fast they travel and how far they reach. Networks are deemed to have an independent ontology from the cultural elements that move through them from node to node (i.e., from one location in a network to another).

A different approach to understanding causal relations between networks and culture relies not on direct associational ties, but on *positions* within broader networks based on the notion of structural equivalence, or the idea that two nodes that are connected with other nodes in the same way are likely to be similar in other ways.[39] For example, Peter Bearman uses blockmodeling techniques to show how the shifting rhetorical orientations of pre–civil war English elites were rooted in changing network positions.[40] Likewise, Roger Gould shows how "participatory identities" in nineteenth-century Parisian insurrections shifted from class to urban community, based on the changing positions of participants in relation to their work, their neighborhood, and the state.[41] These researchers show how actors' positions in relation to other blocks of actors—rather than direct connections themselves—contribute to the generation of shared identities and discourse; that is, network structure plays a causal role in historical shifts in cultural processes and forms.

Other recent work flips the causal arrow in the other direction; rather than showing how networks shape culture, it shows how cultural elements such as tastes and values can shape network structure. For example, Omar Lizardo argues that "highbrow" cultural tastes are more easily converted into exclusionary and solidaristic "strong-tie" networks than tastes for popular culture, which facilitate "weak ties" that bridge locations in social space.[42] Likewise, Vaisey and Lizardo argue that deep-seated, largely unconscious moral worldviews can contribute to the selection of friendship relations, as well as to the cultivation or decay of those ties over time.[43] In both cases, the researchers identify and compare various kinds of cultural elements (drawing on survey responses about tastes and worldviews) and show how they influence different kinds of network structures; they argue that culture causes particular kinds of network formations, rather than the other way around.

At a more macro level, researchers have used cultural data to show how changing networks contribute to large-scale historical shifts. For example, Emily Erikson and Peter Bearman analyze shipping logs, journals, correspondence, and reports to show that the East India Company created a dense global network of ship captains working to advance their own material gain through private trade with the East.[44] This network eventually laid the groundwork for globalization and monopoly trade, leading to the demise of the private trading system that created it. Here, shipping routes gathered from textual records serve as indicators of individual interests that both flow through and generate social networks. They use network measures to show how the relational configuration was changing in ways that were antithetical to the interests of the individual network members at the time.

## USING NETWORK TOOLS TO DESCRIBE RELATIONS IN CULTURAL ARTIFACTS

A second use of network tools in cultural analysis involves using formal network analytic techniques to describe relations within and between cultural artifacts, such as texts, artistic productions, and other kinds of cultural forms. The core idea here is that cultural forms are themselves relationally composed, and these relations can be systematically mapped and measured in ways that provide insight into both the internal structuring and the external embedding of those cultural elements. These approaches generally break down cultural forms into discrete observable elements (e.g., concepts, categories, practices, narratives, events, and genres) and use formal techniques to map their relations to each other or to other kinds of entities.

An early example of this approach was narrative network analysis. In one variant pioneered by Roberto Franzosi, researchers locate "semantic grammars"—grammatical units consisting of subject-verb-object relations—in historical texts such as news reports, aggregating and abstracting from these units to generate network matrices, which can be analyzed using tools such as clustering or blockmodeling.[45] These in turn can be used as part of larger-scale historical comparisons to show shifts in relations and practices, such as repertoires of contention between powerholders and challengers.[46] Another variant developed by Bearman and his colleagues analyzes causal statements within narratives, treating autobiographical or historical narratives as networks of causal arcs to which network measures such as density, path distance, reach, and centrality can be applied.[47]

A second pioneering approach to cultural network analysis can be found in Carley's work on mental models and cognitive mapping.[48] Carley argues that researchers can construct representations of what she calls people's "mental models" from cultural texts by extracting concepts and using network measures such as density, consensus, and conductivity to show the relations among them. This is justified, she argues, because "the meaning of a concept for an individual is embedded in its relationship to other concepts in the individual's mental model."[49] In other work, Carley has examined complex intersections between different kinds and levels of relations, focusing on communication and learning in an "ecology of networks."[50] A parallel line of inquiry was launched by the aforementioned Harrison White, who wrote at length about the interdependency of social categorization and social networks in his book *Identity and Control.*[51]

Equally pathbreaking is the work of John Mohr, who has used network analytic tools such as blockmodeling and Galois lattices to examine relations between discourse and practice in changing institutional fields.[52] He developed a cultural extension of the Simmelian concept of the duality of persons and groups, which had been mathematically elaborated in network terms by Breiger.[53] Breiger's original idea was that person-to-person networks could be captured by looking at the affiliation of individuals with groups. Mohr subsequently borrowed this intuition to examine the historical relationship between identity categories and poverty relief services. He drew on textual data from progressive-era charity directories that grouped charity recipients into morally laden categories (mothers, drifters) that indexed the "deserving" versus the "undeserving" poor. He has also applied blockmodeling techniques to Foucault's notion of institutional power.[54]

Subsequent researchers have similarly built upon the notion of duality in applying formal relational modeling to cultural analysis. Examples include John Levi Martin's use of an entropy-based dispersion measure to examine relations between animals and job occupation in Richard Scarry's children's books; Ann Mische and Philippa Pattison's use of Galois lattices to examine the tripartite relation between organizations, projects, and events in Brazil (discussed in the next chapter); King-To Yeung's lattice-based analysis of the relationship between group meaning-structures and leadership stability in urban communes; and Craig Rawlings and Michael Bourgeois's analysis of the dual association between organizations and credentialing categories in the establishment of institutional niche positions.[55] Similarly, Chris Bail's research shows that nonprofit organizations that produce language that combines multiple thematic elements—what he calls "cultural betweenness"—are more likely to traverse social media networks and generate large, viral conversations that help such groups call attention to their cause.[56]

## TRACING CO-CONSTITUTION OF NETWORKS AND CULTURE VIA INTERACTION

Finally, a third approach to the use of network tools in cultural measurement brings us back to the analysis of social interaction by tracing how culture and networks co-constitute each other through communicative practices. Although the application of network techniques to cultural forms may seem to pull in the direction of comparative "statics" (i.e., snapshots of structure at various points in time), recent research has pushed toward a dynamic understanding of the cultural processes underlying network formation and change. The more micro versions of this work often draw heavily on the work of Erving Goffman, showing how network relations are constituted through performance and discursive interaction. The more macro version employs techniques for big data analysis, while being similarly concerned with communication patterns and the diffusion of public performances of identity and emotion.[57]

On the micro end of this spectrum, Paul McLean draws explicitly on Goffman's notion of "keying" to analyze the rhetorical construction of patronage ties and self-presentation in Renaissance Florence.[58] Through a content analysis of patronage letters—combining close textual reading with multidimensional scaling of discursive elements—McLean shows how patronage-seekers signal the types of relations and selves that they aspire to (through notions such as "friendship," "honor," and "respect"), and thus build networks through the performance of public self-representations. Likewise, as we show in the next chapter, Mische builds on Goffman's work on performance while combining ethnographic and network methodologies to show how Brazilian political activists activate and deactivate key dimensions of their identities as they construct different kinds of "publics" across overlapping organizational networks.[59]

In a move toward formal measurement that preserves the microinteractional focus, Gibson's work—which we discussed earlier in this chapter—combines conversation analytic-techniques with network tools to show how small-group interactions are permeated with different kinds of relations.[60] He uses Goffman's "participation framework"—which focuses on changing relations between speaker, target, and unaddressed recipients—to map 50,000 speaking turns onto network ties, showing how conversational dynamics are affected by relations such as friendship, cowork, or institutional hierarchy. Likewise, Dan McFarland examines the microdynamics of classroom relations, combining up-close observation of how students and teachers "switch" discursively between interaction roles with abstract visualization of the shifting networks composed by these "discursive moves."[61] In this way, he shows how evolving cultural interactions contribute to the stabilization and destabilization of classroom relations.[62] At a more macro level, Bail's work on the online spread of anti-Muslim discourse similarly focuses on how microprocesses of communicative interaction constitute broader patterns of social relations, albeit across electronic networks on a global scale.[63]

In all of these cases, researchers develop measurements of discursive practices in spoken, written, or electronic discourse that signal—and performatively constitute—relations with other actors. These communicative interactions serve as relational units that can be observed, aggregated, compared, and analyzed using network measures. These measures in turn return to the researchers' hermeneutic toolkit, becoming components of broader sociological analyses and arguments.

## SOCIAL FIELDS

### *History of Measurement*

Field analysis represents a very different type of relational approach to the study of culture. In both interactional and network analyses, researchers pay attention to specific connections between individuals in an interaction or to particular nodes that are linked in a network. This implies a focus on questions such as "Who is friends with whom?" "Who sends email to whom?" and "Which organizations are funded by which funding agencies?" In contrast, field analysis pays attention to the ways in which the whole of a social environment may be greater than the sum of its relational parts. This implies a focus on questions such as "Are there larger forces that shape the relationships between multiple social networks?" and "Are there institutional forces that channel or routinize social interactions in more or less predictable ways?" Field theory thus recognizes that elements within a field (such as social networks or social interactions) are influenced by broader macro-level forces, regardless of whether we have any measures of direct connectivity between the elements within the field.

In the study of culture, the term *social field* usually designates a kind of shared area of operations. For example, DiMaggio and Powell define an organizational field as consisting of "those organizations that, in the aggregate, constitute a recognized area of institutional life: key suppliers, resource and product consumers, regulatory agencies, and other organizations that produce similar services or products."[64] Yet the concept of field analysis was originally developed in physics as a way to account for interactions between objects that are not in immediate contact with one another. Gravity is a classic example—objects in a gravity field are affected by lines of force, even though there is no physical contact between them. Other examples include electric or magnetic fields. One can imagine fields of iron filings pulled and pushed in different directions because they are within the same magnetic field.

The original application of field analysis to social phenomena occurred around the time of World War I in Germany, where Ernst Koehler and others associated with the Gestalt psychology laboratory at the University of Berlin began to think about how human perception operated through a kind of field effect. That is, Gestalt psychologists examined how human perception organizes patterns of relations that enable individuals to navigate broader frameworks. Perhaps the most familiar tenet of the Gestalt tradition is that our perception shifts between one holistic organizing framework and another. Rather than experience gradual change from one framework to another, we reorganize elements in our perceptual environment through dramatic shifts. One well-known way to manufacture a Gestalt switch is through an image that contains two subimages; a famous example contains both an image of a young woman's face and the profile of an older woman. It is difficult to simultaneously "see" both, even though they are contained in the same image, although viewers can be taught how to identify the subimage they did not recognize was there at first.

The use of field analysis in the social sciences was further developed by Kurt Lewin, who had been trained at the University of Berlin before moving to Iowa in the early 1930s to escape Nazi Germany. He took the basic principles of Gestalt psychology and applied them to the study of individuals' experience of their social environment. Initially he worked with children, and his goal was to explain how they understood and maneuvered within a set of cognitive mappings of their environment. Like physicists, Lewin sought to understand how forces operated within a field, with some objects attracting the child and other objects generating forces of repulsion, pushing them away. He focused on producing mapping diagrams that were intended to contain all the relevant elements of a person's cognitive field, drawn in such a way that relations among the elements could be made visible. One of his most important contributions was a rigorous mathematical representation of these systems of relations that he called "hodological space"—an approach that he borrowed from the formal mathematics of topology theory (the branch of modern mathematics that measures patterns of relations without consideration of distance or direction).

Roland Warren carried Lewin's approach forward in his formulation of an organizational field as a topological space.[65] Like Lewin, he believed the logic of the whole was greater than the sum of its parts. But Warren was also deeply interested in Lewin's efforts to integrate the duality of subject and object. Thus, he described how the structure of an organizational field affects the value configurations that are held by organizational agents, and how these values shape the kinds of interorganizational systems that emerge. Warren and colleagues developed this insight further in their descriptions of the "institutionalized thought structure" operating in the field of community service organizations.[66] In this pathbreaking study, the subjective dimensions of an organizational environment were given equal weight and consequence to the conventionally studied objective factors (resource dependencies, exchange relationships, network structures, and the like).

Perhaps the most famous field theorist in modern sociology, however, is the French sociologist Pierre Bourdieu. Bourdieu used the field concept as a way to talk about a region of social life that includes all the people who are immediately involved in it, as well as other people and activities that sustain it (and are sustained by it). The field of literature, for example, would thus include writers, but also publishers, agents, literary critics, and others.[67] Other examples that Bourdieu analyzed include the field of higher education and the field of law.[68] Each of these fields represents an organized social space where some groups of people are in more advantageous positions than others. For example, some people tend to be paid better, have more autonomy, enjoy more recognition, and have more control over how things get done in the field. In short, within each field, some have more symbolic power (i.e., a better chance to both achieve and define the good).

Lastly, today, the term *field* is regularly used by the new institutional school of organizational analysts, a group of scholars who seek to explain the character of markets and industries by identifying the impact of taken-for-granted institutional systems of ideas, rules, practices, and conventions. Most contemporary usage of the term can be traced to the aforementioned article by DiMaggio and Powell.[69] In this text, they incorporated concepts from the networks literature and from the work of Bourdieu to extend Warren's original conceptualization of an organizational field. The resulting construct provides a tool for analyzing markets and industries that carries forward many of Lewin's original ideas about how to study social environments.[70]

# METHODOLOGICAL CHOICES AND CHALLENGES

## *Mapping Distributions of Types of Capital*

For Bourdieu, measuring a field involves searching for the system of goods, or capital, that is specific to the field and for the social organization of how that capital is distributed and how it operates. He theorized that the forces that operated in every field were governed by one or more types of capital, or styles and stocks of resources that were accepted as given, and thus as providing the basis for legitimate power and position within the given social arena. Bourdieu distinguished among various kinds of capital—economic, cultural, and social—each of which he defined as a distinctive form of good. But he also highlighted that every field is grounded in its own specific type of capital, which together helps define the core set of practices and understandings that hold sway in the corresponding arenas of discourse and practice, and which ultimately constitutes what is at stake in a given field. Capital empowers its possessors because when one has an amount of field-specific capital, so too does one have the capacity to act with power and force within the field. According to Bourdieu, the inverse is also true; the more power one has within the field, the more capacity that one has to help shape and mold what counts as capital in that social arena.

How does Bourdieu's work help us understand the measurement of culture within fields? In his empirical studies of different fields (e.g., higher education, law, and art), Bourdieu identified not only different forms of capital that operated within these fields, but also a general tendency for this capital to be unevenly distributed across a given field, thus reflecting (and creating) systems of inequality and forms of power. For example, in his study of French research universities, Bourdieu describes how the academic field was largely governed by the competing logics of two types of capital. First, he identifies a logic defined by acclaim in the field of science itself, within the highly contested and socially ordered social space of research.[71] Second, he describes a logic ordered by the accumulation of economic capital that was necessary to sustain the university and the research endeavor itself. In his discussion of the field of law, Bourdieu identifies a variety of competing capitals, including the critical opposition between the capital associated with "the position of the 'theorist' dedicated to pure doctrinal construction against the position of the 'practitioner' concerned only with the realm of its application."[72]

Two things are new here with regard to measurement. One is Bourdieu's focus on treating a taste for specific cultural content as the object of formal analysis. Here, his methodological innovation was sometimes as simple as using survey and interview responses to look for orderings in taste preferences by occupational membership. So, for example, in the very first figure in his book *Distinction*, Bourdieu presents a set of three simple graphs showing how members of various occupational groupings (ranging from manual workers at one end to higher-education teachers and art producers at the other) chose among a list of musical titles: "The interviewer read out a list of sixteen musical works and asked the respondent to name the composer of each . . ."[73] More generally, Bourdieu and his team are able to describe the way in which the field of cultural tastes is sorted across the cultural landscape in a way that also maps onto specific social locations (or "class fractions"), which in this case is indicated by the respondents' location in particular occupations.

Other scholars have since built upon Bourdieu's focus on distributions of taste and preferences as a way of systematically measuring culture from a field perspective. For example, in her now-classic article examining the field of music, Bethany Bryson shows that even people who describe themselves as tolerant and liberal use their taste in music to reinforce boundaries between themselves and categories of people they dislike. They express dismay at heavy metal, country, rap, and gospel—all genres whose fans tend to be less educated on average.[74] Adam Isaiah Green describes how "tiers of desirability" structure collective sexual life, such that more conventionally attractive individuals enjoy positions of relative power and agency while less attractive individuals are often left out of sexual life altogether.[75] Fishman and Lizardo demonstrate that the distribution of taste is also influenced by macro-level forces: the divergent political trajectories of Portugal and Spain triggered distinct pedagogical practices in the two countries, which led Portuguese youth to express a more "omnivorous" cultural taste profile than Spanish youth.[76] Caitlin Daniel demonstrates how economic inequality maps onto young children's food preferences: because children need to try new foods multiple times before liking them, poor parents are wary of food waste and tend to buy what their children already like, while more wealthy parents repeatedly introduce foods that their children learn to like over time.[77]

The use of *correspondence analysis* is a second important measurement innovation of Bourdieu's approach to field analysis. In *Distinction* and other writings, Bourdieu uses multiple correspondence analyses to map relations among kinds of capital (cultural, economic, political), as well as to show what kinds of capital are dominant (i.e., most prized or valued) within different fields or regions of a field. Correspondence analysis involves mapping a complex, multidimensional, categorical data array (in Bourdieu's case, including measures of cultural tastes, educational attainment, occupational status, economic assets, and political alignments) into a lower-dimensional Euclidean space that represents these various kinds of capital in mutually constituting relations to each other.[78] As a variant of factor analysis, correspondence analysis projects a contingency table with cross-tabulations (or alternatively, a binary "indicator matrix") into weighted eigenvector loadings, which can be used to generate two-dimensional (or higher) visualizations of the salient relationships in the data. Correspondence analysis can serve as an alternative to conventional multivariate statistical approaches to categorical data (such as log-linear analysis). Others have followed Bourdieu in fiercely defending correspondence analysis as a relational mapping technique that is truer to the mutually constituting dynamics of social and cultural fields.[79]

The use of correspondence analysis as a way to study cultural fields has become increasingly popular, and a number of new studies have been published that use this approach effectively. For example, Hanquinet has used correspondence analysis as a way to analyze the relationship between cultural tastes, museum attendance, and social stratification. Similarly, Hanquinet, Savage and Callier link correspondence analysis back to locations in physical space as a way to examine the codeterminations of social and geographic spaces in assessing the character of urban life.[80] Also, Roose uses correspondence analysis as a way to look for alternative pathways toward achieving cultural distinction in Belgium,[81] while Teney and Hanquinet use this tool as a way to measure the shifting character of cultural tastes among youth populations.[82] And Friedland, Mohr, Roose, and Gardinali use correspondence analysis as a way to analyze the underlying institutional logics of love among a population of American university students.[83]

## Measuring Configurations of Relations in Institutional Fields

In organizational analysis, researchers have taken a different approach to measuring how the configuration of relations among actors affects the dynamics of institutional fields.[84] New institutionalists began the measurement of fields by using very indirect and impressionistic assessments of the degree to which organizations within a particular field were more or less homogeneous. Over time, much more sophisticated approaches were developed for measuring fields and their effects. A key focus of the new institutionalist project is assessing the ways in which organizational environments exhibit higher or lower levels of structuration, which is used to assess how strong the field effects will likely be. A variety of factors are identified as contributing to strong fields, including the level of interaction between organizations, the level of uncertainty in the field in question, the level of professionalization among staff, the amount of government control, and the levels of resource dependency between the organizations. Recent examples include Fligstein and McAdam's *A Theory of Fields*, which more explicitly integrates field theory with organizational theory and social movement theory.[85] They argue that field change results from protracted conflict between organizational insiders and outside challengers, who often contest the logic of the field. These authors measure these shifts and conflicts via a combination of archival analysis and quantitative study of collective actors, such as social movement organizations.

A somewhat different style of using cultural measures for field analysis has also begun to develop, partially in response to the work of John Levi Martin, who has also embraced field theory as an alternative to mainstream approaches to social explanation.[86] Like Bourdieu, Martin is highly critical of mainstream tendencies to study individuals and their attributes as pieces within a causal logic of explanation. One place where these ideas have been finding empirical footing is the study of social interactional spaces such as sexual fields.[87] Another example of innovation in the measurement of culture in fields is Bail's use of plagiarism detection software to measure not only shifts in social network structures related to public discourse about Islam, but also broader historical shifts in the dominant interpretation within fields over time.[88] Similarly, Foster, Rzhetsky, and Evans use citation analysis techniques to demonstrate how scientific fields evolve through a delicate equilibrium between risky, innovative research and steady, incremental work—the pace of which enables radical paradigm shifts in turn.[89]

## CONCLUSIONS

This chapter set out to examine the measurement of culture in relational contexts such as social interactions, social networks, and social fields. Although the next chapter turns to the ways in which scholars pivot between levels of analysis, we should note that the social structures discussed here have complex relationships to each other. For example, social fields are not static entities that have a monotonic influence upon social networks or social interaction. Instead, much of the work reviewed here illuminates complex feedback loops among fields, networks, and interactions. Although fields may define rules of behavior that shape individual interactions more often than the other way around, social interactions can quickly reshape social networks in ways that can fundamentally change the contours of social fields.

As we noted at the beginning, the relational point of view inherent in all three levels of analysis depicted in this chapter has an uneasy relationship with the measurement of both objects and people's attributes. For Bourdieu, for example, the field concept was important precisely because it afforded him a way to conduct a relational social science in opposition to what he terms the substantialism of most mainstream sociology. Substantialism is a way of thinking about the object of science as the pursuit of the pure nature of things—a quest to understand what the core substances are that make a thing a thing. For him, such substantialism

> treats the properties attached to agents—occupation, age, sex, qualifications—as forces independent of the relationship within which they 'act'. This eliminates the question of what is determinant in the determinant variable and what is determined in the determined variable, in other words, the question of what, among the properties chosen, consciously or unconsciously, through the indicators under consideration, constitutes the pertinent property that is really capable of determining the relationship within which it is determined.[90]

In this strong framing of the relational perspective, conventional statistical methodologies focusing on covariations in attributes are perceived as intrinsically reductionist—and, by implication, flawed. Emirbayer notes, "Variable-based analysis . . . detaches elements (substances with variable attributes) from their spatiotemporal contexts, analyzing them apart from their relations with other elements within fields of mutual determination and flux."[91] To take attributes out of the transactional flow—for example, through logistic regression analysis or other multivariate techniques—commits a kind of ontological distortion that masks the fundamentally relational and processual composition of social life.

This chapter built upon the insights of the relational turn, while remaining agnostic about the interaction between relations and attributes. There are many ways in which social relations and categorical attributes shape and direct each other. Attributes are often shorthand terms for sedimented relationships; relations have attributes associated with both their structure (e.g., strength, weakness, density, and centrality) and their content (the type of tie) that can be systematically and comparatively studied. At the same time, we want to move beyond the dichotomization of structure and process. We believe that systematic attention to the emergence and evolution of social relationships—from the performance of relations in interaction settings to the coupling and decoupling of network ties to the dynamics of cooperation and opposition in larger fields—can advance our understanding of the cultural structuring of social life. The trick, as we show in the next chapter, is how we pivot among modes of measurement and various types of elements—some relational, some seemingly more substantialist—in our work.

# 4

# PIVOTS AND CHOICES IN THE
# PROCESS OF RESEARCH

**T**HUS far, this book has primarily focused upon reviewing ways of measuring culture at multiple levels of analysis. Our gambit was that the measurement of culture provides a window into both an area of work and issues plaguing sociology more generally. After all, if people are meaning-making animals, then the question of measuring meaning is an aspect of the social that may crop up in any study, whatever its substantive concern or level of analysis. For simplicity, we then proceeded to work through some basic categories of the measurement of meaning—from an individual's acts of meaning-making through the artifacts they make and the relationships they sustain.

Yet many of the best projects we have in mind are more than short forays into measurement. A serious, extended research project often requires different modes of engagement at different moments and at different levels of analysis. This chapter brings to life some of the modes of measurement outlined over the last three chapters by following three projects that have pushed the limits of measuring culture in meaningful ways. We demonstrate how leading sociologists of culture have pivoted among various measurement approaches, highlighting critical decision points where researchers plunged into new research sites or modified their research techniques.

To do so, we have chosen three projects—including two that the book's authors took part in or led. The first is Paul DiMaggio and colleagues' project on the "culture wars," worked through numerous publications over the past two decades. The second is a project on Brazilian political activists conducted by Ann Mische, spanning over twenty years, as described in her book *Partisan Publics* and numerous subsequent articles. The third is a joint project developed by John Mohr, Ronald Breiger, and Robin Wagner-Pacifici, in which the authors analyzed discursive themes in National Security Strategy documents using a combination of qualitative and quantitative techniques, trying to find ways to work through discourse-analytic categories via new measurement tools.[1]

We have chosen these specific projects for both intellectual and pedagogical reasons. While we obviously consider these research studies to be exemplary, we considered many other projects. Yet the three projects we chose have a number of unique virtues. First, they show different modes of work. Breiger, Mohr, and Wagner-Pacifici's project is discourse-analytic, and it attempts to realize in measured form what is, in essence, a "poetic reading" of a cultural text; Mische's research is partly an attempt to meld ethnographic work with quantitative network analysis; and DiMaggio's work shows most clearly the relationship between the theoretical and methodological puzzles that emerge in the flow of an empirical question and the different strategies of measurement that ensue.

Throughout the three projects, we attempt to give an "insider's peek" into the *process* of measuring culture. Thus, rather than simply summarizing the research, we opted to interview the researchers. We then reconstructed the trajectory of the research in narrative form, using both the interview and the actual body of work of each researcher (or research team), and then working with the researchers to coedit it afterward.

## DiMaggio AND THE CURIOUS CASE OF THE MISSING CULTURE WARS

In the early 1990s, pundits and academics alike began talking about a polarization of public opinion—a "culture war" brewing between city and country, secular-progressives and traditionalists.[2] Americans were forming camps, we were told, and these camps were pulling the country apart. Against this popular wisdom, DiMaggio developed a long-term research agenda, investigating whether these wars were indeed being fought, and if so, by whom.[3]

DiMaggio's work with various colleagues follows three distinct subprojects. First, he wanted to know whether the polarization pundits spoke of was indeed borne out by evidence. Were Americans truly more polarized? Given that the answer (at least at the time) was negative, the second move was to ask how this illusion of an incredibly polarized polity came about. Why did Americans see themselves as more divided than they were? Were the culture wars an effect not of public opinion, but of mobilization by dedicated politicos?

DiMaggio and his colleagues—notably Bethany Bryson—started by studying polarization in the arts. As DiMaggio recalled,

I got involved in the 1993 sociology of culture module for the General Social Survey [a major public opinion survey], and I was really curious about how people looked at these issues of cultural authority and cultural diversity because there was absolutely no survey research on that, so we added a set of questions that . . . asked, "Do you believe that there's a canon [of arts]?" And . . . the other thing is that I was involved with the world of arts policy in different ways at this time. This was the period in which the National Endowment for the Arts became sort of a punching bag for the right. And as part of that, there was this rhetoric of there being a "culture war" between secular humanists and people of conservative religious faith. And it seemed to me that it was clearly a political project of some people on the right to construct a culture war that would then contribute to an identity that would pull together a whole lot of different attitudes into a single political identity which would make it easier to organize people.

To get at that social-political intuition, DiMaggio and Bryson focused on polarization in attitudes toward the arts using survey measures.[4] As they suspected, they found little evidence of polarization. Most people seemed to reside quite happily in the middle of the distribution; many people were far from coherent in expressing their attitudes. And—to make things worse for the prophets of the culture wars—the highly educated, who were supposed to lead the leftist-elitist charge for high culture, didn't see "cultural diversity" and "the Western canon" as being in tension with each other. Rather than finding culture warriors gearing up for a battle, it seemed that "the ranks of the highly educated will yield few willing conscripts to culture wars in higher education and the arts; and, as the stakes of such wars ultimately matter the most to the highly educated, even the most bellicose generals will find it difficult to raise large armies."[5]

But as DiMaggio and his colleagues delved deeper into the question of polarization, they increasingly realized that what was meant by "polarization" was not very clear—or at least when people talked about "polarization," a number of competing meanings were conflated with each other. In his next project, with Bryson and John Evans, DiMaggio both expanded the scope of the search for polarization to attitudes beyond the arts and deepened the analytic engagement.[6] As Paul put it, "we realized that the definition of polarization was far from clear. But we figured that there are three or four things that it could mean, and is often used to mean." It could mean, first, that people's attitudes have become more dispersed, and thus more polarized (a "dispersion principle"). Second, and perhaps the closest to our everyday intuition, that different camps cluster more tightly in different groups. That is, that the more bimodal the distribution of attitudes, the more polarized they are (what they called a "bimodal principle"). Third, that the more associated different items become with each other, the more polarized they are (a "constraint principle"). Lastly, polarization may mean that the attitudes of specific kinds of people coalesce in specific ways—evangelicals hold one set of attitudes, Catholics another, etc. (a "consolidation principle").

In terms of measurement, the advance here is in noting that given the different intuitions about what polarization may mean, they needed to implement, develop, or borrow various measures. Most interesting and novel is the measure of the "bimodality principle." As DiMaggio recalled, "the biggest methods challenge was operationalizing the situation in which polarization is bimodality, which is in some ways closest to the folk understanding of polarization: that the population divides itself into two different groups, without a whole lot of people in between. It wasn't quite variance, but there wasn't any obvious measure for it. And then one of my colleagues, Howard Taylor, said 'Well, what about kurtosis?' and I said 'What's kurtosis?' and it seemed to be exactly right." Polarization through this lens is not necessarily about becoming more extreme, but rather about how people "cluster into separate camps."[7] Kurtosis thus measures the "dualedness" of a distribution. The higher the kurtosis measure, the more bimodal the distribution.

The different measures in the paper, then, are not primarily a way to be "rigorous" about the measurement of political attitude-polarization, but rather a way to get at different interpretations of the concept. While kurtosis was a novel application of method, it was not particularly "fancy" or mathematically complex—it was simpler, for example, than the method used to measure the "constraint principle" (Cronbach's alpha). Rather, it was a way to get at precise theoretical intuitions rather than collapsing them with measures of variance or skewness, which are empirically and theoretically distinct.

Much as in his work with Bryson on the arts, DiMaggio et al. found little polarization. There was no culture war—at least in terms of public opinion. There was less polarization in the 1990s than in the 1970s of attitudes about a host of issues, including women's rights and racial integration, although there was somewhat more polarization of attitudes toward abortion and some clustering around "Democrat" and "Republican" as salient identities. But all in all, aside from partisan opposition, there simply seemed to be no *there* there.

And yet political culture does not only reside in people's minds. While the question of how people answer such attitude questions is important, it does not address the puzzle of the culture wars, but rather deepens it. As DiMaggio put it, "[W]e all know that political conflict is rarely driven by the general public, so then the question is why is it that people perceive this high degree of polarization. One possibility is that you have a relatively small number of people who are highly committed and mobilized and you then have an increase in conflict-events, and that would give you something that looked like a culture war, and by some definitions might constitute one. And then, the press is writing as if it is a culture war and constructs one for whatever purposes. So, what the survey research paper made me want to do is first the study of events and second the study of media coverage."

The two possibilities led DiMaggio in different empirical directions. Importantly, in terms of this book, both of them moved him from the measurement of attributes to an analysis of cultural objects—to events and texts. First, looking for events that may be understood as reflecting a culture war, he focused on public conflicts at the local level.[8] Choosing Philadelphia as a case, DiMaggio and colleagues collected data on any local event of conflict about the arts, tracking conflicts over a thirty-two-year period (1965–1997). What they found was that although there was no change in the *number* of conflicts that occurred per year, there was change in their *public character*. In the putative "culture war" years in the 1990s, there were more protests and social movement mobilization around conflicts. In other words, conflicts generated more "noise" and thus were more publicly salient. Of course, in terms of measurement, the work is extremely simple: "all of the methodology was defining what an event was. So, there wasn't any interesting math about that, it was all about 'What's a case?' . . . " Still—interesting math or not—the count of events powerfully complements the more mathematically sophisticated analyses of variance, kurtosis, or Cronbach's alpha used in the study of political attitudes.

While DiMaggio's work measuring events didn't call for complex methods, his work on the journalistic front resulted in one of the early uses of topic modeling in sociology. As DiMaggio remembers, "I started downloading and curated a very large set of articles about cultural conflict over the arts. And I ended up with thousands of articles and absolutely not a clue about what to do with them, so they just sat for quite a number of years. But what turned out to be one of the most important decisions going into that study was in how to define what the population was. There would have been two ways of doing it. One would be to look at any conflict over the arts on which there was a report in the newspaper; the other, which we chose, would have been to look at any discussion of any kind of public support for the arts or any kind of public subsidy for the arts that appeared in the newspaper.

And that provided a context that we could actually observe change in the talk about the government's support for the arts, what we later called the 'semantic environment' for that over time."

The methodological breakthrough in this case came by chance. DiMaggio was working with two of his students, Amir Goldberg and Hana Shepherd, on a different problem—the attempt to see whether a given distribution of attitudes was hiding different groups with specific response patterns, and to group people according to the relationship between their survey responses. Until Goldberg came up with the breakthrough that produced "Relational Class Analysis," or RCA,[9] the group felt like they "kept going around and around in circles." In an attempt to get some outside advice, DiMaggio asked a friend in computer science whether someone there might have the statistical chops to help, and the friend recommended his colleague David Blei. He continues:

> So I called him and set up a lunch . . . I described this problem to him. And he's a very nice guy, but he looked about as bored as a really nice guy can look. So I said, "What are you doing?" And he started describing topic modeling. At the time he had just published a couple of papers on it; it was very young and it totally blew my mind.

The work that Blei described to DiMaggio over lunch was Latent Dirichlet Allocation (LDA). By now a well-known measurement strategy, it defines topics as an inductively generated "distribution over a vocabulary."[10] LDA clusters words into topics according to the probability of their cooccurrence.

Beyond its charm as an inductive, reader-neutral analytic strategy, this method shares some affinities to important theoretical precepts, making it especially valuable for cultural sociology. First, the method captures polysemy—the same words can be used in different relational contexts, and will thus appear in different "topics," which in turn can be used to identify and analyze these different uses. Second, it is a "multiple membership" approach. In effect, texts are assumed to be "heteroglossic," exhibiting "a mixture of different voices rather than something to be put into a single category." This second point especially was important for analyzing a genre such as media reports, which often quoted from different sources (including the particular writer's voice) in the same text.

DiMaggio, Blei, and another graduate student of DiMaggio's, Manish Nag, proceeded to analyze the textual corpus that DiMaggio had collected.[11] The results were in line with the intuition that DiMaggio had following the Philadelphia case: "The tone of press coverage of arts funding shifted dramatically in 1989 from largely celebratory to substantially focused on controversy, producing a cloud of negative representations that persisted to varying degrees throughout the 1990s."[12] Moreover, they also found in subsequent analyses that as the focus on controversies continued, there was a thematic shift from "controversies" as a topic to "culture war" as a master topic.[13] That is, a two-step process seemed to occur: first, the arts began to gain more attention in terms of conflict rather than in celebratory terms; second, the controversies themselves became rekeyed into a different topic—as one front in the putative culture wars.

Although spread out over multiple publications, DiMaggio's project thus coalesced around a historical-political narrative: despite no increased polarization in terms of public attitudes, the culture wars of the 1990s were created as a political project by mobilized actors, especially on the right. This mobilization was mirrored by press coverage that increasingly narrated these conflicts as symptomatic of the culture wars that they claimed to represent. It is a story whose outcomes, of course, we are feeling acutely as this book is written.

Simultaneously, this research project gave rise to methodological innovations. And yet the methodological innovations did not fuel the project. While measurement was extremely rudimentary at certain moments in the project, these moments were no less important for the empirical and theoretical story than the moments in which the measurement strategies became more mathematically or algorithmically complex. Methods and theory, in both cases, are interlinked so that, as Paul put it, "every time I think I have a theoretical conundrum, I need to develop a new method, or at least try somebody else's new method, in order to work my way out of it, to do research that reflects a reasonable solution to the theoretical problem. And then, every time I think I have a methodological issue that I've encountered in my research, it always turns out to ride on a theoretical question."

Lastly, DiMaggio's project highlights two important points. First, it underlines the importance of intellectual networks that span disciplines. It is only through poking around and talking to people outside the discipline that DiMaggio found some of the new measurement strategies outlined here. But just as important, tracing the culture wars exemplifies how the unit of analysis changes throughout a measurement project. Moving from personal attitudes to conflict-events, and then to media representations, allowed DiMaggio to tell a more compelling overarching story, precisely because he could shift the location of political culture. And, with each shift, theoretical stories and measurement challenges crystallized in new ways.

## ETHNOGRAPHY AND MEASUREMENT: MISCHE'S PARTISAN PUBLICS

The second case that we follow here comes from one of this book's authors: Ann Mische's *Partisan Publics* project. It is a set of studies that Mische worked on for over twenty years, and which resulted in her dissertation, her first major book, and a series of influential articles. As such, the project is distinct from the others here in two important ways. First, biographically: while the other two projects were crafted by scholars who have built their careers in other projects—and even other modes of knowing—Mische's is a "dissertation project" story. As a genre, its structure is more of an academic's *bildungsroman*—a story of the crystallization of both an idea and of its protagonist. Second, it is a mixed-methods project in the classic sense of the term. While all three projects use diverse modes of measurement, Mische entered the field primarily as an ethnographer—if one with an analytic, mathematically inclined bent. As such, this project allows us to return to the question of interpretation and measurement in interesting new ways.

In retrospect, the most original puzzle in Mische's project emerged well before she even began her graduate career. After majoring in philosophy in college, she received a journalistic grant to go abroad and "follow her nose." She chose to go to Brazil. Fascinated by the scholar-activist Paulo Freire and the education movement, she spent two years in São Paulo, hanging out with activists in the poorer Eastern Zone of the city and writing journalistic memos back home. Yet, the more she became enmeshed in activists' everyday lives, the more she found herself pulled in new and unanticipated directions. As Mische tells it:

> I discovered that people who were involved in the education movement, including young people, secondary school students, were also involved in church groups; they were also involved in the Worker's Party; they were also involved in labor unions, in Afro-Brazilian cultural movements . . . And they were all going from meeting, to meeting, to meeting, across the urban

periphery and across São Paulo. I began to see the interweaving of these networks, to understand it on a visceral, almost experiential, level.

Still, without an analytic language, this "interweaving of networks" remained an embryonic idea, and, for a while, Mische dropped the project. Joining the New School for graduate school in 1990, she immersed herself in theory and ethnography. She began working on futures and the concept of agency with Mustafa Emirbayer and on young people's aspirations in Harlem with ethnographer Terry Williams. She worked closely with Charles Tilly at the New School, as well as taking a theory course with Harrison White at Columbia, just after he published his important book *Identity and Control*.[14] It was a thoroughly "New York" education, at a moment in which—at least from Mische's perspective—a new and exciting relational school seemed to be emerging among different universities in the city.[15]

But, after a couple of years of reading and thinking, when Mische was ready to dive into her dissertation project, she chose to return to Brazil and examine what she had seen and experienced earlier—the intertwined careers, aspirations, and networks of activists—with more analytic clarity. She returned to São Paulo, and—for the first few months of the years that she subsequently spent in the field—focused primarily on participant observation. Once again, she joined youth activists as they traipsed between partisan, religious, student movement and other types of social and political engagement. And once again, she noticed the interplay and tension among these multiple affiliations as they played out in the dramas of those meetings.

Mische's first analytic and methodological breakthrough, as she tells it both in her book and in the interview for this book, came a few months into the fieldwork.[16] As she was running from meeting to meeting, she felt like she needed an additional analytic strategy to capture what was going on. On her way to a weekend-long student movement "encounter," she created a long survey, meant to capture the participation trajectories and the past and present affiliations of the participants in multiple types of groups. She fielded it in three different youth movement meetings in quick succession. These surveys, which soon became her "trademark" in the field, proved to be a crucial analytic and methodological turning point.

As she relates it:

> While I couldn't do intensive fieldnotes at all my meetings, these were some of the meetings where I did really intensive observations. And at those meetings, I noted that the tension between the partisan affiliation of the students and what they were trying to accomplish became really salient. These were not meetings of a political party, these were meetings of a professional student organization, or the black student movement, or a Catholic youth group. And yet the partisan dynamic was really driving it, even though it was unspoken. Because of my previous time in Brazil, I knew what the factional politics were, so I could follow what was going on there. [After collecting the surveys,] I came out of these three meetings with affiliation trajectory data on almost all of the participants, plus intensive observations of a multiday event, along with extended field notes that I wrote up quickly afterwards. . . . The contrast between what I knew about their affiliations through the surveys—including their partisan background—and what was being expressed at the meetings swung into focus.

In other words—and although this was not exactly what the surveys were crafted for—she realized that these data allowed her to "see" a kind of invisible context that shaped both the individual participation of activists and what she termed the "affiliation profile" of the group. This included affiliations that the activists explicitly expressed (or "performed") in those settings, as well as those that were backgrounded or suppressed (but that she knew about through the surveys).[17] The broader affiliation profile, consisting of both visible and hidden identities, was something that she—and the participants themselves—were aware of. But it was only through the juxtaposition of analytic strategies that this relationship, which became the analytical cornerstone of her project, became apparent. Different networks had different structures of overlapping affiliations and different norms about which identities could and couldn't be expressed, which then shaped activists' participation in different ways. As Mische put it in her first publications from the project that examined the relationship between narrative and networks: "more important than their party affiliation per se is the fact that most of these young people represented links with wider networks of youth (and other) organizations, distinguishable by particular structures of ties between groups, as well as by particular styles of civic intervention."[18]

Although this initial insight focused Mische's gaze on affiliation profiles and networks, this was not enough. While affiliation profiles, networks, trajectories, and narratives had all emerged as analytic foci, there was still something "impressionistic" about her attempt to capture what tied all these pieces of data together. This realization was coupled with a momentous time in Brazil's political history. In 1992, the president of Brazil, Fernando Collor de Mello, was impeached and ousted on corruption charges, with an explosion of youth demonstrations as a crucial aspect of the movement for his impeachment. Mische clearly saw that the kinds of activism and mobilizations that she traced had many real-world effects on democratization in Brazil. As the analytic story of her dissertation was slowly crystallizing, the empirical story of her dissertation seemed to be writing itself.

But while the juxtaposition of surveys and ethnographic field-notes was potent, Mische still didn't have a way to formalize her data in a satisfactory way. Thus, her second breakthrough was, in a way, about methods of formalization. It came through a conference she attended in 1995. This was the first conference dedicated to meaning and measurement hosted by the American Sociological Association's (ASA) *Sociology of Culture* section, organized by Ann Swidler and Michèle Lamont. In one of the small breakout panels, Mische met John Mohr, then a young assistant professor at the University of California, Santa Barbara, who explained how he had used Galois lattices to capture the structure of dual relationships. Created in the 1930s as a way to capture the mathematical shape of semantic structures, Galois lattices were further developed in the 1980s in Germany and France. The technique's core insight was a semiotic one: the meaning of discourse can be found in the network of relationships between kinds of objects and kinds of attributes, whatever they are.

Adopting the technique and pushing its insight a step further, Mohr was working on the policies aimed at poverty relief in nineteenth- and early twentieth-century New York. Utilizing Galois lattices, he constructed a formal lattice of categories used to describe "the poor" and the policy interventions aimed at them—capturing the intersections between kinds of actors and kinds of actions. By using Galois lattices, Mohr could both capture the structure hidden in a large textual corpus, and also see—in graphic form—how the relationship between categories of people and policies changed over time. Moreover, Mohr (like Mische) had read and internalized Breiger's "The Duality of Persons and Groups," where Breiger developed network techniques to formalize the Simmelian notion of the mutual co-constitution of persons and groups.[19] Indeed, his use of Galois lattices to examine the relation between discourse and practice was partly inspired by Breiger's development of Simmel's insights in network terms, providing a cultural extension to a structural insight.

This seemed to be what Mische was searching for—a way to formalize and trace the structure of activists' overlapping affiliations and figure out why they mattered. As she wrote later, lattice analysis "makes possible a simultaneous graphical representation of both the 'between set' and the 'within set' implied by a two-data array."[20] And yet this was not exactly what she needed. The kind of relationship she wanted to capture was threefold: it was a relationship between youth activists who belong to multiple groups and went to multiple events. Whereas Galois lattices were primarily developed to capture dual relationships, Mische was fishing for a way to introduce the notion of "event" into the analysis—a tripartite relationship.

Mathematically out of her depth, Mische contacted Philippa Pattison, a sophisticated mathematical psychologist she met through White. Mische wrote to Pattison asking whether there was a way to capture tripartite relationships with Galois lattices. She replied that there was, and that it would be the kind of challenge she would be happy to tackle together with Mische. And while tripartite lattices had already made it into Mische's dissertation work,[21] it was two years later that she and Pattison published their paper explicating the use of this tripartite connection in a new analysis of the coalescence of Brazil's 1992 impeachment movement. The paper starts with a simple bipartite lattice mapping organizations by projects. Yet, as they note, in such a mapping, there was "no temporality in the analysis, only an abstract mapping of discursively ordered relations in the multi-organizational field."[22] While it is always possible to produce multiple snapshots of the same lattice over time, and thus produce a temporal analysis of discourse-through-time made of cinematic-like moving images—something that both Mohr did in his poverty policy project and Mische did later in her book—they were also after a temporality of a different kind: a *temporality of events*.

The analytic "trick" they employed to make such tripartite lattices possible was to treat nodes not as organizations or as projects, but rather to assume that "*each node on a lattice can be seen as describing a particular relational conjuncture*."[23] Doing so allowed Mische and Pattison to look at different kinds of events in which organizations and projects came together, and to see how these were patterned and connected. More empirically, it provided them with "the means to describe and compare the sociocultural composition of local political settings, as well as how the global structuring of such settings changed over the course of the impeachment mobilization."[24] Constructing tripartite lattices for the entire period leading to the impeachment of Collor de Mello, they could trace stages of articulation, denunciation, and mobilization that were marked first by a discursive reformulation, and then by a simplification of the lattice around "civic" (rather than more segmented or partisan) actions. They could also see clearly what kinds of projects had to be silenced in the process. In other words, it gave them a means to capture—in a general way—how civic action developed.

This, then, is a cultural analysis in a situated sense; it allowed them to trace how ideas and identities take shape *within*, and crucially, *through* different settings. Mische describes this as follows:

> So, the question became, "How does the composition of the setting affect what can or can't be said in the setting?" That's why I had to get—not just who was there, not just the individuals or the organizations that were at that setting, but what projects were expressed. In terms of my observations, this is a measurement

issue. Because I had to abstract, I had to find some kind of an indicator for culture. So, the indicator for culture might be the expression of some element of a party platform. Or it could be some mention of an organizational identity . . . As a cultural sociologist, I know this is a thin understanding of identity. But yet it was doing the work of meaning-making, because for me, it was metonymic for a whole bunch of other stuff.

Metonyms, however, cannot simply be assumed into being—even tripartite Galois lattices have their limits. To make good on her own intellectual project, Mische needed to turn back to the narratives that activists told about themselves, their projects, and the very shape of the political arena.[25] Thus, the entire second part of her eventual book—only one chapter of which comes from the dissertation—returns from lattices to the nitty-gritty of mobilization and narratives in action and interaction. Mische follows the political debates and discussions; the ways in which activists themselves worked together to dissect and anticipate them; and how the narratives and very form of civic action evolved over time. In that sense, she moves back from the formalized measurement of meaning to a more interpretive, interactional moment.

This move is important. Measurement can often move *away* from the way that ethnographers sensitive to the production of meaning have long worked. Indeed, had Mische not written the last few chapters of her book, her work could be seen as a way to grasp a different level of analysis and thus *complement* the miniaturism of ethnographic data and theory.[26] But Mische's work takes a different tack. Rather than moving away from interpretation, or complementing it through formal methods, the moment of measurement ends up *amplifying* interpretation. Starting from interpretive ethnography, her research moved into different modes of measurement, only to return to the actors on the ground with new insights; this allowed her to focus on aspects of the situation that actors could often sense only through a glass darkly. In that way, formalization helped make better sense both of what actors said and of what they could *not* have said at particular junctures—something that ethnographers are often aware of but can seldom demonstrate convincingly.

## MEASURING POLITICAL DISCOURSE: WAGNER-PACIFICI, MOHR, AND BREIGER

The last extended research project followed here was developed by Wagner-Pacifici, Mohr, and Breiger (henceforth *BMW*).[27] Compared to the other two projects that we have described— where, even if parts were coauthored, a primary author's vision can be identified—theirs was an experiment in melding minds. It began with what seemed to be a minor puzzle. Invited to give a talk at a conference on legal justice and injustice, Wagner-Pacifici thought that she would analyze some of the National Security Strategy documents making up the "[George W.] Bush doctrine" of foreign affairs and the administration's "preemptive war policy." She read the documents and published a paper about how the 2002 National Security Strategy report has "ways of making [the] violent innocuous."[28]

Yet as she read this and other National Security Strategy reports—and despite her expertise in discourse analysis— Wagner-Pacifici felt that she was missing something. As she put it, the documents were a bizarre amalgam:

> [T]hey are hard to read. Sometimes they read like bureaucratic memos with hierarchies of embedded arguments: "We're going to do this," and, "We're going to do A, B and C," laying things out

there logically. At other times, they're very hortatory: "Freedom is the most beautiful thing in the world and we're free to bring freedom to free people everywhere." Sometimes they're written in a personal voice, the voice of the president; at other times, it's more of an anonymous bureaucratic collective discourse. Sometimes it's very specific: about specific countries or specific people. Other times, it's vague. And then it has all these entities running around in it, and these entities are relational but they're often not specified. The document usually doesn't tell you who our "friends" are, for example. It was just not clear what kind of a document it was, what job it had, and what genre it was composed in. It was fascinating but also very confusing, and I had this intuition that there were relational networks that were embedded in the document. Sometimes they were explicit, but more often they were implicit. And they mapped onto different kinds of relational networks that exist in social and political life.

But Wagner-Pacifici wasn't sure how to get at that intuition empirically—how to get at the relational entities and networks she sensed in the text. And so, when she ran into Mohr at a conference at New York University, a colleague she had known for years, she asked him whether he was interested in pursuing an analysis of the National Security Strategy documents together. He was intrigued by the puzzle and the possibility of writing something with her, and suggested asking Breiger—both a network theorist and a mathematical sociologist—if he wanted to join forces with them and try to develop ways of thinking about these documents. Breiger happily agreed, and the three started to schedule regular conference calls to talk things through, spending almost a decade meeting once every few weeks to analyze the documents together.

The first important move that BMW developed was a melding of theoretical perspectives. As we saw previously, Mohr's earlier work mapped what he and Breiger termed the "duality" of action and the definition of actors. In a series of articles on the welfare reform of the late nineteenth century and social workers' discourse about the poor, he used blockmodeling and then Galois lattices to map the discursive relations between categories and actions, as well as how they have changed over time.[29] While the co-constitution of action and actors was useful and fascinating, Wagner-Pacifici wanted to see whether it could be pushed further. Like Mische in the *Partisan Publics* project, they wanted a tripartite relationship.

Underlying this analytic move, however, was not eventful temporality, but a reading of literary theorist Kenneth Burke's *A Grammar of Motives*.[30] In this work, Burke developed a powerful rhetorical-dramatic tool that he termed the "dramatistic pentad." This pentad—consisting of an agent, scene, act, agency, and purpose—allowed him to parse out the specific discursive structure of literary and philosophical accounts. This influential mode of understanding drama lends itself to the work that Mohr had already done. Seen through Burke's prism, Mohr's work mapped two points in the pentad—the agent and the act—showing how they co-constituted each other and changed over time.

Pushing the analysis one step further, BMW added another point of the pentad: the "scene" of agent-act relations in the National Security Strategy documents. In other words, they analyzed the general contours of the situation in which the agent is defined and acts. The result, written with computer scientist Petko Bogdanov, is thus an attempt to "make use of [these] new advances in computational text analysis and Burkean interpretation to provide a patterned reading of the U.S. 'National Security Strategy' documents."[31]

In terms of measurement, BMW constructed a three-pronged approach that mirrored their theoretical intervention.

They implemented natural language processing methods (such as named-entity recognition) to look for "actors," a relatively straightforward measuring strategy—basically a computer-generated search and organization of nouns. They then used semantic grammar parsers to identify "acts": using software that recognizes parts of speech, they extracted verbs from the text. Overlaying these two measures, BMW constructed a map of relationships between acts and actors. Which kinds of actors engaged in which kinds of acts? Lastly, and most originally, they used topic models to identify "scenes." The result was one of the earliest uses of topic modeling in sociology, published in the same journal issue as DiMaggio, Nag, and Blei's paper, discussed earlier.[32] The assumption that BMW made is that by grouping elements together, a topic model provides the kind of general situation in which the actors are defined and act. Thus, although not a perfect reflection, topic models are "scenes" of a sort.

Put together, such a triple measurement strategy allowed BMW "to isolate the various combinations [of agents and acts] according to the scenic setting in which they co-occur."[33] This, as Mohr put it, provides "the way in which all of these different associations are piled up, and the different kinds of readings associated with it." Graphically, it provided a way of capturing each scene according to different sets of actors and acts. One example is the case of the topic/setting of "conflict."

Beyond what was then the novelty of using topic models, what is most noteworthy in BMW's first article is their focused attempt to use different measuring techniques to capture each of the three aspects of Burke's pentad. It is an attempt to take a known theorization in literary theory and translate it, as faithfully as possible, into an interaction among modes of measurement. In that sense, the paper is reminiscent of DiMaggio, Evans, and Bryson's multiple measures of polarization.[34] Yet here, instead of taking one object and thinking about it through different measures, the point is to take a complex theoretical framework and remain relatively faithful to its complexity and overlaying of different analytic dimensions—to a "poetic reading." And while this isn't a complete translation (after all, there are two more points to Burke's pentad, as well as the ratio between elements in the pentad, which was a crucial aspect of Burke's literary theory), it is an important step in bringing together what we can think of as techniques of measurement and techniques of interpretation.

This first paper and their early thoughts were also, as Breiger put it, "optimistic," in that BMW hoped to show that through different measuring techniques, researchers can—however imperfectly—approximate a poetic reading.[35] This optimism stands in contrast to the second major BMW paper, which operates as a constructive warning, even as it constitutes an empirical intervention. This paper takes a step back from the complex methods increasingly used for text analysis.[36] While big data and measurement techniques are usually understood as modes of "upscaling" our analytic lenses, this was a step toward a "downscaling" of the act of reading—"an effort to come a little closer to close reading," as Breiger noted. Rather than focus on the measurement of empirical patterns, BMW opted to take stock of what measurement too often misses because of the simplifying assumptions that data mining algorithms—and especially topic models—make.

Instead of the distanced models that most measurement of texts seems to assume, the model that BMW envision is termed a "reader in control hermeneutics (RiCH)" reading: a call to recenter deep, poetic, reading. Such a position is based on

the recognition that textual interpretation proceeds from a continual process of moving back and forth from the parts of a text to the whole. A reader simply cannot know and make sense of the whole without knowing the parts and vice versa. The RiCH reading actively engages this movement back and forth between the parts (punctuation, words, sentences, paragraphs, sections) and whole of a text as a reader constantly recalibrates and reinterprets the meanings of the text.[37]

One step toward such a RiCH model involves the central problem of "stop words"—words like *but* and *while* that do not have an independent meaning. For some computer scientists and statisticians developing the models that we end up using in the measurement of culture, these words are deemed "noise." Because they have no meaning of their own, they are considered essentially "meaningless." And yet of course, words such as *but* and modalities such as *would* or *could* are thick with meaning. Thinking practically, in terms of our measurement tools, such words should change the way that topics are constructed. This, then, calls for a back-and-forth between computer-generated reading of the text, as well as human reading that recursively shapes the way that stop words are interpreted, as crucial parts of the analysis.

Moving between human (meaning intensive) reading and formalization techniques, they suggest a hybrid "algorithm" for such work. Thus, for example, we can flag all the sentences that include the stop word *but* and read them intensively. As they illustrate, such formalization shows that the word *but* often operates as a "coordinating conjunction," importantly tying together various elements of discourse and the texts written during Barack Obama's administration, and often acting to signal support of "the international and institutional order."[38] Having identified this rhetorical form, as a second stage, we can then refine the iterative search to see whether we can find the cases in which *but* serves this coordinating function, thus finding "new things to measure" through each iterative round of human and computer-generated reading.

Although couched in the language of algorithms, the analytic critique that BMW make here is reminiscent of Biernacki's critique of the notion of measuring culture.[39] Seemingly inconsequential words, as Biernacki argued, are often the most important in a hermeneutic reading of a text; this includes words like *but, the,* or the modality of *could* or *should.* But where his conclusion is that we should leave behind the ill-advised attempt to measure meaning, the recursive relation offered by BMW is—if cautiously—more optimistic about the possibility of reforming the measurement of culture to help us grasp some of the things that a deep hermeneutic reading provides. Human reading is crucial, and the idea that we can throw away so-called stop words is ill-advised. But it is the interaction between both kinds of reading that animates BMW's imagination.

The third move in BMW's project, currently in progress, returns to Wagner-Pacifici's initial insight—that there is a class of relational entities (like "foes," "friends," or "enemies") that can be traced both within each document and over time. Thus, as BMW put it in a recent presentation, the relevant questions are:

> [W]hat are all these different types of entities doing in these reports (e.g., what does it mean for the US, or any state, to have "friends")? What are the limits of relationships in a National Security Strategy report? What kinds of networks are conceivable? What are inconceivable? What kinds of actors and networks are historically surpassed? What are historically emerging?[40]

Moreover, as BMW recognize, these questions concern events—what things can certain relational entities do, and what can be done *to* them? Events, entities, and relational networks are mutually constitutive. Taking the example of the "ally," BMW note that "it seems that allies can be members of different kinds of *relational networks*, networks that are established, encouraged, and undone across time and space, that have different kinds of expectations loaded onto them, and that are variably organized and empowered."[41]

To capture this through measurement tools, BMW are turning away from the version of topic modeling they used earlier to a more directed "seeded" topic modeling brought to the attention of BMW by Mohr, where the researcher can feed topic "seeds" (or, to use technical language, "lexical priors") to produce a semiguided set of topics.[42] This, then, allows them to begin—for instance—with a category like "ally" and organize the model around it. Combining this approach with the Burke-inspired work that they began with will, they hope, move them toward a way to capture this triple co-constitution of relations, events, and entities in texts, the shifts that occur in them over time, and perhaps even how these shifts come about.

In summary, throughout the BMW collaboration, the team has focused on the melding of techniques of measurement and interpretation. What made the collaboration powerful was partly the constituent parts—bringing together one of sociology's premier theorists and practitioners of discourse analysis, the codeveloper of (among other things) blockmodeling and the theory of "cultural holes," and the primary mover in the social sciences of the project of measuring culture. But beyond this melding of theoretical minds,[43] the collaboration is interesting in another way. Compared to other sustained work in the measurement of culture, there is a reflexive flavor to the BMW collaboration. Although they were motivated by the attempt to better understand the National Security Strategy documents—by an empirical and political puzzle—they became increasingly interested to test, and push, the limits of measurement. As Mohr said, part of the point was "to go from a very conventional content analysis to

[then] try and make content analysis better. It was more about being truly a real-life card-carrying hermeneuticist." A card-carrying hermeneuticist, perhaps, but one with a powerful computing edge.

## CONCLUSIONS

This chapter detailed the unfolding of three projects that provide prominent examples of pivots between measurement tools, as well as the deep interplay of measurement and hermeneutics. But these are only drops in what is increasingly an ocean of projects. There are many other projects and authors, which are no less fascinating and innovative. With the increasing popularity of "computational sociology," with increasing computing power, and with more and more studies of meaning-making on the internet, a whole universe of studies is emerging. Most of these studies, as with most sociological work in general, will not be so prolonged or so multipronged. Most of them will take a well-defined problem and tackle it with readily available tools. This is how normal science works. Still, precisely because the projects depicted in this chapter are far from typical, it can be instructive to look at some of the convergences and divergences between these projects' logics of interpretation and measurement.

First, and probably most important, although measurement necessarily involves a moment of abstraction, the best research by those on the forefront of measurement is not about simplification. Whether it is about capturing an underlying discursive structure (as in BMW's project), following a phenomenon across different instantiations (as in DiMaggio's work), or amplifying the interpretive, interactional data garnered through ethnographic work (as in Mische's), it is more useful to think of measurement as a beat in a rhythm. For a time, we abstract away through formalization. But this beat is preceded by immersion in the data, and itself precedes other moments of immersion.

Second, as each project shows, tools of formalization allow us to address specific problems. While this is a cliché which faculty often tell our students without quite believing it ourselves, there are problems looking for tools, rather than tools looking for problems. Thus, DiMaggio needed to hunt and gather mathematical tools and formalization techniques from other fields; Mische was not sure if what she wanted to do was even possible; and BMW needed to find innovative ways to capture their own triadic structure for discourse analysis. And, again, although we realize full well that most of us in sociology work the other way around—an ethnographer looking for ethnographic problems, a network sociologist for network problems, etc.—it is interesting to note that, at least in the field of measuring culture, the "problem looking for a method" technique is still the mark of some of our most interesting and generative work. This may characterize a young subdiscipline, still experimenting with ways of knowing. Or, perhaps, it is the effect of the dizzying array of formalization techniques that we have at our disposal. Still, as researchers, we need to step aside and ask ourselves: what exactly do we want formalization to do?

At the same time, of course, the three projects described here follow different paths and emerge through different intellectual motivations. For DiMaggio, each iteration of measurement followed a return to the basics—to the question of polarization at hand. Each mode of measurement called for the next. Rather than alternating between qualitative research and measurement, he thus alternates between modes of measurement. For BMW, the goal of formalization was twofold. One—almost playful—was to see just how closely the authors could follow both the moments of measurement and of hermeneutic interpretation. Is there a horizon where interpretive and formal methods become so close as to become indistinguishable? In that sense, formalization is an interpretive dare. In another sense, however, BMW's project was more reminiscent of Mische's, in that its ultimate end was to be able to focus on what is only vaguely captured in a qualitative reading—whether that is the kind of invisible context that shapes identities and projects in particular settings or discursive structures that can escape our reading. In that second sense, there is an ampliative relationship between measurement and interpretive techniques.

There are other ways of thinking about different measures, as well as the alternation between hermeneutic interpretation and formalization. Most research will end up being more limited in scope (more complementary than ampliative), simply because of the time requirements of going back and forth between aspects of the problem and modes of analysis. Yet what makes the best research, we believe, is the attempt to dig into a phenomenon—an attempt that results not in throwing up one's hands in despair, but in a better interpretive understanding of the phenomenon at hand.

# CONCLUSION

## The Future of Measuring Culture

N an ambitious history of humankind, historian Yuval Noah Harari provides an interesting thought experiment: if an alien life form had visited planet Earth when humans first appeared some 200,000 years ago, what would they think of this new species of animal?[1] Humans were far less powerful than the saber-toothed tigers that roamed the planet at the time, and even less powerful than our Neanderthal cousins, who could easily have overpowered us in hand-to-hand combat. The aliens might well conclude that *Homo sapiens* were unlikely to become the most successful species on the planet—if by success, we mean population growth and the ability to control other species. And yet humans have become so skilled at this that our existence has now begun to threaten the very existence of life as we know it— this era's mass extinction is the only extinction on record that will have been caused by a single species. How did we manage to exercise such powerful, creative—and destructive—control?

The answer, Harari concludes, is our capacity to create what he calls "collective fictions"—something that cultural sociologists would more likely specify as some amalgamation of collective narratives, categories, and schemas. We are, as Aristotle saw long ago, a speaking animal capable of rational thought. But, as Aristotle added, we are also an intensely social animal, much like bees or wolves. It is in the intersection of our sociality and our symbolic capabilities that culture emerges. Our stories and our categories are not simply made up in the minds of detached individuals; rather, they are rooted in our shared experiences and material realities, and they necessarily require language—a shared vocabulary of experience.[2]

Other species have the ability to communicate among their members, and some species even build sophisticated tools to navigate their environment. Certain species of animals have their own traditions—specific ways in which subpopulations communicate and do things together.[3] Yet our ability to create and share abstracted categories and narratives and to act upon them collectively does make us unique. Not only do we give form to what philosopher William James called the "blooming, buzzing confusion" that we are assailed with through our senses, but we also do so in a socially coordinated fashion.[4] That is, we have the capacity to share, disseminate, and argue about how to usefully abstract from reality to survive, prosper, and at times destroy both ourselves and the world around us.

In short, we simultaneously shape and are shaped by our collective categories and narratives. This is the classic dialectic of the human condition that sociologists of knowledge have long defined.[5] It's what we do and who we are. And yet we don't construct our narratives as a species. We construct and negotiate our narratives in smaller collectivities, in delimited social contexts, and in particular social situations.[6] While some narratives and practices have diffused widely, there is no human culture common to us all. This interplay between our shared symbolic capacities and the delimited collectivities in which we exercise them is one of the core tensions of any sociology of culture writ large. It is also a tension that is especially poignant because many of the categories and narratives that we construct and live by use other people as their foils.

Given how central such cultural capacities are to who *we* are, this subject has lain at the core of a hermeneutic tradition that spans history, anthropology, cultural studies, psychology, and many other disciplines. These are the giants' shoulders that the measuring culture project stands upon. Yet, historically, a curious thing has happened. Our technological capacity to capture aspects of culture skyrocketed with statistical advances and the revolution ushered in by the advent of survey research in the early twentieth century; more and more actors became interested in these questions—not only academics and other intellectuals, but also others who hoped to reap the profits of culture, such as marketers, propagandists, and governments. Yet at the same time, this explosion of methods and technological power has not yielded much in the way of a better understanding of culture. The translation of technological advances in measurement into the realm of culture has remained impoverished, partially capturing only a sliver of culture.

And thus, as we stand today in the midst of another technological revolution, with the increasing availability of so-called found data and seemingly unbounded technological capacity for analyzing such data, our efforts to use these capacities are still in their early stages. But if technology itself is unlikely to produce increasingly accurate and useful measurements—as we discuss in more detail later in this conclusion—how should we study how humans create, sustain, and revise collective narratives, categories, and shared practices? At the outset of this book, we suggested that this agenda requires acknowledging the duality of measurement and hermeneutics. Studying the process of how humans coordinate with one another to create, sustain, and revise accounts about our world means navigating the tension between our ability to abstract social observations into discrete measurements and to interpret the inevitable errors resulting from these abstractions.[7]

We have argued thus far that cultural sociology is uniquely positioned to develop systematic theories of how to navigate the duality of interpretation and measurement. This book, at its root, is a first effort to formalize this process by taking stock of the history of measuring meaning at multiple levels of analysis, as well as identifying some of the conceptual and practical frontiers that cultural sociologists will have to navigate in the coming years as the field of culture evolves to further influence not only sociology, but other disciplines as well.

## FRONTIERS OF MEASUREMENT: SOME CONCEPTUAL CHALLENGES

*Measuring Culture* proceeded through an analytic separation of three intertwined approaches to measurement—three starting points. We can start with the people who make meaning. This sometimes requires us to bracket the fact that these people are the product of numerous interactions, networks, and materialities. It often, if not always, decontextualizes meaning-making from the situations and environments in which it occurs. Still, it allows us to start in the midst of the world and see what people are up to—how they think, talk, and act. Similarly, we can begin with the materiality of the world, with the stuff that we have meaningfully produced and that acts back upon us. Or we can begin with relationships themselves, which may have existed ontologically prior to objects and individuals—that, after all, is the gambit of the discipline of sociology as a whole—but which often pushes us to gloss over the histories and anticipations of the actors in the relations, as well as the material affordances within which these relations take place.

While we do not think that the separation among these analytic strategies reflects the structure of the social world, these approaches are different in practice; they differ in the modes of measurement that researchers developed to capture each approach, and thus in the insights they provide. An important part of this book's argument is that rather than requiring a unified theory of all culture, it may be more analytically and empirically productive to be nimble in our transitions among approaches in the process of research—what we called the "pivots" of measurement.

Still, being nimble does not mean that there are no overarching questions and challenges that we have to face together. Another advantage of thinking separately about these approaches to culture is that we can start to identify common conceptual challenges that future researchers attempting to measure aspects of culture will need to work through creatively. These are distinct from the specific empirical and theoretical challenges that we surely have to solve—there are too many of these for us to review, and there would be no point to doing so. Rather, these are important empirical and conceptual challenges that cut through different methods.

Chapter 1 focused on measuring culture in people. That is, starting with the actor, we approach culture by studying how people think, talk, and act. The core tension that we identified and outlined was between the deliberate and nondeliberate realms of human thinking and the related inconsistencies between what people think, say, and do. We also argued that the internal logic of this stream of research has raised a new question: how far must cultural sociology go into the subpersonal level of analysis? Neuroscience and cognitive science, for example, have made enormous strides in recent decades, many of which have received cautious (and not-so-cautious) enthusiasm from cultural sociologists.[8] However, at the same time, most cultural sociologists continue to view functional magnetic resonance imaging (fMRI) studies with a degree of skepticism, wondering what we miss or decontextualize as we reach deeper into biological processes.

Next, chapter 2 drew attention to cultural objects. This analytic approach reversed the direction of research presented earlier. If people make meaningful objects, they then encounter them (sometimes literally bumping into them) in their materiality. Thus, we can start from these artifacts in order to study the processes of meaning-making that gave them life, as well as how materiality itself affects the way that meaning is recursively shaped. But one pitfall we face in measuring objects is assuming that meanings are inherent in, or easily discernible from, objects. Meanings are products of people, objects, and contexts. When we consider objects alone, the best we can do is identify potential meanings or meaning structures. To measure cultural objects often means to measure affordances and imagine how they are taken up in actuality. If we want to understand intended meanings or people's interpretations of objects, we argue that we need to find measures that are sensitive to both the qualities of objects and people's interactions with objects in production, circulation, and reception—interactions that are located in particular settings.

Chapter 3 built upon the previous two chapters in order to study social relationships that unfold in micro-level interactions between individuals, as well as in broader social structures such as social networks and fields. And, as with people and objects, some problems keep recurring: how does one determine the boundaries of a social network in such a way that it encompasses the social relationships that shape a given system of meaning, all without becoming so diffuse as to lose its coherence and relevance to the topic at hand? Equally challenging are broader questions about the social fields that encircle and bridge social networks—what shared properties define these fields, and what can we use to demarcate one field from another? What happens, in Gil Eyal's evocative terms, in the space between the fields?[9]

## META-CONCERNS

What threads, if any, connect these questions? Although each of the chapters that we just described addresses many of these challenges, we think that there are two broad questions that consistently crop up in different guises throughout the book: that of potentiality and that of absence.

First is the question of potentiality—latent qualities that might lie dormant in individuals, objects, or relationships, which may or may not be activated and which lead to an array of possible outcomes. As sociologists of culture increasingly argue, much of our meaning-making emerges in interactions with the environment rather than being lodged within us.[10] On an individual level, while it is important to think about people's schemas and dispositions, the situations in which schemas are activated matter, and dispositions are far more plastic and less coherent than most of us seem to assume.[11] Rather than a simple, internalized structure of meaning, it is more useful to think about an array of potentialities that can be actualized differently in specific environments. This is a challenge for experimental designs, but it is not circumscribed to such research, or even to quantitative research more broadly.[12] Across methodologies, the challenge is to develop tools that can help us capture the relationships and patterning of thought, talk, and action across situations.

A similar challenge haunts the study of both cultural objects and relations. As chapter 2 shows, objects' potential to signify is complicated by their material properties. Condoms become bracelets; the color on a sign fades and changes its possible set of meanings.[13] There is a kind of double potentiality in the study of cultural objects—their interpretation and use are contextual, and their material properties as objects are unstable. And relations too have their potentials—whether it is the ways in which interactions assume potential futures, or the way that activists understand their meetings by imagining other meetings.[14]

This challenge of potentiality is important not just as an attempt to capture the possible variation of meaning-making—a distribution of potential instantiations that researchers need to be aware of and that cannot be reduced to so-called measurement error. Rather, it is also because people are often themselves aware of the potential of meaning. To understand and measure cultural accomplishments such as humor or metaphor, we need an understanding of people's awareness of the potential of meaning-making. Moreover, as some of the researchers discussed in this book have developed in their empirical work, in order to understand how people make meaning in the present, we need a deeper understanding of how people imagine their future and the unfolding of their lives.[15] Both subjective and objective potentialities await both more rigorous theorization and the development of tools of measurement.

In other words, the question of potentiality requires us to come to terms with and develop tools to study what can transpire, recognizing the importance of the possible permutations of meaning. A related question is that of absence—the empty spaces of relationships, networks, and fields, as well as what is left unsaid and unthought.

Compared to potentiality, absence has received more attention. After all, we intuitively know that some absences are deeply meaningful—what people do *not* talk about in a meeting or on a date is often the most interesting thing about it; what people don't care enough to think about is as important as what they do focus on.[16] But how do we know what unsaid thing is more important than another? The hermeneutic tradition has spent much energy on the question of such silences and how they can be productively "read," but how would a measurement strategy work? We need a typology of absences. Secrets,[17] for example, can be approached differently than avoidances, which are different still from things that are so taken for granted as to become unremarkable.

This is clear in the case of thought, talk, and action, but it is no less clear in the realm of cultural objects: the fashions that never take off are as important to understanding culture as those that do; the same goes for the objects that remain in the museum's warehouse or never make it there to begin with. Perhaps one of the most interesting critiques that Biernacki posed in his acerbic attack on the entire "measuring culture" project was his argument that in Bearman and Stovel's computational approach to text in their article "Becoming a Nazi," they treated word counts as a straightforward measure of the importance of elements of a story.[18] He reminded us that a word that appears only once—or that even never appears at all—can be the most important one in the story. How could we capture such a luminous absence?

The same applies to relations. Goffman once observed that the most interesting thing about a dinner is who was *not* invited—whom we don't interact with, or those we interact with but fail to mention to people in our social world, structures our social world in important ways.[19] Similarly, one of the most interesting features of a network is where it isn't. Here, of course, there is a burgeoning body of literature ranging from the translation of the "structural hole" concept in network theory to "cultural holes," which look at the absences in networks of cultural tastes, discourses, and logics; to Mische's work combining Galois lattices and ethnography, in which identities that are not expressed shape the public as much as those that do.[20]

Common to both these challenges is our emphasis throughout this book on the crucial importance of the relationship between the hermeneutic and formalist moments in a research project. Without being enmeshed in hermeneutic questions and debates, measurement can gravitate to the easily observable and countable. But this need not be the case. Many of the best measurement projects grasp at least some of the silences as potentialities of culture—sometimes in ways that are as illuminating as the more traditional close reading of texts and actions—but to achieve this, we must not lose sight of the theoretical, hermeneutic impulse.

## RESEARCH PIVOTS

While the questions discussed here are some of the intellectual challenges that we need to solve as part of a broader project of measuring culture, there is a complementary aspect of measuring culture that we need to examine: the eminently practical relationship to projects as they evolve. Theoretical questions, after all, are only important insofar as they allow us to think about our observations in new and interesting ways.

Chapter 4 of this book thus attempted to use a practical register to break down the barriers between approaches and levels of analysis reviewed in previous chapters. We thus interviewed and synthesized the work of authors who conducted what we consider to be exemplary studies—the work of DiMaggio on the culture wars, the investigation by Mische of student activism in Brazil, and the efforts of Wagner-Pacifici, Mohr, and Breiger (BMW) to combine varied computational discourse analysis tools to study issues pertaining to national security.

Reflecting upon the broader themes and commonalities that emerged across the stories of how these three research projects evolved, we identified two overarching practical points. First, each of the teams succeeded in part through interdisciplinary and intra-disciplinary bridging among their members. BMW's collaboration involved an unlikely group of researchers who, while all sociologists, ranged from the deeply hermeneutic tradition in cultural sociology to the most formal theorists in the field; DiMaggio et al.'s research got important traction when he reached out to computer scientists and experts in the field of natural-language processing; and Mische's work greatly benefited from her collaboration with a mathematical psychologist to create tripartite Galois lattices.

The second theme that stands out to us is that none of the research trajectories depicted here begin with hermeneutic approaches and evolve into increasingly formalized proofs or methods. In each of the case studies, there were moments where the push to formalize measurement—to transform narratives, discourses, and ethnographic observations into neatly categorized numbers—only amplified the need for more hermeneutic work. Rather than a call to move beyond the interpretive and hermeneutic, we expect that many of the best research projects going forward should move recursively among modes of analysis.

While we think these examples are suggestive, they leave many questions unanswered. For example, how exactly does one strike the appropriate balance between interpretation and measurement in different projects? Is there a broader pattern to the movement among levels of analysis? In an attempt to catalog how a more diverse group of scholars pivots among different levels of analysis, the authors of this book each completed a survey that documented how they navigate different levels of analysis across time during one of their more prominent research studies. The graphs shown here illustrate the results of this impressionistic exercise. The *x*-axis of each graph describes time intervals within the research project (standardized to account for differences in the duration of the projects); and the *y*-axis describes the level of analysis (where small numbers refer to ethnography, or deep hermeneutic analysis, and large numbers refer to more macro-levels of analysis such as social networks or fields).

Although each of these projects has an interesting narrative about the particular choices that researchers can make in

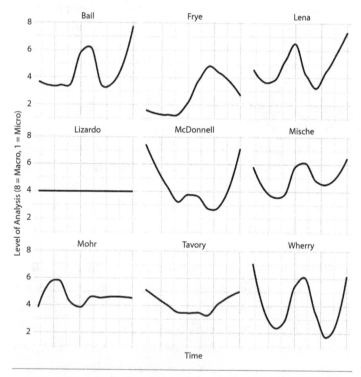

FIGURE 5.1 Pivots in the Level of Analysis in Recent Research Projects by the Coauthors of This Volume. These graphs refer to the following research projects: Bail 2015b; Frye 2017; Lena 2012; Lizardo 2014; McDonnell 2016; Mische 2008; Mohr, Wagner-Pacifici, and Breiger (2013, 2015, 2018; Tavory 2016; Wherry 2011.

navigating various levels of analysis, several brief observations are warranted. While there seems to be many ways to skin a cat, there are some suggestive patterns: Bail's, Lena's, Mische's, and Wherry's studies follow a similar trajectory, where the researchers started at midrange levels of analysis, drifted toward fairly macro-levels of analysis, returned to more micro-levels of analysis, and ultimately concluded once again at macro-levels of analysis. By contrast, McDonnell and Tavory—two of the three ethnographers in this volume—did not start by working inductively from micro-levels of analysis. Instead, their research efforts began at more meso- (or even macro-) levels of analysis, probed intensively at micro-levels of analysis, and ultimately concluded at the meso-levels where they began.

Moreover, not every research project in cultural sociology involves significant pivots in the research process. Thus, an important exception to the shifts described can be seen in Lizardo's work, marked by more "surgical" interventions that did not require him to shift among levels of analysis within the research project, resulting in a flat line in the graph.

There are thus many paths that researchers can take as they develop their research. Yet in most studies, researchers should expect their level of analysis to shift in the process of research, rather than seeing that as a mark of woolly-headed thinking. This is as it should be: struggling with empirical and theoretical questions often forces us to shift analytic lenses midflight.

## COMPUTATIONAL SOCIAL SCIENCE AND THE FUTURE OF MEASURING CULTURE

We conclude this book by highlighting a trend that was featured in several of the preceding chapters: the rapidly increasing amount of data and new analytic tools that can be thought of as the emerging field of computational social science. The growing amount of data that surrounds us is both obvious and dizzying. More data were collected in 2002 than all the previous years of history combined.[21] And, even while we write these conclusions, the amount of data accumulated each day is surpassing that of all data collected in 2002. Most important for cultural sociologists, the data explosion includes a variety of information that is central to the process of meaning-making.[22] The most obvious type of such data is the voluminous text-based data produced each day on social media sites such as Facebook and Twitter. But ongoing efforts to digitally archive virtually every book ever written—alongside vast historical archives—mean that cultural sociologists have the gamut of information sources, ranging from everyday accounts of lives, to literary texts, to cat pictures.

Equally important is that the data revolution is not limited to text. As we noted in chapter 1, these new wellsprings of data contain information about individuals' micro-level actions that can be aggregated into broader social patterns. As chapter 2 notes, they also contain vast troves of audiovisual data, the potential of which has been almost wholly unrealized by cultural sociologists. And as chapter 3 says, such data allow us to investigate interactions, institutions, and meso-level social communities in unprecedented ways.

In addition to the sheer scale of data for studying meaning-making that has recently become available, the field of computational social science is rapidly producing new tools to analyze it. Many of these techniques take advantage of the dramatic increases in computing power that have been developed alongside the remarkable outgrowth of data in recent years.[23] For example, topic models, text networks, and word embeddings have become increasingly valuable for identifying latent themes in text.[24] The field of machine learning is rapidly producing an analogous set of tools for audiovisual data that arguably work even better than the aforementioned tools for text. For example, image detection has become so powerful that it can be used to help diagnose autism early by measuring shifts in children's faces as they watch videos of people interacting.[25]

At the same time, as we explore throughout this book, the new tools being produced in the field of computational social science are more in need of hermeneutics and interpretation than ever. A topic-modeling algorithm will identify latent themes within any corpus of documents, but many of those who have experience with this method will know that, left to their own devices, topic-modeling algorithms can produce very poor—or even nonsensical—interpretations of text. Indeed, much like BMW, computer scientist David Mimno, who is one of the pioneers of topic modeling, describes topic models as "tools for reading."[26] Effective use of topic models depends upon validation by human coders to avoid "reading the tea leaves"—finding spurious, meaningless patterns—that can be created by unsupervised models. The results produced by an algorithm should never be the end game of research: instead, these results should provoke further interpretive analysis.

If readers are excited about the possibilities of computational social science for cultural sociology, they are probably still left wondering: what would good work in this domain look like? The answer to this question, we believe, will often involve the type of research pivoting described in this discussion—tacking back and forth between deep reading, or even observations, and big data. But pivoting need not involve the marriage of qualitative and quantitative approaches either. Survey research on culture could be fruitfully combined with the texts that people produce on social media by creating new research instruments that link responses across different platforms. Text networks can be used to enrich studies of social fields, while experiments designed to capture cultural processes can be embedded into online platforms.[27]

Time will tell whether computational social science represents a watershed moment for cultural sociology—where new possibilities will reconfigure our research and theorizing in fundamental ways—or simply adds another set of tools, data sources, and concepts that will enrich the field. Regardless of which situation unfolds, computational sociologists of culture will face interesting questions: To what extent can machines be taught to interpret meaning on their own? How are different kinds of data produced that are related to offline modes of being in the world? Are there new cultural processes that can be identified at the macro-levels of analysis, such as lengthy historical trends or questions about entire populations instead of just samples? These questions and many others that we might ask will take years to answer. Yet, at the time of this writing, it appears clear that there will be no sociological singularity any time soon. That is, we do not perceive a point where algorithms can overtake human analysts entirely—nor should there be one. Still, to leave the enormous potential of computational methods on the table would come at great cost to the field of cultural sociology, which appears particularly well positioned to take advantage of this opportunity.

## CONCLUDING REMARKS

Over the past several decades, cultural sociology has risen from an obscure section within the American Sociological Association (ASA) to one of the largest and most dynamic subfields in sociology.[28] It has grown so much during this period that cultural sociologists now regularly venture out to forage in nearly every other subfield in the discipline—from medical sociology to the study of crime and conflict. It brings together scholars who are closer to the humanities, as well as some of the most sophisticated computational scholars. It is in part this mix of perspectives, theoretical traditions, and methodologies that gives it its intellectual staying power.

But with its increasing salience come some risks. First, perhaps as with any growing field, the larger it is, the more fragile it potentially becomes. We can easily imagine warring camps emerging in the sociology of culture. Especially worrying to us is the possibility that with the growth of the computational sociology of culture, a rift could appear between the more interpretive among us and those who use quantitative methods and computational approaches. And then, perhaps more than in other subfields of sociology, cultural sociology has grown and evolved thanks to a close dialogue with other fields—anthropology, social psychology, cognitive science, literary theory, and the humanities more generally. And yet, as we survey the landscape of the field today, we observe only a handful of cultural sociologists seriously reaching out to other fields. The more legitimate cultural sociology becomes, perhaps, the less reason there seems to be to go elsewhere.

Such potential developments, we believe, would be tragic. It would both stultify the possibility of progress in the field and lock us in place. Cultural sociology has much to offer, not only in terms of the theories we have produced, but also because of our advances in measuring culture. We need more—not fewer—forays into other fields. In our ideal world, sociologists of culture would continue their previous engagements while also contributing to (and learning from) emerging fields such as computational social science and the digital humanities.

More than a decade ago, Moody and Light used a cocitation analysis to show that sociology traded coherence for centrality in the social sciences.[29] The sociology of culture, in that sense, is only an extreme case of a trend that may define the discipline of sociology as a whole. Yet, while we would surely want to remain central to both social sciences and other fields, we need to think more together, across our methodological commitments. If we do so, we think, there is much to look forward to.

Our shared conversations over four meetings and the collaborative process of writing this book make manifest the promise of *thinking more together* about measurement. The rigorous debates, unexpected points of agreement, and collective attention paid to measuring culture oriented us toward new potentialities, absences, and pivots. Thinking across modes of observation—people, objects, and relations—and hermeneutic and formal methods, we necessarily established common ground, but we also benefited from productive disagreements. In presenting these ideas, we hope that this book sets a foundation of consensus for cultural sociologists to build upon. *Measuring Culture*, then, truly is an introduction: the start of a much longer conversation, but a start that also models the bridging work that we encounter across disciplines, as well as among ourselves.

# NOTES

## ACKNOWLEDGMENTS

1. These included two ASA Culture Section miniconferences on the topic of "Meaning and Measurement" (in 1995 at George Mason, and in 2003 at Emory), and four conferences on "The Cultural Turn" at the University of California, Santa Barbara, from 1997 to 2003, coorganized by Mohr and Friedland.
2. McDonnell, Bail, and Tavory 2017.

## INTRODUCTION: WHY MEASURE CULTURE?

1. Wagner-Pacifici 2010: 109.
2. For the study of social class and identity, see, e.g., Lamont 1992; for an example of a study that links health outcomes to semiotics, see Tavory and Swidler 2009; for an exemplary cultural study of violence, see Wagner-Pacifici 2005.
3. Fine 1979. See also Mohr and Ghaziani 2014; Ghaziani 2009.
4. Ricoeur 1973.
5. Burke 1945.
6. Smith 2005.
7. Geertz 1973.
8. In one notable example, Lamont and White (2008) conducted a major report on standards for evidence in qualitative research that was commissioned by the National Science Foundation in the United States.

Though this report discusses research on meaning-making, the authors' broader goal was to elucidate standards for scientific evidence in qualitative research to aid grant reviewers, *not* to calibrate qualitative methods for the measurement of meaning-making in detail.

9. We note that the theoretical genealogy of modern cultural sociology can also be traced to other neo-Kantian traditions within continental philosophy that became popular in the early twentieth century (Adorno 1997, 2003; Cassirer 1953), as well as to early pragmatist traditions in the United States (e.g., Dewey 1929; James 1907).

10. Jacobs 1961.

11. Thomas and Znaniecki 1918.

12. Converse 2009.

13. Stouffer, Suchman, DeVinney, Star, and Williams 1949.

14. Lasswell and Leites 1949; Lasswell, Lerner, and Pool 1952.

15. Mohr and Rawlings 2018.

16. Katz and Lazarsfeld 1955.

17. Kroeber and Parsons 1958: 583.

18. Blumer 1969; Berger and Luckmann 1966; Garfinkel 1967.

19. Eyal, Hart, Onculer, Oren, and Rossi 2010; Lamont 1992; Lamont and Fournier 1992; Lamont and Molnár 2002; Peterson 1976; Peterson and Berger 1975; Griswold 1986, 1987b; Alexander and Smith 1993; Swidler 1986; Friedland and Alford 1991; Powell and DiMaggio 1991; Zucker 1991; for the phenomenological and ethnomethodological resonances of such work, see Heritage 1984.

20. White 1992.

21. White 2008b; Tilly 1978; Krinsky and Mische 2013.

22. For a review, see Mische 2011.

23. Lazer and Radford 2017.

24. McFarland, Lewis, and Goldberg 2016.

25. Mohr, Wagner-Pacifici, and Breiger 2015.

26. Bail 2014.

27. Jacobs and Spillman 2005.

28. Jerolmack and Khan 2014; Cerulo 2014; Vaisey 2014.

29. Rorty 1979.

30. Becker 2007.

31. Mohr, Wagner-Pacifici, and Breiger 2015.

## 1. MEASURING CULTURE IN PEOPLE

1. Rueschemeyer 2006.
2. Schmaus 2004.
3. Brekhus 2007.
4. Schütz 1967.
5. Berger and Luckmann 1966.
6. Douglas 1986.
7. Nisbett and Wilson 1977; Wegner and Wheatley 1999.
8. Anderson, Goel, Huber, Malhotra, and Watts 2014.
9. Zaller 1992.
10. Wuthnow 1989.
11. Brekhus 2007.
12. Martin 2010.
13. However, see Inkeles 1969.
14. Swidler 2008.
15. Miles 2015; Vaisey 2009; Vaisey and Lizardo 2010.
16. Douglas 1986.
17. Nisbett and Wilson 1977; Lizardo et al. 2016; Vaisey 2009.
18. Miles 2019.
19. Rumelhart and Ortony 1982; Goldberg and Stein 2018.
20. DiMaggio 1997.
21. Vaisey 2009.
22. Lizardo et al. 2016.
23. Gawronski and Bodenhausen 2006.
24. Giddens 1979; Bourdieu 1990.
25. See Pugh 2013.
26. Cerulo 2018; McDonnell 2014; Moore 2017; Pugh 2013; Vaisey and Miles 2014.
27. Miles, Charron-Chénier, and Schleifer 2019; Moore 2017.
28. Miles et al. 2019.
29. Fazio and Olson 2003.
30. Srivastava and Banaji 2011.
31. Greenwald and Farnham 2000.
32. Leschziner 2015; Pugh 2013.
33. Moore 2017.
34. Cunningham, Zelazo, Packer, and Van Bavel 2007.

35. Miles 2015.

36. Schwartz 2012: 8.

37. Miles 2019.

38. Nosek, Hawkins, and Frazier 2011.

39. Miles et al. 2019.

40. Mische n.d.; Winchester 2016.

41. Vila-Henninger 2015.

42. Cunningham et al. 2007.

43. Cunningham and Zelazo 2007.

44. Cerulo 2018.

45. Bartlett 1932.

46. D'Andrade 1991.

47. Goldberg and Stein 2018; Leschziner 2019.

48. Goldberg 2011.

49. Goldberg's approach is related to a measurement tradition in social science concerned with the formal structure of belief systems inaugurated by Converse (1964) and more recently developed by Martin (1999, 2002) and Boutyline and Vaisey (2017). This line of work deals with whether attitudes are tightly or loosely organized (e.g., have high levels of constraint), and thus the unit of analysis is the cluster of beliefs. In Goldberg's approach, the goal is to partition people into clusters based on shared schemas, and thus the unit of analysis is the individual.

50. Baldassarri and Goldberg 2014.

51. Note that both respondents would also be classified as not sharing the same schema as a respondent who rated the genres 0, 2, 0 (country lover, but otherwise neutral).

52. See Goldberg (2011). Recent research has shown that not all methods of extracting schemas from vectors of responses are equally valid. Boutyline (2017) shows that the absolute value of the Pearson correlation between response vectors outperforms relationality as a criterion for measuring schematic distance between two people (with zero meaning completely disjointed and one meaning complete sharing of schemas). He refers to his approach as "Correlational Class Analysis (CCA)." Boutyline further argues that both RCA and CCA may be variants of a more general analytic strategy that he refers to as "Schematic Class Analysis."

53. Baldassarri and Goldberg 2014; Daenekindt, de Koster, and van der Waal 2017; DiMaggio, Sotoudeh, Goldberg, and Shepherd 2018; Boutyline 2017; Daenekindt 2017; Goldberg 2011; DiMaggio and Goldberg 2018.

54. In recent work, Hunzaker and Valentino (2019) recommend moving beyond the indirect relational strategy pioneered by Goldberg and toward a direct relational approach to measuring all the pairwise associations between concepts that constitute people's schematic understanding of a given domain (e.g., food, politics, music, etc.).

55. See Mills 1940: 904.

56. de Saussure 1964.

57. Foucault 1970.

58. Boden and Zimmerman 1991; Fairclough 1992; Wuthnow 1989.

59. Habermas 1984.

60. Benney and Hughes 1956: 137.

61. Brenner 1981: 115.

62. Becker and Geer 1957; Benney and Hughes 1956;Briggs 1986; Deutscher, Pestello, and Pestello 1993.

63. Jerolmack and Khan 2014: 178.

64. Cerulo 2014; Vaisey 2014.

65. Indeed, in the introduction of their article on the attitudinal fallacy, Jerolmack and Khan (2014) quote Pugh (2013: 50), acknowledging that interviews can "discern the emotional landscape of desire, morality, and expectations."

66. Vaisey 2010; Reynolds and Baird 2010; Strand and Winston 2008; Young 2006.

67. Hanson 1994; Hardie 2015; Schneider and Stevenson 2000; Schoon and Ng-Knight 2017.

68. Frye and Trinitapoli 2015; Johnson-Hanks, Bachrach, Morgan, and Kohler 2011; Hardie 2014; MacLeod 2018; Silva 2013.

69. Mische 2014: 441.

70. Frye 2012; Pimlott-Wilson 2015.

71. Illouz 2008; Pagis 2016; Silva 2013.

72. Harding 2010.

73. Frye 2012.

74. Frye 2012: 1565.

75. Ewick and Silbey 1995; Frye 2017; Jacobs 2002; Polletta 2009; Small 2004; Somers 1994; Wherry 2011.

76. Tilly 2002: 39.

77. Ewick and Silbey 1995.

78. Polletta 2015.

79. Franzosi 1998.

80. Polletta 2009: 12.

81. Lena and Lindemann 2014.

82. Polletta 2009: 93.

83. Abend 2014.

84. Frye 2017; Rosen 2017.

85. Polletta, Chen, Gardner, and Motes 2011; Simko 2012; Somers 1994.

86. Polletta 2009.

87. Cerulo 1998; Polletta, Trigoso, Adams, and Ebner 2013; Rambotti 2017.

88. Bail 2015a; Rosen 2017.

89. Polletta et al. 2013.

90. In addition to the focus group discussions, the authors conducted a survey in which they asked respondents to read each scenario and answer open-ended questions about it afterward.

91. Rosen 2017.

92. Rosen 2017: 276.

93. Bourdieu 1990; Dalton 2004; Gross 2009; Joas 1996; Sewell 2005; Swidler 2001; Whitford 2002.

94. Sewell 2005; Bourdieu 1990.

95. Bourdieu 1990.

96. Polanyi 1958.

97. Polanyi 1958, see also Collins 2010.

98. Karmiloff-Smith 1995.

99. Dreyfus 1996; Mauss 1973.

100. Eliasoph and Lichterman 2003; Khan and Jerolmack 2013.

101. On the distinction between "experience-near" and "experience-distant" strategies, see Geertz 1983.

102. Du Bois 1899; Thomas and Znaniecki 1918.

103. Bourdieu 1990.

104. Wacquant 2004: 59.

105. Mears 2013.

106. Bail 2014; Bruch, Feinberg, and Lee 2016; Evans and Aceves 2016; Lewis and Kaufman 2018; Wagner-Pacifici, Mohr, and Breiger 2015.

107. Desmond 2007; Mears 2013; Wacquant 2004.

108. Wacquant 2004.

109. Wacquant 2004: 3.

110. Wacquant 2015: 5, emphasis in the original.

111. Wacquant 2015: 59.

112. Desmond 2007.
113. Desmond 2007: 284,
114. Desmond 2007: 267.
115. Mears 2011.
116. Mears 2011: 7.
117. Mears 2011: 105.
118. Collins and Kusch 1999.
119. Vallacher and Wegner 2014.
120. Weber 1958.
121. Collins 1983.
122. Eagle and Pentland 2006; Anderson et al. 2014.
123. McFarland, Jurafsky, and Rawlings 2013.
124. Collins 2004.
125. Ingram and Morris 2007.
126. Ingram and Morris 2007: 566.
127. Lewis 2016.
128. Pugh 2013.
129. Hochschild 1983.
130. Illouz 2008.
131. E.g. Carter 2005; Lamont et al. 2016; Simi, Blee, DeMichele, and Windisch 2017.
132. Carter 2005; Tannen 1993.
133. Latour 1993.

## 2. MEASURING CULTURE IN OBJECTS

1. Barthes 1967.
2. Wolff 1992.
3. Thanks to Clayton Childress for this metaphor.
4. Jerolmack and Tavory 2014.
5. Lizardo 2016; Wuthnow and Witten 1988.
6. Becker 2007; Taylor, Stoltz, and McDonnell 2019.
7. Becker 2007.
8. Latour 1992; 2005.
9. Swidler 1986; Vaisey 2009.
10. Griswold 1986.
11. McDonnell 2010.

12. Paramei 2005.
13. Douglas 1966.
14. Wallach 2006.
15. See also Biernacki 2012.
16. Hutchison 2006.
17. Rose-Greenland 2016.
18. White and White 1965.
19. DeNora 1995.
20. Simmel 1997: 110f.
21. Elias 1982; Simmel 1997; DeSoucey 2010; Johnston and Baumann 2009; Visser 1991; Ferguson 2004; Rao et al. 2005; Hennion 2015; Leschziner 2015.
22. Leschziner and Dakin 2008.
23. Synnott 1991; Low 2005; Simmel 1908; Berger and Luckmann 1966: 203.
24. Low 2005; Synnott 1991.
25. Mangione 2016.
26. Polanyi 1958.
27. Sennett 2008.
28. Klett 2014; Nowak and Bennett 2014.
29. Espeland and Sauder 2009; Lena 2012.
30. Elias 1982: 55f.
31. We note that at least two forms of categorization are taking place here: items that belong on tables, and constellations of behaviors that are civilized. Given our attention to objects in this chapter, we focus on the former, even though the objective of many studies of classification is to illuminate the relationship between social organization and systems of classification. We encourage the reader to bear this in mind.
32. Sahlins 1976.
33. Blumer 1969.
34. Mears 2014.
35. Godart and Mears 2009.
36. Lena 2006.
37. DiMaggio 1987: 441.
38. Zelizer 2000: 818. For recent work on modeling and measuring the social meanings of money, see Bandelj, Wherry, and Zelizer (2017).
39. Thus, for example, Bandelj, Wherry, and Zelizer (2017) have brought together work from behavioral economics, development economics,

cognitive psychology, and other fields to specify some of the challenges to modeling how the social meanings of money function in financial decision-making.

40. Baumann 2001: 415.
41. Durkheim 1915; Weber 1958.
42. DiMaggio 1987; Traugott 1995; Anderson 1983; Ferguson 2004; Lieberson 2000.
43. Lamont and Molnár 2002.
44. Bowker and Star 1999: 297; Star and Griesemer 1989.
45. Becker 2007.
46. Wagner-Pacifici and Schwartz 1991.
47. Wagner-Pacifici and Schwartz 1991: 382.
48. McDonnell 2016.
49. Domínguez Rubio 2016.
50. Kopytoff 1986.
51. Domínguez Rubio 2014.
52. McDonnell 2016.
53. Lang and Lang 1988.
54. Latour 1992.
55. Griswold 1986, 2012.
56. Griswold 2000; McDonnell 2016.
57. Childress 2017.
58. White and White 1965.
59. Crane 1992; DiMaggio 1982; Griswold 1981; Hirsch 1972; Peterson 1976, 1990.
60. Peterson and Berger 1975.
61. Lopes 1992: 65, 66.
62. Dowd 2004.
63. Anand and Peterson 2000.
64. De Laat 2014; Lena 2006.
65. Cf. Waksman 2009; Walser 1993.
66. Lena 2015: 150.
67. Askin and Mauskapf 2017.
68. Becker 1982.
69. Wohl 2017.
70. Leschziner 2015; Ottenbacher and Harrington 2007.
71. Lena and Pachucki 2013.

72. Fields 2014.
73. Fields 2014: 159.
74. Fields 2014: 160.
75. Rogers 2010.
76. Chanan 1995.
77. Bielby and Harrington 2002.
78. Lee and Peterson 2004; Manuel and Shepherd 2003; Ryan and Peterson 1993.
79. Becker 1982.
80. Crane 1997; Dowd 2004, 2006; Lena 2006; Manuel 1993.
81. Ferguson 1998.
82. Hebdige 1979; O'Brien 2018; Willis 1977.
83. McDonnell 2010.
84. Hobsbawm and Ranger 1983.
85. Schwartz 1996.
86. Kuipers 2015.
87. Hannerz 1992.
88. Ginzburg 1979.
89. DiMaggio 1982, 1983; Levine 1988.
90. Carroll, Khessina, and McKendrick 2010.
91. Grazian 2003.
92. Wherry 2008, 2011. For recent examples from India, see Ranganathan (2018).
93. Peterson 2005: 1089.
94. Horkheimer and Adorno 2006; Schudson 1999.
95. Bourdieu 1984; Coulangeon 2016; Peterson and Kern 1996.
96. Douglas and Isherwood 2002.
97. Csikszentmihalyi and Rochberg-Halton 1981.
98. Hebdige 1979; Childress and Friedkin 2012; Long 2003; Alexander 2004; Collins 2004. See also Grindstaff and Turow (2006) for a review.
99. Griswold 1987a; Radway 1984; Katz and Liebes 1990; Shively 1992; Childress and Friedkin 2012; Long 2003.
100. Belk 1988.
101. Belk 1988: 160.
102. Holt 1997b.
103. Holt 1997a.
104. E.g., Jenkins 2006, 2012; Hebdige 1983; Miller 2008.

105. Csikszentmihalyi and Rochberg-Halton 1981; Miller 2008.

106. Miller 2008; Miller and Woodward 2012.

107. Griswold 1987a; Schudson 1989; Swidler 1992.

108. Rossman 2012.

109. McDonnell, Bail, and Tavory 2017; Schudson 1989.

110. See Bail (2015b) and McDonnell et al. (2017) for critiques of teleological tendencies.

111. McDonnell 2014.

112. Bail 2016.

113. Griswold 1987a.

114. Griswold 1987b; Gell 1998.

115. McDonnell 2016.

116. Baxandall 1972.

## 3. MEASURING CULTURE IN SOCIAL RELATIONSHIPS

1. See especially the edited volume by Wellman and Berkovitz (1988), which collects several important early essays.

2. White, Boorman, and Breiger 1976: 732.

3. Erickson 1988: 99.

4. Emirbayer and Goodwin 1994: 1414.

5. Emirbayer 1997: 282, emphasis in the original.

6. Tavory and Timmermans 2014.

7. Blumer 1969.

8. Garfinkel 1967.

9. Fine 1995.

10. Schegloff 1993.

11. Davis 1959.

12. Glaser and Strauss 1964.

13. Drew and Heritage 1992.

14. E.g., Gibson 2003, 2005.

15. Becker 1998.

16. Roy 1952; see also Becker 2016.

17. Moskos 2008.

18. Lara-Millán 2014: 873–874.

19. Heritage, Robinson, Elliott, Beckett, and Wilkes 2007.

20. See also Maynard, Freese, and Schaeffer 2010; Stivers and Majid 2007.
21. Gibson 2012.
22. Bail 2014.
23. Additionally, as Menchik and Tian (2008) show, interaction also takes place paratextually.
24. Bail, Brown, and Mann 2017.
25. Moreno 1934.
26. Heider 1946; Cartwright and Harary 1956; Davis 1963, 1967.
27. Simmel 1950.
28. Mayo 1933; Roethlisberger and Dickson 1939.
29. Warner and Lunt 1941a, 1941b; Davis, Gardner, and Gardner 1941.
30. Barnes 1954, 1969; Mitchell 1969; Bott 1957.
31. Scott 2000: 27.
32. Bott 1957; Jones 2018.
33. Lee 1969; Granovetter 1973.
34. Nadel 1957.
35. Lorrain and White 1971; White et al. 1976; Emirbayer and Goodwin 1994.
36. For reviews, see DiMaggio 2011; Erikson 2013; Fuhse 2009; Kirchner and Mohr 2010; Mische 2011; Mohr 1998; Pachucki and Breiger 2010.
37. Katz and Lazarsfeld 1955; Coleman, Katz, and Menzel 1966; Burt 1987, 1992, 2004, 2005; see also Valente 1995.
38. Granovetter 1978; Kim and Bearman 1997; Marwell, Oliver, and Prahl 1988; Oliver and Myers 2003; Goel, Anderson, Hofman, and Watts 2015; Watts 1999.
39. Lorrain and White 1971.
40. Bearman 1993.
41. Gould 1995.
42. Lizardo 2006.
43. Vaisey and Lizardo 2010.
44. Erikson and Bearman 2006.
45. Franzosi 1997, 2004.
46. E.g. Tilly 1997, 2008; Tilly and Wood 2003; Wada 2004.
47. Bearman, Faris, and Moody 1999; Bearman and Stovel 2000.
48. Carley 1993, 1994; Carley and Kaufer 1993; Carley and Palmquist 1992.
49. Carley and Palmquist 1992: 602.
50. E.g., Carley 1999.

51. White 1992, 2008a.
52. Mohr 1994; Mohr and Duquenne 1997.
53. Mohr 1974, 2000. See also Breiger 1974.
54. Mohr and Neely 2009.
55. Martin 2000; Mische and Pattison 2000; Yeung 2005; Rawlings and Bourgeois 2004.
56. Bail 2016.
57. See, e.g., Bail 2016.
58. McLean 1998, 2007.
59. Mische 2008, 2015.
60. Gibson 2003, 2005.
61. McFarland 2001, 2004.
62. See also Diehl and McFarland 2012; Moody, McFarland, and Bender-deMoll 2005.
63. Bail 2015b.
64. DiMaggio and Powell 1983: 148.
65. Warren 1967.
66. Warren, Rose, and Bergunder 1974.
67. Bourdieu 1996.
68. Bourdieu 1986, 1988.
69. DiMaggio and Powell 1983.
70. McDonough, Ventresca, and Outcalt 1999.
71. Bourdieu 1988.
72. Bourdieu 1987: 821.
73. Bourdieu 1984: 23.
74. Bryson 1996.
75. Green 2008.
76. Fishman and Lizardo 2013.
77. Daniel 2016.
78. Benzécri 1973; Clausen 1998; Greenacre 1983, 2007.
79. Flemmen, Jarness, and Rosenlund 2018.
80. Hanquinet 2013; Hanquinet, Savage and Callier 2012.
81. Roose 2014.
82. Teney and Hanquinet 2012.
83. Friedland, Mohr, Roose, and Gardinali 2014.
84. DiMaggio and Powell 1983.
85. Fligstein and McAdam 2012.

86. Martin 2003, 2011.
87. Green 2013; Martin and George 2006.
88. Bail 2015b.
89. Foster, Rzhetsky, and Evans 2015.
90. Bourdieu 1984: 22.
91. Emirbayer 1997: 288.

# 4. PIVOTS AND CHOICES IN THE PROCESS OF RESEARCH

1. Interviews with Breiger, DiMaggio, Mische, Mohr, and Wagner-Pacifici were conducted by Iddo Tavory. Throughout the chapter, where quotation marks are used without reference to a specific bibliographical item, the quote is from one of the interviews.
2. Hunter 1992.
3. See DiMaggio 2003.
4. See DiMaggio and Bryson (2007). We note that the project was conducted in the mid-1990s, and so while it was published later than much of the research cited here, it should thus be understood as the first in this series.
5. DiMaggio and Bryson 2007: 264.
6. DiMaggio, Evans, and Bryson 1996.
7. DiMaggio, Evans, and Bryson 1996: 694.
8. See DiMaggio, Cadge, Robinson, and Steensland 2001.
9. Goldberg 2011.
10. DiMaggio, Nag, and Blei 2013: 578.
11. DiMaggio et al. 2013; DiMaggio, Nag, and Blei 2015.
12. DiMaggio et al. 2013: 602.
13. DiMaggio et al. 2015.
14. White 1992.
15. Mische 2011.
16. See Mische 2008.
17. Here, Mische built on the methodological innovations of Eliasoph (1998) and Lichterman (1999) by observing variations in the expression and suppression of identities and relations across settings.
18. Mische 1995: 144.
19. Breiger 1974.

20. Mische and Pattison 2000: 170.
21. Mische 1998.
22. Mische and Pattison 2000: 173.
23. Mische and Pattison 2000: 177, emphasis in the original.
24. Mische and Pattison 2000: 179.
25. Mische 2008, 2015.
26. Stolte, Alan, and Cook 2001.
27. This acronym was chosen strictly for alphabetical order.
28. Wagner-Pacifici 2008.
29. Mohr 1994; Mohr and Duquenne 1997.
30. Burke 1945.
31. Mohr, Wagner-Pacifici, and Breiger 2013: 674.
32. DiMaggio et al. 2013.
33. Mohr et al. 2013: 686.
34. DiMaggio et al. 1996.
35. Mohr et al. 2015; see also Wagner-Pacifici et al. 2015.
36. Breiger 2015; Breiger, Wagner-Pacifici, and Mohr 2018.
37. Breiger, Wagner-Pacifici, and Mohr 2018: 107.
38. Breiger, Wagner-Pacifici, and Mohr 2018: 110.
39. Biernacki 2012.
40. Wagner-Pacifici, Mohr, and 2018.
41. Wagner-Pacifici, Mohr, and Breiger 2018, italics in the original.
42. Jagarlamudi, Daumé, and Udupa 2012.
43. Lizardo 2018.

## CONCLUSION: THE FUTURE OF MEASURING CULTURE

1. Harari 2014.
2. Dor 2015.
3. Avital and Jablonka 2000.
4. James 1890: 462.
5. Such studies include Berger and Luckmann (1966).
6. Fine 1979.
7. See Frye (2017) for one recent investigation of this tension.
8. Lizardo, Sepulvado, Stoltz, and Taylor 2019; Norton 2019.
9. Eyal 2013.

10. Martin 2010.
11. For instance, see Lahire 2011; Wood, Stoltz, Van Ness, and Taylor 2018.
12. Trouille and Tavory 2019.
13. McDonnell 2016.
14. Tavory 2018; Mische 2008.
15. See Frye 2012; Mische 2009; Tavory 2016.
16. Zerubavel 2006, 2015.
17. E.g., Cowan 2014.
18. Biernacki 2012; Bearman and Stovel 2000.
19. Swidler 2010; Tavory 2016.
20. Bail 2016; Lizardo 2014; Pachucki and Breiger 2010; Mische 2008.
21. Bail 2014.
22. Edelman, Wolff, Montagne, and Bail 2020.
23. Salganik 2017.
24. In a recent contribution, Kozlowski, Taddy, and Evans (2019) make the sociological case for word embeddings as the royal road to capturing "the geometry of culture" in a way that respects relational understandings of meaning in language.
25. Campbell et al. 2018.
26. Mimno 2015.
27. See Salganik, Dodds, and Watts 2006; Salganik and Watts 2008; Bail, Brown, and Mann 2017.
28. Jacobs and Spillman 2005.
29. Moody and Light 2006.

# BIBLIOGRAPHY

Abend, Gabriel. 2014. *The Moral Background: An Inquiry into the History of* *Business Ethics*. Princeton, NJ: Princeton University Press.

Adorno, Theodor. 1997. *Aesthetic Theory*. London: A&C Black.

Adorno, Theodor. 2003. *Negative Dialectics*. New York: Routledge.

Alexander, Jeffrey C. 2004. "Cultural Pragmatics: Social Performance Between Ritual and Strategy." *Sociological Theory* 22(4): 527–73.

Alexander, Jeffrey C., and Philip Smith. 1993. "The Discourse of American Civil Society: A New Proposal for Cultural Studies." *Theory and Society* 22(2): 151–207.

Anand, Narasimhan, and Richard A. Peterson. 2000. "When Market Information Constitutes Fields: Sensemaking of Markets in the Commercial Music Industry." *Organization Science* 11(3): 270–84.

Anderson, Ashton, Sharad Goel, Gregory Huber, Neil Malhotra, and Duncan J. Watts. 2014. "Political Ideology and Racial Preferences in Online Dating." *Sociological Science* 1: 28–40.

Anderson, Benedict. 1983. *Imagined Communities: Reflections on the Origin and Spread of Nationalism*. London: Verso.

Askin, Noah, and Michael Mauskapf. 2017. "What Makes Popular Culture Popular? Product Features and Optimal Differentiation in Music." *American Sociological Review* 82(5): 910–44.

Avital, Eytan, and Eva Jablonka. 2000. *Animal Traditions: Behavioural Inheritance in Evolution*. Cambridge: Cambridge University Press.

Bail, Christopher A. 2014. "The Cultural Environment: Measuring Culture with Big Data." *Theory and Society* 43(3–4): 465–82.

Bail, Christopher A. 2015a. "The Public Life of Secrets: Deception, Disclosure, and Discursive Framing in the Policy Process." *Sociological Theory* 33(2): 97–124.

Bail, Christopher A. 2015b. *Terrified: How Anti-Muslim Fringe Organizations Became Mainstream*. Princeton, NJ: Princeton University Press.

Bail, Christopher A. 2016. "Combining Natural Language Processing and Network Analysis to Examine How Advocacy Organizations Stimulate Conversation on Social Media." *Proceedings of the National Academy of Sciences* 113(42): 11823–28.

Bail, Christopher A., Taylor W. Brown, and Marcus Mann. 2017. "Channeling Hearts and Minds: Advocacy Organizations, Cognitive-Emotional Currents, and Public Conversation." *American Sociological Review* 82(6): 1188–1213.

Bail, Christopher A., Lisa Argyle, Taylor Brown, John Bumpuss, Haohan Chen, Mary Beth Fallin-Hunzaker, Marcus Mann, Friedolin Merhout, and Alexander Volfovsky. 2018. "Exposure to Opposing Views Can Increase Political Polarization: Evidence from a Large-Scale Field Experiment on Social Media." *Proceedings of the National Academy of Sciences* 155(37): 9216–221.

Baldassarri, Delia, and Amir Goldberg. 2014. "Neither Ideologues nor Agnostics: Alternative Voters' Belief System in an Age of Partisan Politics." *American Journal of Sociology* 120(1): 45–95.

Bandelj, Nina, Frederick F. Wherry, and Viviana A. Zelizer, eds. 2017. *Money Talks: How Money Really Works*. Princeton, NJ: Princeton University Press.

Barnes, John A. 1954. "Class and Committees in a Norwegian Island Parish." *Human Relations* 7(1): 39–58.

Barnes, John A. 1969. "Graph Theory and Social Networks: A Technical Comment on Connectedness and Connectivity." *Sociology* 3(2): 215–32.

Barthes, Roland. 1967. *The Fashion System*. Berkeley: University of California Press.

Bartlett, Frederic. 1932. *Remembering: A Study in Experimental and Social Psychology*. Cambridge: Cambridge University Press.

Baumann, Shyon. 2001. "Intellectualization and Art World Development: Film in the United States." *American Sociological Review* 66(3): 404–26.

Baxandall, Michael. 1972. *Painting and Experience in Fifteenth-Century Italy: A Primer in the Social History of Pictorial Style*. Oxford: Oxford University Press.

Bearman, Peter S. 1993. *Relations into Rhetorics: Local Elite Social Structure in Norfolk, England: 1540–1640.* New Brunswick, NJ: Rutgers University Press.

Bearman, Peter S., and Katherine Stovel. 2000. "Becoming a Nazi: A Model for Narrative Networks." *Poetics* 27(2–3): 69–90.

Bearman, Peter S., Robert Faris, and James Moody. 1999. "Blocking the Future: New Solutions for Old Problems in Historical Social Science." *Social Science History* 23(4): 501–33.

Becker, Howard S. 1982. *Art Worlds.* Berkeley: University of California Press.

Becker, Howard S. 1998. *Tricks of the Trade: How to Think About Your Research While You're Doing It.* Chicago: University of Chicago Press.

Becker, Howard S. 2007. *Telling About Society.* Chicago: University of Chicago Press.

Becker, Howard S. 2016. *Evidence.* Chicago: University of Chicago Press.

Becker, Howard, and Blanche Geer. 1957. "Participant Observation and Interviewing: A Comparison." *Human Organization* 16(3): 28–32.

Belk, Russell W. 1988. "Possessions and the Extended Self." *Journal of Consumer Research* 15(2): 139–68.

Benney, Mark, and Everett C. Hughes. 1956. "Of Sociology and the Interview: Editorial Preface." *American Journal of Sociology* 62(2): 137–42.

Benzécri, Jean-Paul. 1973. *L'Analyse Des Données. Volume II. L'Analyse Des Correspondances.* Paris: Dunod.

Berger, Peter L., and Thomas Luckmann. 1966. *The Social Construction of Reality: A Treatise in the Sociology of Knowledge.* New York: Anchor.

Bielby, D. D., and C. L. Harrington. 2002. "Markets and Meanings: The Global Syndication of Television Programming." In *Global Culture: Arts, Media, Policy, and Globalization*, ed. D. Crane, N. Kawashima, and K. Kawasaki, 215–32. New York: Routledge.

Biernacki, Richard. 2012. *Reinventing Evidence in Social Inquiry: Decoding Facts and Variables.* New York: Palgrave MacMillan.

Blumer, Herbert. 1969. *Symbolic Interactionism: Perspective and Method.* Englewood Cliffs, NJ: Prentice-Hall.

Boden, Deirdre, and Donald H. Zimmerman. 1991. *Talk and Social Structure: Studies in Ethnomethodology and Conversation Analysis.* Berkeley: University of California Press.

Bott, Elizabeth. 1957. *Family and Social Network.* London: Tavistock.

Bourdieu, Pierre. 1984. *Distinction: A Social Critique of the Judgement of Taste.* Cambridge, MA: Harvard University Press.

Bourdieu, Pierre. 1987. "The Force of Law: Toward a Sociology of the Juridical Field." *Hastings Law Journal* 38: 805–54.

Bourdieu, Pierre. 1988. *Homo Academicus*. Stanford, CA: Stanford University Press.

Bourdieu, Pierre. 1990. *The Logic of Practice*. Palo Alto, CA: Stanford University Press.

Bourdieu, Pierre. 1996. *The Rules of Art: Genesis and Structure of the Literary Field*. Stanford, CA: Stanford University Press.

Boutyline, Andrei. 2017. "Improving the Measurement of Shared Cultural Schemas with Correlational Class Analysis: Theory and Method." *Sociological Science* 4: 353–93.

Boutyline, Andrei, and Stephen Vaisey. 2017. "Belief Network Analysis: A Relational Approach to Understanding the Structure of Attitudes." *American Journal of Sociology* 122(5): 1371–447.

Bowker, Geoffrey C., and Susan Leigh Star. 1999. *Sorting Things Out: Classification and Its Consequences*. Cambridge, MA: MIT Press.

Breiger, Ronald L. 1974. "The Duality of Persons and Groups." *Social Forces* 53(2): 181–90.

Breiger, Ronald L. 2015. "Scaling Down." *Big Data & Society* 2(2): https://doi.org/10.1177/2053951715602497.

Breiger, Ronald L., Robin Wagner-Pacifici, and John W. Mohr. 2018. "Capturing Distinctions While Mining Text Data: Toward Low-Tech Formalization for Text Analysis." *Poetics* 68: 104–19.

Brekhus, Wayne. 2007. "The Rutgers School: A Zerubavelian Culturalist Cognitive Sociology." *European Journal of Social Theory* 10(3): 448–64.

Brenner, Michael. 1981. *Social Method and Social Life*. London: Academic Press.

Briggs, Charles L. 1986. *Learning How to Ask: A Sociolinguistic Appraisal of the Role of the Interview in Social Science Research*. Cambridge: Cambridge University Press.

Bruch, Elizabeth, Fred Feinberg, and Kee Yeun Lee. 2016. "Extracting Multistage Screening Rules from Online Dating Activity Data." *Proceedings of the National Academy of Sciences* 113(38): 10530–535.

Bryson, Bethany. 1996. " 'Anything But Heavy Metal': Symbolic Exclusion and Musical Dislikes." *American Sociological Review* 61(5): 884–99.

Burke, Kenneth. 1945. *A Grammar of Motives*. New York: Prentice-Hall.

Burt, Ronald S. 1987. "Social Contagion and Innovation: Cohesion Versus Structural Equivalence." *American Journal of Sociology* 92(6): 1287–335.

Burt, Ronald S. 1992. *Structural Holes: The Social Structure of Competition.* Cambridge, MA: Harvard University Press.

Burt, Ronald S. 2004. "Structural Holes and Good Ideas." *American Journal of Sociology* 110(2): 349–99.

Burt, Ronald S. 2005. *Brokerage and Closure: An Introduction to Social Capital.* Oxford: Oxford University Press.

Campbell, Kathleen, Kimberly L. H. Carpenter, Jordan Hashemi, Steven Espinosa, Samuel Marsan, Jana Schaich Borg, Zhuoqing Chang, Qiang Qiu, Saritha Vermeer, Elizabeth Adler, Mariano Tepper, Helen L. Egger, Jeffery P. Baker, Guillermo Sapiro, and Geraldine Dawson. 2018. "Computer Vision Analysis Captures Atypical Attention in Toddlers with Autism." *Autism* 23(3): 619–28.

Carley, Kathleen M. 1993. "Coding Choices for Textual Analysis: A Comparison of Content Analysis and Map Analysis." *Sociological Methodology* 23: 75–126.

Carley, Kathleen M. 1994. "Extracting Culture Through Textual Analysis." *Poetics* 22(4): 291–312.

Carley, Kathleen M. 1999. "On the Evolution of Social and Organizational Networks." Special Issue on Networks in and Around Organizations, ed. D. Knoke and S. Andrews. *Research in the Sociology of Organizations* 16: 3–30.

Carley, Kathleen M., and David S. Kaufer. 1993. "Semantic Connectivity: An Approach for Analyzing Symbols in Semantic Networks." *Communication Theory* 3(3): 183–213.

Carley, Kathleen M., and Michael Palmquist. 1992. "Extracting, Representing, and Analyzing Mental Models." *Social Forces* 70(3): 601–36.

Carroll, Glenn R., Olga M. Khessina, and David G. McKendrick. 2010. "The Social Lives of Products: Analyzing Product Demography for Management Theory and Practice." *Academy of Management Annals* 4(1): 157–203.

Carter, Prudence L. 2005. *Keepin' It Real: School Success Beyond Black and White.* Oxford: Oxford University Press.

Cartwright, Dorwin, and Frank Harary. 1956. "Structural Balance: A Generalization of Heider's Theory." *Psychological Review* 63(5): 277–93.

Cassirer, Ernst. 1953. *The Philosophy of Symbolic Forms: The Phenomenology of Knowledge.* New Haven, CT: Yale University Press.

Cerulo, Karen A. 1998. *Deciphering Violence: The Cognitive Structure of Right and Wrong.* New York: Routledge.

Cerulo, Karen A. 2014. "Reassessing the Problem." *Sociological Methods & Research* 43(2): 219–26.

Cerulo, Karen A. 2018. "Scents and Sensibility: Olfaction, Sense-Making, and Meaning Attribution." *American Sociological Review* 83(2): 361–89.

Chanan, Michael. 1995. *Repeated Takes: A Short History of Recording and Its Effects on Music.* London: Verso.

Childress, C. Clayton, and Noah E. Friedkin. 2012. "Cultural Reception and Production: The Social Construction of Meaning in Book Clubs." *American Sociological Review* 77(1): 45–68.

Childress, Clayton. 2017. *Under the Cover: The Creation, Production, and Reception of a Novel.* Princeton, NJ: Princeton University Press.

Clausen, Sten Erik. 1998. *Applied Correspondence Analysis: An Introduction.* London: SAGE Publications.

Coleman, James S., Elihu Katz, and Herbert Menzel. 1966. *Medical Innovation: A Diffusion Study.* New York: Bobbs-Merrill.

Collins, Harry. 2010. *Tacit and Explicit Knowledge.* Chicago: University of Chicago Press.

Collins, Harry, and Martin Kusch. 1999. *The Shape of Actions: What Humans and Machines Can Do.* Cambridge, MA: MIT Press.

Collins, Randall. 1983. "Micromethods as a Basis for Macrosociology." *Urban Life* 12(2): 184–202.

Collins, Randall. 2004. "Rituals of Solidarity and Security in the Wake of Terrorist Attack." *Sociological Theory* 22(1): 53–87.

Converse, Jean N. 2009. *Survey Research in the United States: Roots and Emergence, 1890–1960.* New Brunswick, NJ: Transaction.

Converse, Philip E. 1964. "The Nature of Belief Systems in Mass Publics." In *Ideology and Discontent,* ed. David E. Apter, 206–61. London: The Free Press of Glencoe.

Coulangeon, Philippe. 2016. *The Sociology of Cultural Participation in France Thirty Years After Distinction.* London: Routledge.

Cowan, Sarah. 2014. "Secrets and Misperceptions: The Creation of Self-Fulfilling Illusions." *Sociological Science* 1: 466–92.

Crane, Diana. 1992. *The Production of Culture: Media and the Urban Arts.* London: SAGE Publications.

Crane, Diana. 1997. "Globalization, Organizational Size, and Innovation in the French Luxury Fashion Industry: Production of Culture Theory Revisited." *Poetics* 24(6): 393–414.

Csikszentmihalyi, Mihaly, and Eugene Rochberg-Halton. 1981. *The Meaning of Things: Domestic Symbols and the Self.* Cambridge: Cambridge University Press.

Cunningham, William A., and Philip David Zelazo. 2007. "Attitudes and Evaluations: A Social Cognitive Neuroscience Perspective." *Trends in Cognitive Sciences* 11(3): 97–104.

Cunningham, William A., Philip David Zelazo, Dominic J. Packer, and Jay J. Van Bavel. 2007. "The Iterative Reprocessing Model: A Multilevel Framework for Attitudes and Evaluation." *Social Cognition* 25(5): 736–60.

Daenekindt, Stijn. 2017. "On the Structure of Dispositions. Transposability of and Oppositions Between Aesthetic Dispositions." *Poetics* 62(1): 43–52.

Daenekindt, Stijn, Willem de Koster, and Jeroen van der Waal. 2017. "How People Organise Cultural Attitudes: Cultural Belief Systems and the Populist Radical Right." *West European Politics* 40(4): 791–811.

Dalton, Benjamin. 2004. "Creativity, Habit, and the Social Products of Creative Action: Revising Joas, Incorporating Bourdieu." *Sociological Theory* 22(4): 603–22.

D'Andrade, Roy G. 1991. "The Identification of Schemas in Naturalistic Data." In *Person Schemas and Maladaptive Interpersonal Patterns*, ed. M. J. Horowitz, 279–301. Chicago: University of Chicago Press.

Daniel, Caitlin. 2016. "Economic Constraints on Taste Formation and the True Cost of Healthy Eating." *Social Science & Medicine* 148: 34–41.

Davis, Allison, Burleigh B. Gardner, and Mary R. Gardner. 1941. *Deep South.* Chicago: University of Chicago Press.

Davis, Fred. 1959. "The Cabdriver and His Fare: Facets of a Fleeting Relationship." *American Journal of Sociology* 65(2): 158–65.

Davis, James A. 1963. "Structural Balance, Mechanical Solidarity, and Interpersonal Relations." *American Journal of Sociology* 68(4): 444–62.

Davis, James A. 1967. "Clustering and Structural Balance in Graphs." *Human Relations* 20(2): 181–87.

de Laat, Kim. 2014. "Innovation and Diversity Redux: Analyzing Musical Form and Content in the American Recording Industry, 1990–2009." *Sociological Forum* 29(3): 673–97.

DeNora, Tia. 1995. *Beethoven and the Construction of Genius: Musical Politics in Vienna, 1792–1803.* Berkeley: University of California Press.

de Saussure, Ferdinand. 1964. *Course in General Linguistics.* 2nd ed. London: Peter Owen.

Desmond, Matthew. 2007. *On the Fireline: Living and Dying with Wildland Firefighters*. Chicago: University of Chicago Press.

DeSoucey, Michaela. 2010. "Gastronationalism: Food Traditions and Authenticity Politics in the European Union." *American Sociological Review* 75(3): 432–55.

Deutscher, Irwin, Fred P. Pestello, and H. Frances P. Pestello. 1993. *Sentiments and Acts*. Piscataway, NJ: Transaction Publishers.

Dewey, John. 1929. *Experience and Nature*. LaSalle, IL: Open Court Publishing.

Diehl, David, and Daniel A. McFarland. 2012. "Classroom Ordering and the Situational Imperatives of Routine and Ritual." *Sociology of Education* 85(4): 326–49.

DiMaggio, Paul J. 1982. "Cultural Entrepreneurship in Nineteenth-Century Boston: The Creation of an Organizational Base for High Culture in America." *Media, Culture, & Society* 4(1): 33–50.

DiMaggio, Paul J. 1983. "Can Culture Survive the Marketplace?" *Journal of Arts Management and Law* 13(1): 61–87.

DiMaggio, Paul J. 1987. "Classification in Art." *American Sociological Review* 52(4): 440–55.

DiMaggio, Paul J. 1997. "Culture and Cognition." *Annual Review of Sociology* 23(1): 263–87.

DiMaggio, Paul J. 2003. "The Myth of the Culture War: The Disparity Between Private Opinion and Public Politics." In *The Fractious Nation? Unity and Division in Contemporary American Life*, ed. J. Rieder, 79–97. Berkeley: University of California Press.

DiMaggio, Paul J. 2011. "Cultural Networks." In *SAGE Handbook of Social Network Analysis*, ed. J. Scott and P. J. Carrington, 286–301. London: SAGE Publications.

DiMaggio, Paul J., and Bethany Bryson. 2007. "Public Attitudes Towards Cultural Authority and Cultural Diversity in Higher Education and the Arts." In C. N. Blake, ed., *The Arts of Democracy. Art, Public Culture and the State*, 243–74. Philadelphia: University of Pennsylvania Press.

DiMaggio, Paul J., and Amir Goldberg. 2018. "Searching for *Homo Economicus*: Variation in Americans' Construals of and Attitudes toward Markets." *European Journal of Sociology* 59(2): 151–89.

DiMaggio, Paul J., and Walter W. Powell. 1983. "The Iron Cage Revisited: Institutional Isomorphism and Collective Rationality in Organizational Fields." *American Sociological Review* 48(2): 147–60.

DiMaggio, Paul J., Wendy Cadge, Lynn Robinson, and Brian Steensland. 2001. "The Role of Religion in Public Conflicts over the Arts in the Philadelphia Area, 1965–1997." In *Crossroads: Art and Religion in American Life*, ed. A. Arthurs and G. Wallach, 103–38. New York: New Press.

DiMaggio, Paul J., John Evans, and Bethany Bryson. 1996. "Have Americans' Social Attitudes Become More Polarized?" *American Journal of Sociology* 102(3): 690–755.

DiMaggio, Paul J., Manish Nag, and David Blei. 2013. "Exploiting Affinities Between Topic Modeling and the Sociological Perspective on Culture: Application to Newspaper Coverage of U.S. Government Arts Funding." *Poetics* 41(6): 570–606.

DiMaggio, Paul J., Manish Nag, and David Blei. 2015. "Defining and Measuring Cultural Change: The Evolving Environment of Representations of U.S. Arts Policy, 1986–1997." Paper presented at the American Sociological Association Meeting, Chicago, August.

DiMaggio, Paul J., Ramina Sotoudeh, Amir Goldberg, and Hana Shepherd. 2018. "Culture Out of Attitudes: Relationality, Population Heterogeneity and Attitudes Toward Science and Religion in the U.S." *Poetics* 68(1): 31–51.

Domínguez Rubio, Fernando. 2014. "Preserving the Unpreservable: Docile and Unruly Objects at MoMA." *Theory and Society* 43(6): 617–45.

Domínguez Rubio, Fernando. 2016. "On the Discrepancy Between Objects and Things: An Ecological Approach." *Journal of Material Culture*. 21(1): 59–86.

Dor, Daniel. 2015. *The Instruction of Imagination: Language as a Social Communication Technology*. Oxford: Oxford University Press.

Douglas, Mary. 1966. *Purity and Danger: An Analysis of Concepts of Pollution and Taboo*. London and New York: Routledge & Kegan Paul.

Douglas, Mary. 1986. *How Institutions Think*. Syracuse, NY: Syracuse University Press.

Douglas, Mary, and Baron Isherwood. 2002. *The World of Goods: Towards an Anthropology of Consumption*. London: Routledge.

Dowd, Timothy J. 2004. "Concentration and Diversity Revisited: Production Logics and the U.S. Mainstream Recording Market, 1940–1990." *Social Forces* 82(4): 1411–55.

Dowd, Timothy J. 2006. "From 78s to MP3s: The Embedded Impact of Technology in the Market for Prerecorded Music." In *The Business of*

*Culture: Strategic Perspectives on Entertainment and Media*, ed. J. Lampel, J. Shamsie, and T. K. Lant, 205–26. Mahwah, NJ: Lawrence Erlbaum.

Drew, Paul, and John Heritage. 1992. "Analyzing Talk at Work: An Introduction." In *Talk at Work: Interaction in Institutional Settings*, ed. P. Drew and J. Heritage, 3–66. Cambridge: Cambridge University Press.

Dreyfus, Hubert L. 1996. "The Current Relevance of Merleau-Ponty's Phenomenology of Embodiment." *Electronic Journal of Analytical Philosophy* 4(4): 1–16.

Du Bois, W. E. B. 1899. *The Philadelphia Negro*. New York: Schocken.

Durkheim, Émile. 1915. *The Elementary Forms of the Religious Life Trans from the French*. George Allen and Unwin.

Eagle, Nathan, and Alex S. Pentland. 2006. "Reality Mining: Sensing Complex Social Systems." *Personal and Ubiquitous Computing* 10(4): 255–68.

Edelman, Achim, Tom Wolff, Danielle Montagne, and Christopher A. Bail. 2020. "Computational Social Science." *Annual Review of Sociology* 46.

Elias, Norbert. 1982. *The Civilizing Process: State Formation and Civilization. Vol. 2*. Oxford, UK: Blackwell.

Eliasoph, Nina. 1998. *Avoiding Politics: How Americans Produce Apathy in Everyday Life*. Cambridge: Cambridge University Press.

Eliasoph, Nina, and Paul Lichterman. 2003. "Culture in Interaction." *American Journal of Sociology* 108(4): 735–94.

Emirbayer, Mustafa. 1997. "Manifesto for a Relational Sociology." *American Journal of Sociology* 103(2): 281–317.

Emirbayer, Mustafa, and Jeff Goodwin. 1994. "Network Analysis, Culture, and the Problem of Agency." *American Journal of Sociology* 99(6): 1411–54.

Erickson, Bonnie H. 1988. "The Relational Basis of Attitudes." In *Social Structures: A Network Approach*, ed. B. Wellman and S. D. Berkowitz, 99–121. Cambridge: Cambridge University Press.

Erikson, Emily. 2013. "Formalist and Relationalist Theory in Social Network Analysis." *Sociological Theory* 31(3): 219–42.

Erikson, Emily, and Peter S. Bearman. 2006. "Malfeasance and the Foundations for Global Trade: The Structure of English Trade in the East Indies, 1601–1833." *American Journal of Sociology* 112(1): 195–230.

Espeland, Wendy, and Michael Sauder. 2009. "Rating the Rankings." *Contexts* 8(2): 16–21.

Evans, James A., and Pedro Aceves. 2016. "Machine Translation: Mining Text for Social Theory." *Annual Review of Sociology* 42(1): 21–50.

Ewick, Patricia, and Susan S. Silbey. 1995. "Subversive Stories and Hege-
monic Tales: Toward a Sociology of Narrative." *Law & Society Review*
29(2): 197–226.

Eyal, Gil. 2013. "Spaces Between Fields." In *Pierre Bourdieu and Historical
Analysis*, ed. P. Gorski, 852–58. Durham, NC: Duke University Press.

Eyal, Gil, Brendan Hart, Emine Onculer, Neta Oren, and Natasha Rossi.
2010. *The Autism Matrix: The Social Origins of the Autism Epidemic*.
Cambridge, UK: Polity Press.

Fairclough, Norman. 1992. "Discourse and Text: Linguistic and Intertextual
Analysis Within Discourse Analysis." *Discourse & Society* 3(2): 193–217.

Fazio, Russell H., and Michael A. Olson. 2003. "Implicit Measures in Social
Cognition Research: Their Meaning and Use." *Annual Review of Psychology* 54(1): 297–327.

Ferguson, Priscilla Parkhurst. 1998. "A Cultural Field in the Making: Gastronomy in 19th-Century France." *American Journal of Sociology* 104(3):
597–641.

Ferguson, Priscilla Parkhurst. 2004. *Accounting for Taste: The Triumph of French
Cuisine*. Chicago: University of Chicago Press.

Fields, Corey D. 2014. "Not Your Grandma's Knitting: The Role of Identity
Processes in the Transformation of Cultural Practices." *Social Psychology
Quarterly* 77(2): 150–65.

Fine, Gary Alan. 1979. "Small Groups and Culture Creation: The Idiocul-
ture of Little League Baseball Teams." *American Sociological Review* 44(5):
733–45.

Fine, Gary Alan. 1995. *A Second Chicago School? The Development of a Postwar
American Sociology*. Chicago: University of Chicago Press.

Fishman, Robert M., and Omar Lizardo. 2013. "How Macro-Historical
Change Shapes Cultural Taste: Legacies of Democratization in Spain
and Portugal." *American Sociological Review* 78(2): 213–39.

Flemmen, Magne, Vegard Jarness, and Lennart Rosenlund. 2018. "Social
Space and Cultural Class Divisions: The Forms of Capital and Contemporary Lifestyle Differentiation." *British Journal of Sociology* 69(1): 124–53.

Fligstein, Neil, and Doug McAdam. 2012. *A Theory of Fields*. Oxford: Oxford
University Press.

Foster, Jacob G., Andrey Rzhetsky, and James A. Evans. 2015. "Tradition
and Innovation in Scientists' Research Strategies." *American Sociological
Review* 80(5): 875–908.

Foucault, Michel. 1970. *The Order of Things: An Archeology of the Human Sciences.* New York: Pantheon Books.

Franzosi, Roberto. 1997. "Mobilization and Counter-Mobilization Processes: From the 'Red Years' (1919–20) to the 'Black Years' (1921–22) in Italy." *Theory and Society* 26(2–3): 275–304.

Franzosi, Roberto. 1998. "Narrative Analysis—Or Why (and How) Sociologists Should Be Interested In Narrative." *Annual Review of Sociology* 24(1): 517–54.

Franzosi, Roberto. 2004. *From Words to Numbers: Narrative, Data, and Social Science.* Cambridge: Cambridge University Press.

Friedland, Roger, and Robert R. Alford. 1991. "The New Institutionalism in Organizational Analysis." In *The New Institutionalism in Organizational Analysis*, ed. W. W. Powell and P. J. DiMaggio, 232–63. Chicago and London: University of Chicago Press.

Friedland, Roger, John W. Mohr, Henk Roose, and Paolo Gardinali. 2014. "The Institutional Logics of Love: Measuring Intimate Life." *Theory and Society* 43(3–4): 333–70.

Frye, Margaret. 2012. "Bright Futures in Malawi's New Dawn: Educational Aspirations as Assertions of Identity." *American Journal of Sociology* 117(6): 1565–1624.

Frye, Margaret. 2017. "Cultural Meanings and the Aggregation of Actions: The Case of Sex and Schooling in Malawi." *American Sociological Review* 82(5): 945–76.

Frye, Margaret, and Jenny Trinitapoli. 2015. "Ideals as Anchors for Relationship Experiences." *American Sociological Review* 80(3): 496–525.

Fuhse, Jan A. 2009. "The Meaning Structure of Social Networks." *Sociological Theory* 27(1): 51–73.

Garfinkel, Harold. 1967. *Studies in Ethnomethodology.* Englewood Cliffs, NJ: Prentice-Hall.

Gawronski, Bertram, and Galen V Bodenhausen. 2006. "Associative and Propositional Processes in Evaluation: An Integrative Review of Implicit and Explicit Attitude Change." *Psychological Bulletin* 132(5): 692–731.

Geertz, Clifford. 1973. *The Interpretation of Cultures: Selected Essays.* New York: Basic Books.

Geertz, Clifford. 1983. *Local Knowledge: Further Essays in Interpretive Anthropology.* New York: Basic Books.

Gell, Alfred. 1998. *Art and Agency: Anthropological Theory.* Oxford, UK: Clarendon Press.

Ghaziani, Amin. 2009. "An "Amorphous Mist"? The Problem of Measurement in the Study of Culture." *Theory and Society* 38(6): 581–612.

Gibson, David R. 2003. "Participation Shifts: Order and Differentiation in Group Conversation." *Social Forces* 81(4): 1335–80.

Gibson, David R. 2005. "Taking Turns and Talking Ties: Networks and Conversational Interaction." *American Journal of Sociology* 110(6): 1561–97.

Gibson, David R. 2012. *Talk at the Brink: Deliberation and Decision During the Cuban Missile Crisis*. Princeton, NJ: Princeton University Press.

Giddens, Anthony. 1979. *Central Problems in Social Theory: Action, Structure, and Contradiction in Social Analysis*. Berkeley: University of California Press.

Ginzburg, Carlo. 1979. *The Cheese and the Worms: The Cosmos of a Sixteenth-Century Miller*. Baltimore: Johns Hopkins University Press.

Glaser, Barney G., and Anselm L. Strauss. 1964. "Awareness Contexts and Social Interaction." *American Sociological Review* 29(5): 669–79.

Godart, Frédéric C., and Ashley Mears. 2009. "How Do Cultural Producers Make Creative Decisions? Lessons from the Catwalk." *Social Forces* 88(2): 671–92.

Goel, Sharad, Ashton Anderson, Jake Hofman, and Duncan J. Watts. 2015. "The Structural Virality of Online Diffusion." *Management Science* 62(1): 180–96.

Goldberg, Amir. 2011. "Mapping Shared Understandings Using Relational Class Analysis: The Case of the Cultural Omnivore Reexamined." *American Journal of Sociology* 116(5): 1397–1436.

Goldberg, Amir, and Sarah K. Stein. 2018. "Beyond Social Contagion: Associative Diffusion and the Emergence of Cultural Variation." *American Sociological Review* 83(5): 897–932.

Gould, Roger. 1995. *Insurgent Identities: Class, Community, and Insurrection in Paris from 1848 to the Commune*. Chicago: Chicago University Press.

Granovetter, Mark. 1973. "The Strength of Weak Ties." *American Journal of Sociology* 78(6): 1360–80.

Granovetter, Mark. 1978. "Threshold Models of Collective Behavior." *American Journal of Sociology* 83(6): 1420–43.

Grazian, David. 2003. *Blue Chicago: The Search for Authenticity in Urban Blues Clubs*. Chicago: University of Chicago Press.

Green, Adam Isaiah. 2008. "The Social Organization of Desire: The Sexual Fields Approach." *Sociological Theory* 26(1): 25–50.

Green, Adam Isaiah, ed. 2013. *Sexual Fields: Toward a Sociology of Collective Sexual Life*. Chicago: University of Chicago Press.

Greenacre, Michael. 1983. *Theory and Applications of Correspondence Analysis*. London: Academic Press.

Greenacre, Michael. 2007. *Correspondence Analysis in Practice*. 2nd ed. London: Chapman & Hall/CRC.

Greenwald, Anthony G., and Shelly D. Farnham. 2000. "Using the Implicit Association Test to Measure Self-Esteem and Self-Concept." *Journal of Personality and Social Psychology* 79(6): 1022–38.

Grindstaff, Laura, and Joseph Turow. 2006. "Video Cultures: Television Sociology in the 'New TV' Age." *Annual Review of Sociology* 32(1): 103–25.

Griswold, Wendy. 1981. "American Character and the American Novel: An Expansion of Reflection Theory in the Sociology of Literature." *American Journal of Sociology* 86(4): 740–65.

Griswold, Wendy. 1986. *Renaissance Revivals: City Comedy and Revenge Tragedy in the London Theater, 1576–1980*. Chicago: University of Chicago Press.

Griswold, Wendy. 1987a. "The Fabrication of Meaning: Literary Interpretation in the United States, Great Britain, and the West Indies." *American Journal of Sociology* 92(5): 1077–1117.

Griswold, Wendy. 1987b. "A Methodological Framework for the Sociology of Culture." *Sociological Methodology* 17: 1–35.

Griswold, Wendy. 2000. *Bearing Witness: Readers, Writers, and the Novel in Nigeria*. Princeton, NJ: Princeton University Press.

Griswold, Wendy. 2012. *Cultures and Societies in a Changing World*. London: SAGE Publications Ltd.

Gross, Neil. 2009. "A Pragmatist Theory of Social Mechanisms." *American Sociological Review* 74(3): 358–79.

Habermas, Jürgen. 1984. *The Theory of Communicative Action. Vol. 1: Reason*. Boston: Beacon Press.

✱ Hannerz, Ulf. 1992. *Cultural Complexity: Studies in the Social Organization of Meaning*. New York: Columbia University Press.

Hanquinet, Laurie. 2013. "Visitors to Modern and Contemporary Art Museums: Towards a New Sociology of 'Cultural Profiles.'" *Sociological Review* 61(4): 790–813.

Hanquinet, Laurie, Mike Savage, and Louise Callier. 2012. "Elaborating Bourdieu's Field Analysis in Urban Studies: Cultural Dynamics in Brussels." *Urban Geography* 33(4): 508–29.

Hanson, Sandra L. 1994. "Lost Talent: Unrealized Educational Aspirations and Expectations Among U.S. Youths." *Sociology of Education* 67(3): 159–83.

Harari, Yuval Noah. 2014. *Sapiens: A Brief History of Humankind*. New York: Random House.

Hardie, Jessica Halliday. 2014. "The Consequences of Unrealized Occupational Goals in the Transition to Adulthood." *Social Science Research* 48: 196–211.

Hardie, Jessica Halliday. 2015. "The Best Laid Plans: Social Capital in the Development of Girls' Educational and Occupational Plans." *Social Problems* 62(2): 241–65.

Harding, David J., 2010. *Living the Drama: Community, Conflict, and Culture among Inner-City Boys*. University of Chicago Press.

Hebdige, Dick. 1979. *Subculture: The Meaning of Style*. London: Routledge.

Hebdige, Dick. 1983. "Travelling Light: One Route into Material Culture." *RAIN* (59): 11–13.

Heider, Fritz. 1946. "Attitudes and Cognitive Organization." *Journal of Psychology* 21(1): 107–12.

Hennion, Antoine. 2015. "Paying Attention: What Is Tasting Wine About?" In *Moments of Valuation: Exploring Sites of Dissonance*, ed. A. B. Antal, M. Hutter, and D. Stark, 37–56. Oxford: Oxford University Press.

Heritage, John. 1984. *Garfinkel and Ethnomethodology*. Cambridge, UK: Polity Press.

Heritage, John, Jeffrey D. Robinson, Marc N. Elliott, Megan Beckett, and Michael Wilkes. 2007. "Reducing Patients' Unmet Concerns in Primary Care: The Difference One Word Can Make." *Journal of General Internal Medicine* 22(10): 1429–33.

Hirsch, Paul M. 1972. "Processing Fads and Fashions: An Organization-Set Analysis of Cultural Industry Systems." *American Journal of Sociology* 77(4): 639–59.

Hobsbawm, Eric, and Terence Ranger, eds. 1983. *The Invention of Tradition*. Cambridge: Cambridge University Press.

Hochschild, Arlie Russell. 1983. *The Managed Heart*. Berkeley: University of California Press.

Holt, Douglas B. 1997a. "Distinction in America? Recovering Bourdieu's Theory of Tastes from Its Critics." *Poetics* 25(2–3): 93–120.

Holt, Douglas B. 1997b. "Poststructuralist Lifestyle Analysis: Conceptualizing the Social Patterning of Consumption in Postmodernity." *Journal of Consumer Research* 23(4): 326–50.

Horkheimer, Max, and Theodor W. Adorno. 2006. "The Culture Industry: Enlightenment as Mass Deception." In *Media and Cultural Studies: Keyworks*, ed. D. Kellner and M. G. Durham, 41–72. Oxford: Blackwell.

Hunter, James D. 1992. *Culture Wars: The Struggle to Define America*. New York: Basic Books.

Hunzaker, M. B. Fallin, and Lauren Valentino. 2019 "Mapping Cultural Schemas: From Theory to Method." *American Sociological Review* 84(5): 950–81.

Hutchison, Coleman. 2006. "Breaking the Book Known as Q." *PMLA* 121(1): 33–66.

Illouz, Eva. 2008. *Saving the Modern Soul: Therapy, Emotions, and the Culture of Self-Help*. Berkeley: University of California Press.

Ingram, Paul, and Michael W. Morris. 2007. "Do People Mix at Mixers? Structure, Homophily, and the 'Life of the Party.'" *Administrative Science Quarterly* 52(4): 558–85.

Inkeles, Alex. 1969. "Making Men Modern: On the Causes and Consequences of Individual Change in Six Developing Countries." *American Journal of Sociology* 75(2): 208–25.

Jacobs, Jane. 1961. *The Death and Life of Great American Cities*. New York: Random House.

Jacobs, Mark D., and Lyn Spillman. 2005. "Cultural Sociology at the Crossroads of the Discipline." *Poetics* 33(1): 1–14.

Jacobs, Ronald N. 2002. "The Narrative Integration of Personal and Collective Identity in Social Movements." In *Narrative Impact: Social and Cognitive Foundations*, ed. M. C. Green, J. J. Strange, and T. C. Brock, 205–28. Mahwah, NJ: Lawrence Erlbaum.

Jagarlamudi, Jagadeesh, Hal Daumé III, and Raghavendra Udupa. 2012. "Incorporating Lexical Priors into Topic Models." In *EACL '12 Proceedings of the 13th Conference of the European Chapter of the Association for Computational Linguistics*, 204–13. Avignon, France.

James, William. 1890. *The Principles of Psychology*. New York: Henry Holt and Company.

James, William. 1907. *Pragmatism*. Ed. B. Kuklick. Cambridge, MA: Hackett.

Jenkins, Henry. 2006. *Fans, Bloggers, and Gamers: Exploring Participatory Culture*. New York: New York University Press.

Jenkins, Henry. 2012. *Textual Poachers: Television Fans and Participatory Culture*. London: Routledge.

Jerolmack, Colin, and Shamus Khan. 2014. "Talk Is Cheap: Ethnography and the Attitudinal Fallacy." *Sociological Methods & Research* 43(2): 178–209.

Jerolmack, Colin, and Iddo Tavory. 2014. "Nonhumans and the Constitution of the Social Self." *Sociological Theory* 32(1): 64–77.

Joas, Hans. 1996. *The Creativity of Action*. Chicago: University of Chicago Press.

Johnson-Hanks, Jennifer A., Christine A. Bachrach, S. Philip Morgan, and Hans-Peter Kohler. 2011. *Understanding Family Change and Variation*. Dordrecht: Springer Netherlands.

Johnston, Josée, and Shyon Baumann. 2009. *Foodies: Democracy and Distinction in the Gourmet Foodscape*. London: Routledge.

Jones, Alasdair. 2018. "Revisiting Bott to Connect the Dots: An Exploration of the Methodological Origins of Social Network Analysis." *Forum Qualitative Sozialforschung/Forum: Qualitative Social Research* 19(2), doi: 10.17169/fqs-19.2.2905.

Karmiloff-Smith, Annette. 1995. *Beyond Modularity: A Developmental Perspective on Cognitive Science*. Cambridge, MA: MIT Press.

Katz, Elihu, and Paul F. Lazarsfeld. 1955. *Personal Influence: The Part Played by People in the Flow of Mass Communications*. Glencoe, IL: Free Press.

Katz, Elihu, and Tamar Liebes. 1990. "Interacting with 'Dallas': Cross Cultural Readings of American TV." *Canadian Journal of Communication* 15(1): 45–66.

Khan, Shamus, and Colin Jerolmack. 2013. "Saying Meritocracy and Doing Privilege." *Sociological Quarterly* 54(1): 9–19.

Kim, Hyojoung, and Peter S. Bearman. 1997. "The Structure and Dynamics of Movement Participation." *American Sociological Review* 62(1): 70–93.

Kirchner, Corinne, and John W. Mohr. 2010. "Meanings and Relations: An Introduction to the Study of Language, Discourse and Networks." *Poetics* 38(6): 555–66.

Klett, Joseph. 2014. "Sound on Sound: Situating Interaction in Sonic Object Settings." *Sociological Theory* 32(2): 147–61.

Kopytoff, Igor. 1986. "The Cultural Biography of Things." In A. Appadurai, ed., *The Social Life of Things*, 64–91. Cambridge: Cambridge University Press.

Kozlowski, Austin C., Matt Taddy, and James A. Evans. 2019. "The Geometry of Culture: Analyzing the Meanings of Class Through Word Embeddings." *American Sociological Review* 84(5): 905–45.

Krinsky, John, and Ann Mische. 2013. "Formations and Formalisms: Charles Tilly and the Paradox of the Actor." *Annual Review of Sociology* 39: 1–26.

Kroeber, Alfred L., and Talcott Parsons. 1958. "The Concepts of Culture and of Social System." *American Sociological Review* 23(5): 582–83.

Kuipers, Giselinde. 2015. "How National Institutions Mediate the Global: Screen Translation, Institutional Interdependencies, and the Production of National Difference in Four European Countries." *American Sociological Review* 80(5): 985–1013.

Lahire, Bernard. 2011. *The Plural Actor*. London: Polity Press.

Lamont, Michèle. 1992. *Money, Morals, and Manners: The Culture of the French and American Upper-Middle Class*. Chicago and London: University of Chicago Press.

Lamont, Michèle, and Marcel Fournier, eds. 1992. *Cultivating Differences: Symbolic Boundaries and the Making of Inequality*. Chicago: University of Chicago Press

Lamont, Michèle, and Virág Molnár. 2002. "The Study of Boundaries in the Social Sciences." *Annual Review of Sociology* 28(1): 167–95.

Lamont, Michèle, and Patricia White. 2008. "Workshop on Interdisciplinary Standards for Systematic Qualitative Research: Cultural Anthropology, Law and Social Science, Political Science, and Sociology Programs." National Science Foundation supported workshop.

Lamont, Michèle, Graziella Moraes Silva, Jessica Welburn, Joshua Guetzkow, Nissim Mizrachi, Hanna Herzog, and Elisa Reis. 2016. *Getting Respect: Responding to Stigma and Discrimination in the United States, Brazil, and Israel*. Princeton, NJ: Princeton University Press.

Lang, Gladys Engel, and Kurt Lang. 1988. "Recognition and Renown: The Survival of Artistic Reputation." *American Journal of Sociology* 94(1): 79–109.

Lara-Millán, Armando. 2014. "Public Emergency Room Overcrowding in the Era of Mass Imprisonment." *American Sociological Review* 79(5): 866–87.

Lasswell, Harold D., and Nathan Leites. 1949. *Language of Politics: Studies in Quantitative Semantics*. New York: George W. Stewart.

Lasswell, Harold D., Daniel Lerner, and Ithiel DeSola Pool. 1952. *The Comparative Study of Symbols*. Stanford, CA: Stanford University Press.

Latour, Bruno. 1992. "Where Are the Missing Masses? The Sociology of a Few Mundane Artifacts." In *Shaping Technology/Building Society: Studies in Sociotechnical Change*, ed. W. E. Bijker and J. Law, 225–58. Cambridge, MA: MIT Press.

Latour, Bruno. 1993. *The Pasteurization of France*. Cambridge, MA: Harvard University Press.

Latour, Bruno. 2005. "From Realpolitik to Dingpolitik or How to Make Things Public." In *Making Things Public: Atmospheres of Democracy*, ed. B. Latour and P. Weibel, 14–41. Cambridge, MA: MIT Press.

Lazer, David, and Jason Radford. 2017. "Data ex Machina: Introduction to Big Data." *Annual Review of Sociology* 43(1): 19–39.

Lee, Nancy Howell. 1969. *The Search for an Abortionist*. Chicago: University of Chicago Press.

Lee, Steve S., and Richard A. Peterson. 2004. "Internet-Based Virtual Music Scenes: The Case of P2 and Alt.Country Music." In *Music Scenes: Local Translocal and Virtual*, ed. Andy Bennett and Richard A. Peterson, 187–204. Nashville: Vanderbilt University Press.

Lena, Jennifer C. 2006. "Social Context and Musical Content of Rap Music, 1979–1995." *Social Forces* 85(1): 479–95.

Lena, Jennifer C. 2012. *Banding Together: How Communities Create Genres in Popular Music*. Princeton, NJ: Princeton University Press.

Lena, Jennifer C. 2015. "Genre: Relational Approaches to the Sociology of Music." In *Routledge International Handbook of the Sociology of Art and Culture*, ed. L. Hanquinet and M. Savage, 149–60. New York: Routledge.

Lena, Jennifer C., and Danielle J. Lindemann. 2014. "Who Is an Artist? New Data for an Old Question." *Poetics* 43: 70–85.

Lena, Jennifer C., and Mark C. Pachucki. 2013. "The Sincerest Form of Flattery: Innovation, Repetition, and Status in an Art Movement." *Poetics* 41(3): 236–64.

Leschziner, Vanina. 2015. *At the Chef's Table: Culinary Creativity in Elite Restaurants*. Palo Alto, CA: Stanford University Press.

Leschziner, Vanina. 2019. "The Specter of Schemas: Uncovering the Meanings and Uses of 'Schemas' in Sociology." Paper presented at the 114th Annual Meeting of the American Sociological Association, New York, August.

Leschziner, Vanina, and Andrew Dakin. 2008. "Theorizing Cuisine from Medieval to Modern Times: Cognitive Structures, the Biology of Taste, and Culinary Conventions." *Ideas* 346–76.

Levine, Lawrence W. 1988. *Highbrow/Lowbrow: The Emergence of Cultural Hierarchy in America*. Cambridge, MA: Harvard University Press.

Lewis, Kevin. 2016. "Preferences in the Early Stages of Mate Choice." *Social Forces* 95(1): 283–320.

Lewis, Kevin, and Jason Kaufman. 2018. "The Conversion of Cultural Tastes into Social Network Ties." *American Journal of Sociology* 123(6): 1684–1742.

Lichterman, Paul. 1999. "Talking Identity in the Public Sphere: Broad Visions and Small Spaces in Sexual Identity Politics." *Theory and Society* 28: 101–41.

Lieberson, Stanley. 2000. *A Matter of Taste: How Names, Fashions, and Culture Change*. New Haven, CT: Yale University Press.

Lizardo, Omar. 2006. "How Cultural Tastes Shape Personal Networks." *American Sociological Review* 71(5): 778–807.

Lizardo, Omar. 2014. "Omnivorousness as the Bridging of Cultural Holes: A Measurement Strategy." *Theory and Society* 43(3–4): 395–419.

Lizardo, Omar. 2016. "Cultural Theory." In *Handbook of Contemporary Sociological Theory*, ed. S. Abrutyn, 99–120. New York: Springer.

Lizardo, Omar. 2018. "Social Theory Tomorrow: A Collaborative Miniaturism Proposal." *ASA Culture Section Newsletter* 30(1): 9–11.

Lizardo, Omar, Robert Mowry, Brandon Sepulvado, Dustin S. Stoltz, Marshall A. Taylor, Justin Van Ness, and Michael L. Wood. 2016. "What Are Dual Process Models? Implications for Cultural Analysis in Sociology." *Sociological Theory* 34(4): 287–310.

Lizardo, Omar, Brandon Sepulvado, Dustin S. Stoltz, and Marshall A. Taylor. 2019. "What Can Cognitive Neuroscience Do for Cultural Sociology?" American Journal of Cultural Sociology. https://doi.org/10.1057/s41290 -019-00077-8

Long, Elizabeth. 2003. *Book Clubs: Women and the Uses of Reading in Everyday Life*. Chicago: University of Chicago Press.

Lopes, Paul D. 1992. "Innovation and Diversity in the Popular Music Industry, 1969 to 1990." *American Sociological Review* 57(1): 56–71.

Lorrain, François, and Harrison C. White. 1971. "Structural Equivalence of Individuals in Social Networks." *Journal of Mathematical Sociology* 1(1): 49–80.

Low, Kelvin E. Y. 2005. "Ruminations on Smell as a Sociocultural Phenomenon." *Current Sociology* 53(3): 397–417.

MacLeod, Jay. 2018. *Ain't No Makin' It: Aspirations and Attainment in a Low-Income Neighborhood*. New York: Routledge.

Mangione, Gemma. 2016. "Making Sense of Things: Constructing Aesthetic Experience in Museum Gardens and Galleries." *Museum and Society* 14(1): 33–51.

Manuel, Peter. 1993. *Cassette Culture: Popular Music and Technology in North India*. Chicago, IL: University of Chicago Press.

Manuel, Peter, and John Shepherd. 2003. "Urbanization." In *Continuum Encyclopedia of Popular Music of the World. Vol. I: Media, Industry, and Society*, ed. J. Shepherd, D. Horn, D. Laing, P. Oliver, and P. Wicke, 385–89. London: Continuum.

Martin, John Levi. 1999. "Entropic Measures of Belief System Constraint." *Social Science Research*, 28(1): 111–34.

Martin, John Levi. 2000. "What Do Animals Do All Day? The Division of Labor, Class Bodies, and Totemic Thinking in the Popular Imagination." *Poetics* 27: 195–231.

Martin, John Levi. 2002. "Power, Authority, and the Constraint of Belief Systems." *American Journal of Sociology* 107(4): 861–904.

Martin, John Levi. 2003. "What Is Field Theory?" *American Journal of Sociology* 109(1): 1–49.

Martin, John Levi. 2010. "Life's a Beach But You're an Ant, and Other Unwelcome News for the Sociology of Culture." *Poetics* 38(2): 228–43.

Martin, John Levi. 2011. *The Explanation of Social Action*. Chicago: University of Chicago Press.

Martin, John Levi, and Matt George. 2006. "Theories of Sexual Stratification: Toward an Analytics of the Sexual Field and a Theory of Sexual Capital." *Sociological Theory* 24(2): 107–32.

Marwell, Gerald, Pamela E. Oliver, and Ralph Prahl. 1988. "Social Networks and Collective Action: A Theory of the Critical Mass. III." *American Journal of Sociology* 94(3): 502–34.

Mauss, Marcel. 1973. "Techniques of the Body." *Economy and Society* 2(1): 70–88.

Maynard, Douglas W., Jeremy Freese, and Nora Cate Schaeffer. 2010. "Calling for Participation: Requests, Blocking Moves, and Rational (Inter)action in Survey Introductions." *American Sociological Review* 75(5): 791–814.

Mayo, Elton. 1933. *The Human Problems of an Industrial Civilization*. Cambridge, MA: MacMillan.

McDonnell, Terence E. 2010. "Cultural Objects as Objects: Materiality, Urban Space, and the Interpretation of AIDS Campaigns in Accra, Ghana." *American Journal of Sociology* 115(6): 1800–52.

McDonnell, Terence E. 2014. "Drawing out Culture: Productive Methods to Measure Cognition and Resonance." *Theory and Society* 43(3–4): 247–74.

McDonnell, Terence E. 2016. *Best Laid Plans: Cultural Entropy and the Unraveling of AIDS Media Campaigns*. Chicago: University of Chicago Press.

McDonnell, Terence E., Christopher A. Bail, and Iddo Tavory. 2017. "A Theory of Resonance." *Sociological Theory* 35(1): 1–14.

McDonough, Patricia M., Marc J. Ventresca, and Charles Outcalt. 1999. "Field of Dreams: Understanding Sociohistorical Changes in College Access, 1965–1995." In *Higher Education: Handbook of Theory and Research*, ed. J. C. Smart. New York: Agathon.

McFarland, Daniel A. 2001. "Student Resistance: How the Formal and Informal Organization of Classrooms Facilitate Everyday Forms of Student Defiance." *American Journal of Sociology* 107(3): 612–78.

McFarland, Daniel A. 2004. "Resistance as a Social Drama: A Study of Change-Oriented Encounters." *American Journal of Sociology* 109(6): 1249–1318.

McFarland, Daniel A., Dan Jurafsky, and Craig M. Rawlings. 2013. "Making the Connection: Social Bonding in Courtship Situations." *American Journal of Sociology* 118(6): 1596–1649.

McFarland, Daniel A., Kevin Lewis, and Amir Goldberg. 2016. "Sociology in the Era of Big Data: The Ascent of Forensic Social Science." *The American Sociologist* 47(1): 12–35.

McLean, Paul D. 1998. "A Frame Analysis of Favor Seeking in the Renaissance: Agency, Networks, and Political Culture." *American Journal of Sociology* 104(1): 51–91.

McLean, Paul D. 2007. *The Art of the Network*. Durham, NC: Duke University Press.

Mears, Ashley. 2011. *Pricing Beauty: The Making of a Fashion Model*. Berkeley: University of California Press.

Mears, Ashley. 2013. "Ethnography as Precarious Work." *The Sociological Quarterly* 54(1): 20–34.

Mears, Ashley. 2014. "Aesthetic Labor for the Sociologies of Work, Gender, and Beauty." *Sociology Compass* 8(12): 1330–43.

Menchik, Daniel A., and Xiaoli Tian. 2008. "Putting Social Context into Text: The Semiotics of E-mail Interaction." *American Journal of Sociology* 114(2): 332–70.

Miles, Andrew. 2015. "The (Re)genesis of Values: Examining the Importance of Values for Action." *American Sociological Review* 80(4): 680–704.

Miles, Andrew. 2019. "An Assessment of Methods for Measuring Automatic Cognition." In *Oxford Handbook of Cognitive Sociology*, ed. W. Brekhus and G. Ignatow. Oxford: Oxford University Press.

Miles, Andrew, Raphaël Charron-Chénier, and Cyrus Schleifer. 2019. "Measuring Automatic Cognition: Advancing Dual-Process Research in Sociology." *American Sociological Review* 84(2): 308–33.

Miller, Daniel. 2008. *The Comfort of Things*. Cambridge, UK: Polity Press.

Miller, Daniel, and Sophie Woodward. 2012. *Blue Jeans: The Art of the Ordinary*. Berkeley: University of California Press.

Mills, C. Wright. 1940. *Situated Actions and Vocabularies of Motive*. Vol. 5.

Mimno, David. 2015. "Topic Models Without the Randomness: New Perspectives on Deterministic Algorithms." Paper presented in the New Directions in Analyzing Text as Data Conference, New York, February.

Mische, Ann. n.d. "Finding the Future in Deliberative Process: A Pragmatist Reappraisal of the Dual Process Model." (Working paper).

Mische, Ann. 1995. "Projecting Democracy: The Formation of Citizenship Across Youth Networks in Brazil." *International Review of Social History* 40(S3): 131–58.

Mische, Ann. 1998. *Projecting Democracy: Contexts and Dynamics of Youth Activism in the Brazilian Impeachment Movement*. Unpublished dissertation. The New School for Social Research, New York.

Mische, Ann. 2008. *Partisan Publics: Communication and Contention Across Brazilian Youth Activist Networks*. Princeton, NJ: Princeton University Press.

Mische, Ann. 2009. "Projects and Possibilities: Researching Futures in Action." *Sociological Forum* 24(3): 694–704.

Mische, Ann. 2011. "Relational Sociology, Culture, and Agency." In *SAGE Handbook of Social Network Analysis*, ed. J. Scott and P. J. Carrington, 80–97. London: SAGE Publications.

Mische, Ann. 2014. "Measuring Futures in Action: Projective Grammars in the Rio + 20 Debates." *Theory and Society* 43(3–4): 437–64.

Mische, Ann. 2015. "Fractal Arenas: Dilemmas of Style and Strategy in a Brazilian Student Congress." In *Players and Arenas: The Interactive Dynamics of Protest*, ed. J. M. Jasper and J. W. Duyvendak, 55–79. Amsterdam: Amsterdam University Press.

Mische, Ann, and Philippa Pattison. 2000. "Composing a Civic Arena: Publics, Projects, and Social Settings." *Poetics* 27(2–3): 163–94.

Mitchell, J. Clyde. 1969. "The Concept and Use of Social Networks." In J. C. Mitchell, ed., *Social Networks in Urban Situations*. Manchester, UK: Manchester University Press.

Mohr, John W. 1994. "Soldiers, Mothers, Tramps, and Others: Discourse Roles in the 1907 New York City Charity Directory." *Poetics* 22(4): 327–57.

Mohr, John W. 1998. "Measuring Meaning Structures." *Annual Review of Sociology* 24(1): 345–70.

Mohr, John W. 2000. "Introduction: Structures, Institutions, and Cultural Analysis." *Poetics* 27(2–3): 57–68.

Mohr, John W., and Vincent Duquenne. 1997. "The Duality of Culture and Practice: Poverty Relief in New York City, 1888–1917." *Theory and Society* 26(2/3): 305–56.

Mohr, John W., and Amin Ghaziani. 2014. "Problems and Prospects of Measurement in the Study of Culture." *Theory and Society* 43(3–4): 225–46.

Mohr, John W., and Brooke Neely. 2009. "Modeling Foucault: Dualities in Institutional Fields." Special Issue on Ideology and Organizational Institutionalism, ed. R. Meyer, K. Sahlin-Andersson, M. Ventresca, and P. Walgenbach. *Research in the Sociology of Organizations* 27: 203–56.

Mohr, John W., and Craig M. Rawlings. 2018. "Formal Models of Culture." In *Routledge Handbook of Cultural Sociology*, ed. L. Grindstaff, M.-C. Lo, and J. R. Hall, 85–94. Abingdon, UK: Routledge.

Mohr, John W., Robin Wagner-Pacifici, and Ronald L. Breiger. 2013. "Graphing the Grammar of Motives in National Security Strategies: Cultural Interpretation, Automated Text Analysis, and the Drama of Global Politics." *Poetics* 41(6): 670–700.

Mohr, John W., Robin Wagner-Pacifici, and Ronald L. Breiger. 2015. "Toward a Computational Hermeneutics." *Big Data & Society* 2(2): 2053951715613801.

Moody, James, and Ryan Light. 2006. "A View from Above: The Evolving Sociological Landscape." *The American Sociologist* 37(2): 67–86.

Moody, James, Daniel A. McFarland, and Skye Bender-deMoll. 2005. "Dynamic Network Visualization." *American Journal of Sociology* 110(4): 1206–41.

Moore, Rick. 2017. "Fast or Slow: Sociological Implications of Measuring Dual-Process Cognition." *Sociological Science* 4: 196–223.

Moreno, Jacob. 1934. *Who Shall Survive?* New York: Beacon Press.

Moskos, Peter. 2008. *Cop in the Hood: My Year Policing Baltimore's Eastern District*. Princeton, NJ: Princeton University Press.

Nadel, Siegfried F. 1957. *The Theory of Social Structure*. London: Cohen and West.

Nisbett, Richard E., and Timothy D. Wilson. 1977. "Telling More Than We Can Know: Verbal Reports on Mental Processes." *Psychological Review* 84(3): 231–59.

Norton, Matthew. 2019. "Meaning on the Move: Synthesizing Cognitive and Systems Concepts of Culture." *American Journal of Cultural Sociology* 7(1): 1–28.

Nosek, Brian A., Carlee Beth Hawkins, and Rebecca S. Frazier. 2011. "Implicit Social Cognition: From Measures to Mechanisms." *Trends in Cognitive Sciences* 15(4): 152–59.

Nowak, Raphaël, and Andy Bennett. 2014. "Analyzing Everyday Sound Environments: The Space, Time, and Corporality of Musical Listening." *Cultural Sociology* 8(4): 426–42.

O'Brien, John. 2018. *Keeping It Halal: The Everyday Lives of Muslim Teenage Boys*. Princeton, NJ: Princeton University Press.

Oliver, Pamela E., and Daniel J. Myers. 2003. "Networks, Diffusion, and Cycles of Collective Action." In *Social Movements and Networks: Relational Approaches to Collective Action*, ed. M. Diani and D. McAdam, 173–203. Oxford: Oxford University Press.

Ottenbacher, Michael, and Robert J. Harrington. 2007. "The Innovation Development Process of Michelin-Starred Chefs." *International Journal of Contemporary Hospitality Management* 19(6): 444–60.

Pachucki, Mark A., and Ronald L. Breiger. 2010. "Cultural Holes: Beyond Relationality in Social Networks and Culture." *Annual Review of Sociology* 36(1): 205–24.

Pagis, Michal. 2016. "Fashioning Futures: Life Coaching and the Self-Made Identity Paradox." *Sociological Forum* 31(4): 1083–103.

Paramei, Galina V. 2005. "Singing the Russian Blues: An Argument for Culturally Basic Color Terms." *Cross-Cultural Research* 39(1): 10–38.

Peterson, Richard A. 1976. "The Production of Culture." *American Behavioral Scientist* 19(6): 669–84.

Peterson, Richard A. 1990. "Why 1955? Explaining the Advent of Rock Music." *Popular Music* 9(01): 97–116.

Peterson, Richard A. 2005. "In Search of Authenticity." *Journal of Management Studies* 42(5): 1083–98.

Peterson, Richard A., and David G. Berger. 1975. "Cycles in Symbol Production: The Case of Popular Music." *American Sociological Review* 40(2): 158–73.

Peterson, Richard A., and Roger M. Kern. 1996. "Changing Highbrow Taste: From Snob to Omnivore." *American Sociological Review* 61(5): 900–907.

Pimlott-Wilson, Helena. 2015. "Parental Responsibility for Paid Employment and Social Reproduction: Children's Experiences in Middle-Class and Working-Class Households in England." *Environment and Planning A: Economy and Space* 47(9): 1892–1906.

Polanyi, Michael. 1958. *Personal Knowledge: Towards a Post Critical Epistemology*. Chicago: University of Chicago Press.

Polletta, Francesca. 2009. *It Was Like a Fever: Storytelling in Protest and Politics*. Chicago: University of Chicago Press.

Polletta, Francesca. 2015. "Characters in Political Storytelling." *Storytelling, Self, Society* 11(1): 34–55.

Polletta, Francesca, Pang Ching Bobby Chen, Beth Gharrity Gardner, and Alice Motes. 2011. "The Sociology of Storytelling." *Annual Review of Sociology* 37(1): 109–30.

Polletta, Francesca, Monica Trigoso, Britni Adams, and Amanda Ebner. 2013. "The Limits of Plot: Accounting for How Women Interpret Stories of Sexual Assault." *American Journal of Cultural Sociology* 1(3): 289–320.

Powell, Walter W., and Paul J. DiMaggio, eds. 1991. *The New Institutionalism in Organizational Analysis*. Chicago: University of Chicago Press.

Pugh, Allison J. 2013. "What Good Are Interviews for Thinking About Culture? Demystifying Interpretive Analysis." *American Journal of Cultural Sociology* 1(1): 42–68.

Radway, Janice A. 2009. *Reading the Romance: Women, Patriarchy, and Popular Literature*. Chapel Hill: University of North Carolina Press.

Rambotti, Simone. 2017. "Narratives of a Dying Woman: Contentious Meaning at the End of Life." *Socius: Sociological Research for a Dynamic World* 3(1). https://doi.org/10.1177/2378023117748111.

Ranganathan, Aruna. 2018. "The Artisan and His Audience: Identification with Work and Price Setting in a Handicraft Cluster in Southern India." *Administrative Science Quarterly* 63(3): 637–67.

Rao, Hayagreeva, Philippe Monin, and Rodolphe Durand. 2005. "Border Crossing: Bricolage and the Erosion of Categorical Boundaries in French Gastronomy." *American Sociological Review* 70(6): 968–91.

Rawlings, Craig M., and Michael D. Bourgeois. 2004. "The Complexity of Institutional Niches: Credentials and Organizational Differentiation in a Field of U.S. Higher Education." *Poetics* 32(6): 411–46.

Reynolds, John R., and Chardie L. Baird. 2010. "Is There a Downside to Shooting for the Stars? Unrealized Educational Expectations and Symptoms of Depression." *American Sociological Review* 75(1): 151–72.

Ricoeur, Paul. 1973. "The Model of the Text: Meaningful Action Considered as a Text." *New Literary History* 5(1): 91–117.

Roethlisberger, Fritz J., and William J. Dickson. 1939. *Management and the Worker*. Cambridge, MA: Harvard University Press.

Rogers, Everett M. 2010. *Diffusion of Innovations*. New York: Simon and Schuster.

Roose, Henk. 2014. "Getting Beyond the Surface: Using Geometric Data Analysis in Cultural Sociology." In *Handbook of the Sociology of Art and Culture*, ed. L. Hanquinet and M. Savage, 174–90. London: Routledge.

Rorty, Richard. 1979. *Philosophy and the Mirror of Nature*. Princeton, NJ: Princeton University Press.

Rose-Greenland, Fiona. 2016. "Color Perception in Sociology." *Sociological Theory* 34(2): 81–105.

Rosen, Eva. 2017. "Horizontal Immobility: How Narratives of Neighborhood Violence Shape Housing Decisions." *American Sociological Review* 82(2): 270–96.

Rossman, Gabriel. 2012. *Climbing the Charts: What Radio Airplay Tells Us About the Diffusion of Innovation*. Princeton, NJ, and Oxford: Princeton University Press.

Roy, Donald. 1952. "Quota Restriction and Goldbricking in a Machine Shop." *American Journal of Sociology* 57(5): 427–42.

Rueschemeyer, Dietrich. 2006. "Why and How Ideas Matter." In *Oxford Handbook of Contextual Political Analysis*, ed. R. Goodin and C. Tilly, 227–51. Oxford: Oxford University Press.

Rumelhart, David E., and Andrew Ortony. 1982. "The Representation of Knowledge in Memory." *Journal for the Study of Education and Development* 5(19–20): 115–58.

Ryan, John, and Richard A. Peterson. 1993. "Occupational and Organizational Consequences of the Digital Revolution in Music Making." *Current Research on Occupations and Professions* 8: 173–201.

Sahlins, Marshall D. 1976. *The Use and Abuse of Biology: An Anthropological Critique of Sociobiology*. Ann Arbor: University of Michigan Press.

Salganik, Matthew J. 2017. *Bit by Bit: Social Research in the Digital Age*. Princeton, NJ: Princeton University Press.

Salganik, Matthew J., Peter Sheridan Dodds, and Duncan J. Watts. 2006. "Experimental Study of Inequality and Unpredictability in an Artificial Cultural Market." *Science* 311(5762): 854–56.

Salganik, Matthew J., and Duncan J. Watts. 2008. "Leading the Herd Astray: An Experimental Study of Self-Fulfilling Prophecies in an Artificial Cultural Market." *Social Psychology Quarterly* 71(4): 338–55.

Schegloff, Emanuel A. 1993. "Reflections on Quantification in the Study of Conversation." *Research on Language & Social Interaction* 26(1): 99–128.

Schmaus, Warren. 2004. *Rethinking Durkheim and His Tradition*. Cambridge: Cambridge University Press.

Schneider, Barbara L., and David Stevenson. 2000. *The Ambitious Generation: America's Teenagers, Motivated But Directionless*. New Haven, CT: Yale University Press.

Schoon, Ingrid, and Terry Ng-Knight. 2017. "Co-Development of Educational Expectations and Effort: Their Antecedents and Role as Predictors of Academic Success." *Research in Human Development* 14(2): 161–76.

Schudson, Michael. 1989. "How Culture Works." *Theory and Society* 18(2): 153–80.

Schudson, Michael. 1999. "Delectable Materialism: Second Thoughts on Consumer Culture." In *Consumer Society in American History*, ed. L. Glickman, 341–58. Ithaca, NY: Cornell University Press.

Schütz, Alfred. 1967. *The Phenomenology of the Social World*. Evanston, IL: Northwestern University Press.

Schwartz, Barry. 1996. "Memory as a Cultural System: Abraham Lincoln in World War II." *American Sociological Review* 61(5): 908–27.

Schwartz, Shalom H. 2012. "An Overview of the Schwartz Theory of Basic Values." *Online Readings in Psychology and Culture* 2(1): 1–20.

Scott, John. 2000. *Social Network Analysis: A Handbook*. 2nd ed. London: SAGE Publications.

Sennett, Richard. 2008. *The Craftsman*. New Haven, CT: Yale University Press.

Sewell, William H. 2005. "The Concept(s) of Culture." In *Practicing History: New Directions in Historical Writing After the Linguistic Turn*, ed. G. M. Spiegel, 76–95. New York: Routledge.

Shively, JoEllen. 1992. "Cowboys and Indians: Perceptions of Western Films Among American Indians and Anglos." *American Sociological Review* 57(6): 725–34.

Silva, Jennifer M. 2013. *Coming up Short: Working-Class Adulthood in an Age of Uncertainty*. Oxford: Oxford University Press.

Simi, Pete, Kathleen Blee, Matthew DeMichele, and Steven Windisch. 2017. "Addicted to Hate: Identity Residual Among Former White Supremacists." *American Sociological Review* 82(6): 1167–87.

Simko, Christina. 2012. "Rhetorics of Suffering: September 11 Commemorations as Theodicy." *American Sociological Review* 77(6): 880–902.

Simmel, Georg. 1908. *Sociologie*. Leipzig: Duncker & Humblot.

Simmel, Georg. 1950. *The Sociology of Georg Simmel*. Glencoe, IL: Free Press.

Simmel, Georg. 1997. *Simmel on Culture: Selected Writings By Georg Simmel*. Ed. D. Frisby and M. Featherstone. London: SAGE Publications.

Small, Mario Luis. 2004. *Villa Victoria: The Transformation of Social Capital in a Boston Barrio*. Chicago: University of Chicago Press.

Smith, Phillip. 2005. *Why War? The Cultural Logic of Iraq, the Gulf War, and Suez*. Chicago: University of Chicago Press.

Somers, Margaret R. 1994. "The Narrative Constitution of Identity: A Relational and Network Approach." *Theory and Society* 23(5): 605–49.

Srivastava, Sameer B., and Mahzarin R. Banaji. 2011. "Culture, Cognition, and Collaborative Networks in Organizations." *American Sociological Review* 76(2): 207–33.

Star, Susan Leigh, and James R. Griesemer. 1989. "Institutional Ecology, 'Translations' and Boundary Objects: Amateurs and Professionals in Berkeley's Museum of Vertebrate Zoology, 1907–39." *Social Studies of Science* 19(3): 387–420.

Stivers, Tanya, and Asifa Majid. 2007. "Questioning Children: Interactional Evidence of Implicit Bias in Medical Interviews." *Social Psychology Quarterly* 70(4): 424–41.

Stolte, John F., Gary Alan, and Karen S. Cook. 2001. "Sociological Miniaturism: Seeing the Big Through the Small in Social Psychology." *Annual Review of Sociology* 27(1): 387–413.

Stouffer, Samuel A., Edward A. Suchman, Leland C. DeVinney, Shirley A. Star, and Robin M. Williams Jr. 1949. *Studies in Social Psychology in World War II: The American Soldier. Vol. 1, Adjustment During Army Life*. Princeton, NJ: Princeton University Press.

Strand, Steve, and Joe Winston. 2008. "Educational Aspirations in Inner City Schools." *Educational Studies* 34(4): 249–67.

Swidler, Ann. 1986. "Culture in Action: Symbols and Strategies." *American Sociological Review* 51(2): 273–86.

Swidler, Ann. 1992. "Inequality and American Culture." *American Behavioral Scientist* 35(4–5): 606–29.

Swidler, Ann. 2001. "What Anchors Cultural Practices." In *The Practice Turn in Contemporary Theory*, ed. K. K. Cetina, T. R. Schatzki, and E. von Savigny, 74–92. London: Routledge.

Swidler, Ann. 2008. "Comment on Stephen Vaisey's 'Socrates, Skinner, and Aristotle: Three Ways of Thinking About Culture in Action.'" *Sociological Forum* 23(3): 614–18.

Swidler, Ann. 2010. "Remembering Erving Goffman." Retrieved December 29, 2019, from http://cdclv.unlv.edu/archives/interactionism/goffman/swidler _10.html.

Synnott, Anthony. 1991. "A Sociology of Smell." *Canadian Review of Sociology/Revue Canadienne de Sociologie* 28(4): 437–59.

Tannen, Deborah, ed. 1993. *Gender and Conversational Interaction*. Oxford: Oxford University Press.

Tavory, Iddo. 2016. *Summoned: Identification and Religious Life in a Jewish Neighborhood*. Chicago: University of Chicago Press.

Tavory, Iddo. 2018. "Between Situations: Anticipation, Rhythms, and the Theory of Interaction." *Sociological Theory* 36(2): 117–33.

Tavory, Iddo, and Ann Swidler. 2009. "Condom Semiotics: Meaning and Condom Use in Rural Malawi." *American Sociological Review* 74(2): 171–89.

Tavory, Iddo, and Stefan Timmermans. 2014. *Abductive Analysis: Theorizing Qualitative Research*. Chicago: University of Chicago Press.

Taylor, Marshall A., Dustin S. Stoltz, and Terence E. McDonnell. 2019. "Binding Significance to Form: Cultural Objects, Neural Binding, and Cultural Change." *Poetics* 73: 1–16.

Teney, Celine, and Laurie Hanquinet. 2012. "High Political Participation, High Social Capital? A Relational Analysis of Youth Social Capital and Political Participation." *Social Science Research* 41(5): 1213–26.

Thomas, William Isaac, and Florian Znaniecki. 1918. *The Polish Peasant in Europe and America*. Chicago: University of Chicago Press.

Tilly, Charles. 1978. *From Mobilization to Revolution*. Reading, MA: Addison Wesley.

Tilly, Charles. 1997. "Parliamentarization of Popular Contention in Great Britain 1758–1834." *Theory and Society* 26: 245–73.

Tilly, Charles. 2002. *Stories, Identities, and Political Change*. Lanham, MD: Rowman & Littlefield.

Tilly, Charles. 2008. *Contentious Performances*. Cambridge: Cambridge University Press.

Tilly, Charles, and Leslie Wood. 2003. "Contentious Connections in Great Britain 1828–34." In *Social Movements and Networks: Relational Approaches to Collective Action*, ed. D. McAdam and M. Diani, 147–72. Oxford: Oxford University Press.

Traugott, Mark, ed. 1995. *Repertoires and Cycles of Collective Action*. Durham, NC: Duke University Press.

Trouille, David and Iddo Tavory. 2019. "Shadowing: Warrants for Intersituational Variation in Ethnography." *Sociological Methods & Research* 48(3): 534–60.

Vaisey, Stephen. 2009. "Motivation and Justification: A Dual-Process Model of Culture in Action." *American Journal of Sociology* 114(6): 1675–1715.

Vaisey, Stephen. 2010. "What People Want: Rethinking Poverty, Culture, and Educational Attainment." *ANNALS of the American Academy of Political and Social Science* 629(1): 75–101.

Vaisey, Stephen. 2014. "The 'Attitudinal Fallacy' Is a Fallacy." *Sociological Methods & Research* 43(2): 227–31.

Vaisey, Stephen, and Omar Lizardo. 2010. "Can Cultural Worldviews Influence Network Composition?" *Social Forces* 88(4): 1595–1618.

Vaisey, Stephen, and Andrew Miles. 2014. "Tools from Moral Psychology for Measuring Personal Moral Culture." *Theory and Society* 43(3–4): 311–32.

Valente, Thomas W. 1995. *Network Models of the Diffusion of Innovations*. Cresskill, NJ: Hampton Press.

Vallacher, Robin R., and Daniel M. Wegner. 2014. *A Theory of Action Identification*. Hove, UK: Psychology Press.

Vila-Henninger, Luis Antonio. 2015. "Toward Defining the Causal Role of Consciousness: Using Models of Memory and Moral Judgment from Cognitive Neuroscience to Expand the Sociological Dual-Process Model." *Journal for the Theory of Social Behaviour* 45(2): 238–60.

Visser, Margaret. 1991. *The Rituals of Dinner: The Origins, Evolution, Eccentricities and Meaning of Table Manners*. New York: Grove Weidenfeld.

Wacquant, Loïc. 2004. *Body & Soul: Notebooks of an Apprentice Boxer*. Oxford: Oxford University Press.

Wacquant, Loïc. 2015. "For a Sociology of Flesh and Blood." *Qualitative Sociology* (38)1: 1–11

Wada, Takeshi. 2004. "Event Analysis of Claim Making in Mexico: How Are Social Protests Transformed into Political Protests?" *Mobilization: An International Quarterly* 9(3): 241–57.

Wagner-Pacifici, Robin. 2005. *The Art of Surrender*. Chicago: University of Chicago Press.

Wagner-Pacifici, Robin. 2008. "The Innocuousness of State Lethality in an Age of National Security." *South Atlantic Quarterly* 107(3): 459–83.

Wagner-Pacifici, Robin. 2010. "The Cultural Sociological Experience of Cultural Objects." In *Handbook of Cultural Sociology*, ed. J. R. Hall, L. Grindstaff, and M.-C. Lo, 109–17. Abingdon, UK: Routledge.

Wagner-Pacifici, Robin, and Barry Schwartz. 1991. "The Vietnam Veterans Memorial: Commemorating a Difficult Past." *American Journal of Sociology* 97(2): 376–420.

Wagner-Pacifici, Robin, John W. Mohr, and Ronald L. Breiger. 2015. "Ontologies, Methodologies, and New Uses of Big Data in the Social and Cultural Sciences." *Big Data & Society* 2(2): 2053951715613810.

Wagner-Pacifici, Robin, John Mohr and Ronald Breiger. 2018. "Varieties of Relational Experience in Security Strategy: Networks of Discourse." Networks in the Global World Conference, St. Petersburg, Russia, July.

Waksman, Steve. 2009. *This Ain't the Summer of Love: Conflict and Crossover in Heavy Metal and Punk*. Berkeley: University of California Press.

Wallach, Hanna M. 2006. "Topic Modeling: Beyond Bag-of-Words." In *Proceedings of the 23rd International Conference on Machine Learning*, 977–84. Pittsburgh, PA.

Walser, Robert. 1993. *Running with the Devil: Power, Gender, and Madness in Heavy Metal Music*. Hanover, CT: Wesleyan University Press.

Warner, W. Lloyd, and Paul S. Lunt. 1941a. *The Social Life of a Modern Community*. New Haven, CT: Yale University Press.

Warner, W. Lloyd, and Paul S. Lunt. 1941b. *The Status System of a Modern Community*. New Haven, CT: Yale University Press.

Warren, Roland L. 1967. "The Interorganizational Field as a Focus for Investigation." *Administrative Science Quarterly* 12(3): 396–419.

Warren, Roland L., Stephen M. Rose, and Ann F. Bergunder. 1974. *The Structure of Urban Reform: Community Decision Organizations in Stability and Change*. Lexington, MA: Lexington Books.

Watts, Duncan J. 1999. "Networks, Dynamics, and the Small-World Phenomenon." *American Journal of Sociology* 105(2): 493–527.

Weber, Max. 1958. *Essays in Sociology.* Oxford: Oxford University Press.

Wegner, Daniel M., and T. Wheatley. 1999. "Apparent Mental Causation: Sources of the Experience of Will." *The American Psychologist* 54(7): 480–92.

Wellman, Barry and S.D. Berkowitz, eds. 1988. *Social Structures: A Network Approach.* Cambridge: Cambridge University Press.

Wherry, Frederick F. 2008. *Global Markets and Local Crafts: Thailand and Costa Rica Compared.* Baltimore: Johns Hopkins University Press.

Wherry, Frederick F. 2011. *The Philadelphia Barrio: The Arts, Branding, and Neighborhood Transformation.* Chicago: Chicago University Press.

White, Harrison C. 1992. *Identity and Control: A Structural Theory of Social Action.* Princeton, NJ: Princeton University Press.

White, Harrison C. 2008a. *Identity and Control: How Social Formations Emerge.* 2nd ed. Princeton, NJ: Princeton University Press.

White, Harrison C. 2008b. "Preface: 'Catnets' Forty Years Later." *Sociologica* 2(1): doi: 10.2383/26575.

White, Harrison C., and Cynthia A. White. 1965. *Canvases and Careers.* New York: Wiley.

White, Harrison C., Scott A. Boorman, and Ronald L. Breiger. 1976. "Social Structure from Multiple Networks. I. Blockmodels of Roles and Positions." *American Journal of Sociology* 81(4): 730–80.

Whitford, Josh. 2002. "Pragmatism and the Untenable Dualism of Means and Ends: Why Rational Choice Theory Does Not Deserve Paradigmatic Privilege." *Theory and Society* 31(3): 325–63.

Willis, Paul. 1977. *Learning to Labour.* London: Routledge.

Winchester, Daniel. 2016. "A Hunger for God: Embodied Metaphor as Cultural Cognition in Action." *Social Forces* 95(2): 585–606.

Wohl, Hannah. 2017. "The Muse at Work: Processes of Creative Experimentation." Paper presented at the *Annual Meeting of the American Sociological Association*, Montreal, August.

Wolff, Janet. 1992. "Excess and Inhibition: Interdisciplinarity in the Study of Art." In *Cultural Studies*, ed. Lawrence Grossberg, Cary Nelson, and Paula Treichler, 706–18. New York: Routledge.

Wood, Michael Lee, Dustin S. Stoltz, Justin Van Ness, and Marshall A. Taylor. 2018. "Schemas and Frames." *Sociological Theory* 36(3): 244–61.

Wuthnow, Robert. 1989. *Meaning and Moral Order: Explorations in Cultural Analysis.* Berkeley: University of California Press.

Wuthnow, Robert, and Marsha Witten. 1988. "New Directions in the Study of Culture." *Annual Review of Sociology* 14(1): 49–67.

Yeung, King-To. 2005. "What Does Love Mean? Exploring Network Culture in Two Network Settings." *Social Forces* 84(1): 391–420.

Young, Alford A., Jr. 2006. *The Minds of Marginalized Black Men: Making Sense of Mobility, Opportunity, and Future Life Chances.* Princeton, NJ: Princeton University Press.

Zaller, John. 1992. *The Nature and Origins of Mass Opinion.* Cambridge: Cambridge University Press.

Zelizer, Viviana A. 2000. "The Purchase of Intimacy." *Law & Social Inquiry* 25(3): 817–48.

Zerubavel, Eviatar. 2006. *The Elephant in the Room: Silence and Denial in Everyday Life.* New York: Oxford University Press.

Zerubavel, Eviatar. 2015. *Hidden in Plain Sight: The Social Structure of Irrelevance.* New York: Oxford University Press.

Zucker, Lynne G. 1991. "Postscript: Microfoundations of Institutional Thought." In *The New Institutionalism in Organizational Analysis*, ed. W. W. Powell and P. J. DiMaggio, 103–6. Chicago: University of Chicago Press.

# INDEX

* Triangulation → part observer
* Senti and class
* Tightness and Congruence (paper)
* Discourse Analysis
* Name Nick Names (religious vs. —)
* Schemas and masculinity

Pig
Teams

CPSIA information can be obtained
at www.ICGtesting.com
Printed in the USA
LVHW091112110920
665536LV00007B/10

9 780231 180290